MASS MEDIA AND POLITICAL TRANSITION: THE HONG KONG PRESS IN CHINA'S ORBIT

THE GUILFORD COMMUNICATION SERIES

Editors
Theodore L. Glasser
Department of Communication, Stanford University

Howard E. Sypher
Department of Communication Studies, University of Kansas

Advisory Board

Charles Berger	**Peter Monge**	**Michael Schudson**
James W. Carey	**Barbara O'Keefe**	**Ellen Wartella**

MASS MEDIA AND POLITICAL TRANSITION: THE HONG KONG
PRESS IN CHINA'S ORBIT
Joseph Man Chan and Chin-Chuan Lee

STUDYING INTERPERSONAL INTERACTION
Barbara M. Montgomery and Steve Duck, *Editors*

VOICES OF CHINA: THE INTERPLAY OF POLITICS AND
JOURNALISM
Chin-Chuan Lee, *Editor*

CASE STUDIES IN ORGANIZATIONAL COMMUNICATION
Beverly Davenport Sypher, *Editor*

COMMUNICATION AND CONTROL: NETWORKS AND THE NEW
ECONOMIES OF COMMUNICATION
G. J. Mulgan

Forthcoming

THE JOURNALISM OF OUTRAGE: INVESTIGATIVE REPORTING AND
AGENDA BUILDING IN AMERICA
David L. Protess, Fay Lomax Cook, Jack C. Doppelt, James S.
Ettema, Margaret T. Gordon, Donna R. Leff, and Peter Miller

MASS MEDIA AND POLITICAL TRANSITION: THE HONG KONG PRESS IN CHINA'S ORBIT

Joseph Man Chan
Chinese University of Hong Kong

Chin-Chuan Lee
University of Minnesota

THE GUILFORD PRESS
New York   London

© 1991 The Guilford Press
A Division of Guilford Publications, Inc.
72 Spring Street, New York, NY 10012

Printed in the United States of America

This book is printed on acid-free paper.

Last digit is print number: 9 8 7 6 5 4 3 2 1

Library of Congress Cataloging-in-Publication Data

Chan, Joseph Man.
    Mass media and political transition : the Hong Kong press in
China's orbit / Joseph Man Chan and Chin-Chuan Lee.
        p.   cm.—(The Guilford communication series)
    Includes bibliographical references and index.
    ISBN 0-89862-313-8
    1. Journalism—Political aspects—Hong Kong. 2. Press—Hong
Kong—History—20th century. 3. Press and politics—Hong Kong.
4. Hong Kong—International status. 5. Hong Kong—Politics and
government. I. Li, Chin-ch'üan, 1946– II. Title. III. Series.
    PN5449.H56C47   1991
    079'.51—dc20   91-8931
                                                       CIP

We dedicate this book to our two loving families,
without whose support it could not have been written.

Our thoughts are with the people of Hong Kong who, like us,
are trying to decipher the meaning of the new political era.
We honor those courageous young souls
who sacrificed themselves in Tiananmen Square
to save more lives of future generations.
Even though world memory is fading away,
we have not forgotten them.

Preface

Hong Kong is a unique living laboratory. In 1997 Britain will relinquish this last colonial stronghold to the People's Republic of China to become a special capitalist region of socialist China. In fact, since 1984 the Sino-British Joint Declaration has set Hong Kong's political transition in motion. This transition approximates a powerful "stimulus" in a natural "field experiment" for observing the dynamic interplay of journalism and politics over time.

Central to our concern has been the changing role of the media in the sociopolitical transition: How does the ideologically polarized press shift its journalistic paradigms to realign itself with the new power structure? This project covers the period from 1982 when the future of Hong Kong first became an issue, to the aftermath of the Tiananmen crackdown with its impact still being painfully felt in Hong Kong. It is now the moment to bring our project to a temporary closure, although our study may continue into 1997 and beyond.

Chapter 1 provides the background of the transition. The omnipotent "China factor" has shaped Hong Kong's patterns of political communication and press–party structure. The press has gravitated swiftly, though grudgingly, toward the emerging dualistic power structure since the transition commenced. In Chapter 2, we argue that as relations of social power undergo metamorphoses, journalistic paradigms shift accordingly to accord with the reconstituted power structure. We outline a framework for understanding the conditions and processes of such paradigm shifts.

Political transition has allowed a dualistic power structure to emerge, consisting of the British colonial regime and Xinhua (New China) News Agency which is China's command post in Hong Kong. Since both power centers are besieged with a legitimation crisis, they have toiled to coopt the Hong Kong press through offers of inducements and cultivation of consciousness (see Chapter 3). In return, the press has accommodated this cooptative pressure by reallocating organizational resources and by forging a viable working tie with the power centers (see Chapter 4).

Three case studies then follow. Chapter 5 traces the striking shifts of journalistic paradigms, which vary with press ideology before and after the Sino-British Joint Declaration. The press, having previously toed the British line to maintain the status quo, now succumbs to the eventuality of China's takeover. The focus of political discourse has shifted from Sino-British rifts to the strain between China's central control and Hong Kong's local autonomy. To illustrate, Chapter 6 shows that almost all but the Communist press stood opposed to a nuclear power plant on the China–Hong Kong border for fear of safety lapses. Although China proceeded with the project, it seems paradigmatic of the press patterns that will arise in future clashes.

With the clock ticking toward the year 1997, the Hong Kong press has watched Beijing's moves with immense apprehension. When Beijing crushed the democracy movement in 1989, the Hong Kong press united in a vehement condemnation of China (see Chapter 7). Journalistic paradigms reverted temporarily to their pre-1984 anti-Communist frameworks. These paradigm reshifts, however dramatic, can only take place within a definite and circumscribed boundary. The press cannot advocate abrogating the Joint Declaration but, at best, urge China to live up to the letter and spirit of the "one country, two systems" policy as espoused in the Declaration. Implications for comparative studies are offered in Chapter 8.

This project has a long history. We first worked on the concept of journalistic paradigms in the early 1980s when Chan was a graduate student and Lee a young faculty member at the Chinese University of Hong Kong.[1] Blessed once more with the good fortune of partnership at the University of Minnesota between 1982 and 1986, we tried to conceptualize Hong Kong's political transition from the perspective of communication. Meanwhile, Lee had written a number of published articles and unpublished conference papers,[2] which, fueled by our intensive discussion, led to the development of an analytical framework.[3] In a work that won him a Kyoon Hurr Dissertation Award of the International Communication Association in 1987, Chan undertook the task of fleshing out empirically the theoretical observations we had previously outlined.[4] Since then a flurry of activities involving substantial revision and fresh studies have occurred back and forth across the Pacific Ocean, made possible by faxing and field visits. The book is truly collaborative; we share equally the fruits of the labor and, also, the deficiencies that remain.

JOSEPH MAN CHAN
Hong Kong

CHIN-CHUAN LEE
Minneapolis

NOTES

1. Joseph Man Chan and Chin-Chuan Lee, "Journalistic Paradigm on Civil Protests: A Case Study in Hong Kong," in Andrew Arno and Wimal Dissanayake, eds., *The News Media in National and International Conflict* (Boulder, CO: Westview Press, 1984).

2 Chin-Chuan Lee, "The Partisan Press in Hong Kong: Between British Colonial Rule and Chinese Politics," (Paper presented at the annual convention of the Association for Education in Journalism and Mass Communication, Memphis, 2–7 August 1985); "Constructing Partisan Realities by the Press: A Riot in Hong Kong," (Paper presented at the annual convention of the Midwest Political Science Association, Chicago, 18–20 April 1985); "Partisan Press Coverage of Government News in Hong Kong," *Journalism Quarterly*, 62, no. 4 (1985): pp. 770–776; "The Right and Left of the Hong Kong Press," *Pai Hsing Semimonthly*, 15 January 1985; "Hong Kong's Power Transition and Mass Media," *Pai Hsing Semimonthly*, 16 March 1986.

3. Chin-Chuan Lee and Joseph Man Chan, "Journalistic Paradigms in Flux: The Press and Political Transition in Hong Kong," *Bulletin of the Institute of Ethnology Academia Sinica*, no. 63 (Spring 1987), 109–131. The paper was drafted in 1985 and presented at the annual convention of the International Communication Association, Chicago, 22–26 August 1986, and at the conference on "Communication, Politics, and Culture in East Asia," University of Minnesota, 8–9 May 1986.

4. Joseph Man Chan, "Shifting Journalistic Paradigms: Mass Media and Political Transition in Hong Kong" (Ph.D. diss., University of Minnesota, 1986).

Acknowledgments

In the course of this research we have owed many people many debts. We are, first, indebted to Phil Tichenor for his sage counsel and encouragement. Over the years we have picked the brains of Leonard Chu, Clement So, Siu-kai Lau, Hsin-chi Kuan, Roy Carter, Ted Glasser, Joseph Galaskiewicz, David Cooperman, Bob Craig, Doug McLeod, Young-chul Yoon, Sandra Braman, Erwin Atwood, Alex Edelstein, Don Gillmor, and the late Jerry Kline. While we appreciate the pressure they put on us for clarifying countless conceptual ambiguities, they are in no way responsible for the imperfection that remains. We are grateful to the numerous informants whose public recognition must be withheld, due to a prior promise of anonymity. We have been fortunate to have had the skilled editorial assistance of Laurie Dennis and Allison Campbell, while the enthusiasm of Seymour Weingarten, Ted Glasser, and Anna Brackett at the Guilford Press has been contagious.

We extend our profound gratitude to the University of Minnesota for a faculty grant-in-aid (to Lee) and a McMillan dissertation travel grant (to Chan); to the Chinese University of Hong Kong for a grant in support of the research reported in Chapter 6, and another grant in support of Chan to work on the manuscript in Minneapolis in the simmering summer of 1989; to the Institute of Ethnology at Academia Sinica for hosting Lee as a visiting scholar during the academic year 1986–1987; and to the China Times Center for Media and Social Studies for providing Lee with summer relief time and other assistance to complete the manuscript.

Appreciation is expressed for permission to reprint, in whole or in part and with revisions, the following works:

Chapters 1 & 2: Chin-Chuan Lee and Joseph Man Chan, "Journalistic Paradigms in Flux: The Press and Political Transition in Hong Kong," *Bulletin of the Institute of Ethnology Academia Sinica*, no. 63 (Spring, 1987): pp. 109–131.

Chapters 1 & 3: Chin-Chuan Lee and Joseph Man Chan, "Government Management of the Press in Hong Kong," *Gazette*, 46, no. 2 (1990): pp. 125–139.

Chapter 2: Joseph Man Chan and Chin-Chuan Lee, "Journalistic

Paradigm on Civil Protests: A Case Study in Hong Kong," in Andrew Arno and Wimal Dissanayake, eds., *The News Media in National and International Conflict* (Boulder, CO: Westview Press, 1984).

Chapter 3: Chin-Chuan Lee, "Partisan Press Coverage of Government News in Hong Kong," *Journalism Quarterly*, 62, no. 4 (1985): pp. 770–776.

Chapter 4: Joseph Man Chan and Chin-Chuan Lee, "Press Ideology and Organizational Control in Hong Kong," *Communication Research*, 15, no. 2 (1988): pp. 185–197.

Chapter 5: Joseph Man Chan and Chin-Chuan Lee, "Shifting Journalistic Paradigms: Editorial Stance and Political Transition in Hong Kong," *China Quarterly*, no. 117 (1989): pp. 98–118.

Chapter 7: Chin-Chuan Lee and Joseph Man Chan, "The Hong Kong Press in China's Orbit: Thunder of Tiananmen," in Chin-Chuan Lee, ed., *Voices of China: The Interplay of Politics and Journalism* (New York: Guilford Press, 1990).

Contents

MASS MEDIA AND POLITICAL TRANSITION: THE HONG KONG PRESS IN CHINA'S ORBIT

Chapter 1

Political Transition: Hong Kong Returns to China

Where can one find a mixture of modern economy and archaic polity in which the media are free yet restrained, apolitical yet partisan, timid yet bold, and culturally proud yet politically loath? Where can one find a people—and press—ambivalent about being emancipated by the motherland from the colonial grip and powerless to decide their own fate? Where can one find a press breathlessly fighting against impossible odds, powerfully swept by the political wind, and reluctantly succumbing to a *fait accompli?* Where can one find a would-be ruler patiently and skillfully cultivating press support and suddenly having its efforts undone by events not entirely within its control?

The place is Hong Kong—a land of contradictions. It is a social observer's "dream" laboratory: where one can participate in history while it is being written, test theories while witnessing the very scenes on which they are based.

This book aims to elucidate the complex contradictions of Hong Kong's mass media as they experience the momentous political transition from a known colonial rule to an uncertain sociopolitical experiment. To wit, what was once "a barren island with hardly a house upon it"—as British Foreign Secretary Lord Palmerston contemptuously described it in 1842 when Britain captured Hong Kong from China under gunboat—has defied all textbook lessons to claim glittering prosperity.[1] By all indications, this tiny colony is undeniably an uneasy envy, a strange "miracle," and an ugly goose laying golden eggs. But in 1997 Britain will hand over this last colonial stronghold to the People's Republic of China (PRC) to become a capitalist region of socialist China.

Colonial humiliation will become a thing of the past for China as Hong Kong returns to the embrace of the motherland. Will the goose turn pretty but lay no eggs, and the press become—against its will— politically active and morally righteous? How will Hong Kong's "free" press clash with China's mouthpiece press? China promises that Hong Kong will be left alone, for at least 50 years. But can China junk its past record from memory and put its unrelenting turmoil under control? How can China bolster its credibility in Hong Kong? These are no easy questions. But, like it or not, the process of political transition is irreversible, vigorously under way since 1984 and continuing to unfold with full force and unexpected twists. Neither the public nor the press can afford to sit idly. They have to cope with the change, weigh alternatives, and grope for the future. This book will tell the story of the Hong Kong press, in China's orbit, both as a testing ground for theories of social communication and as a guide post to what the future may hold for this transition. To begin, let us set the stage.

HONG KONG AND CHINA

The island of Hong Kong and the Kowloon peninsula were ceded in perpetuity to Britain in 1842 and 1860 respectively.[2] The New Territories, about five-sixths of the colony in all, were leased in 1898 for a 99–year term.[3] The June 30, 1997, expiration date of the New Territories lease is getting uncomfortably close. The British cannot possibly manage the "theoretically ceded" island of Hong Kong and the Kowloon peninsula without annexation of the leased New Territories. China refused to yield to Britain's proposed lease extension, forcing Britain to forfeit Hong Kong to China on July 1, 1997.

The Manchurian Qing dynasty that ceded Hong Kong to Britain has long faded into history, overthrown by a Nationalist revolution that established the first Chinese republic in 1911. A Communist revolution soon replaced the Nationalists with a second "people's republic" in 1949, hoisting the flags of nationalism and anti-imperialism. During these tidal waves of revolutionary change in China, the British Empire was disembodied and forced out of all of its colonies except Hong Kong. Amazingly, the People's Republic of China swallowed its national pride and Communist ideology and has allowed the existence of an annoying British colony on its doorstep. Despite its glittering prosperity, however, this tiny colony has always been a "borrowed place" living on "borrowed time." What has been borrowed is now due.

Why has China waited so patiently and for so long to reclaim Hong Kong? For decades, China has scornfully attacked Moscow as "revisionists" deviating from the true tenets of Marxist–Leninism. In return, Moscow has traded insults by humiliating China for having the profitable imperialist pimple on the border that could have easily been scratched out if China had the mind to do so. China could have reabsorbed the territory at any time after 1949, if not long before. If military might was not preferred, China could have instigated sustained urban terrorism.[4] "What it takes [for China to reclaim the territory]," a high-ranking Hong Kong official was quoted as saying, "is a phone call." But none of those possibilities came to pass even when Sino-British relations tread treacherous waters.

Mao's rise to power touched off an acrimonious debate over "who lost China" in the United States. The British were particularly fearful of China's imminent takeover of Hong Kong; as Sir Alexander Gratham (Governor of Hong Kong from 1947 to 1958) said in a 1954 speech, Communist China was the most likely source of invasion, yet the "barbarous Communism" could not conquer a civilized China. The People's Republic of China was, however, almost totally isolated from the outside world, especially after the U.S. imposition of an all-out embargo against Communist countries in the wake of the Korean War. Faced with international ostracism, Chairman Mao Zedong and Premier Zhou Enlai decided early on that China's policy toward Hong Kong would be based on "long-term calculation and full-scale utilization."[5] China has organized no violent mass movement to change Hong Kong's colonial status, while taking pains to declare that the question would be settled "when conditions are ripe" with no set date.[6]

When Nationalist riots broke out in Kowloon in 1956, Zhou Enlai sternly warned that China could not permit such disorders on its doorstep. His demand that Hong Kong not be turned into an anti-China base amounted, in actuality, to acquiescence of British rule. Even in the tense year of 1967 when radical riots erupted on the island as a spinoff of China's Cultural Revolution with rhetoric vowing to drive British imperialists out of Hong Kong, the Communist army did not march across the border.

The United Nations, at China's request, removed Hong Kong and Macao, regarded as part of Chinese territory, from the list of "colonial territories" in 1972. In May 1974, as the Cultural Revolution raged on, the Chinese authorities told former Prime Minister Edward Heath that China did not regard Hong Kong as a obstacle to Sino-British relations.[7] Corollary to this development was that China, claiming that the condition was "not ripe," declined three separate offers made by Portugal between 1974 and 1977 to return Macao to the Chinese motherland. As soon as the radical Maoist era ended, post-Mao leaders denounced the ultraleftist policy that had been pursued in Hong Kong during the previous decade.

If Mao the radical could bear the embarrassments of a colonial

TABLE 1–1. China's Net Foreign Exchange Earnings from Hong Kong (in Million U.S. Dollars)

Source of earning	1977	1978	1979	1980
Trade surplus	1,741.4	2,259.5	3,034.1	4,407.2
Remittance and other unrequited transfers	394.9	477.3	562.9	673.7
Travel and tourism	223.5	367.5	819.4	951.8
Investment profits	367.8	461.0	609.9	824.9
Total	2,727.6	3,565.3	5,026.3	6,857.6
Share in China's total foreign exchange earnings	29.3%	31.7%	31.8%	36.5%

Source: Y. C. Jao, "Hong Kong's Role in Financing China's Modernization," in A. J. Youngson, ed., *China and Hong Kong: The Economic Nexus* (Hong Kong: Oxford University Press, 1984). Reprinted with permission of the publisher.

Hong Kong for practical gains, there seemed little reason to think that Deng the pragmatic, who needed Hong Kong to benefit China's modernization program, would seek to alter the status quo. But this assumption has proved wishful. With political goals taking precedence over economic benefits, Deng saw Hong Kong as a missing piece ready to be put back into China's puzzle when the colonial lease expires in 1997. He was intent on making Hong Kong a showcase, a lure, a "demonstration station," to persuade Taiwan into unifying with the motherland under the grand banner of a "one country, two systems" scheme. Moreover, with China breaking out of international isolation and pursuing a "reform and open" policy, Deng did not think that China's takeover would ruin Hong Kong's economy. (We shall return in Chapter 5 to describe the rancorous negotiations that led to the final Sino-British Joint Declaration, as well as their implications for the press.)

In any event, Mao's early assessment regarding China's long-term economic dependence on the colony proved a foresight. A significant part of China's much-needed foreign exchange earnings are derived from Hong Kong.[8] Table 1–1 shows that China garnered $2,727.6 million in foreign exchange from Hong Kong in 1977, which amounted to 29.3% of China's total foreign exchange earnings. The figures soared to $6,857.6 million, or 36.5% of China's net total foreign earnings, in 1980. These earnings came from four major sources: trade surpluses, remittances and other unrequited transfers, travel and tourism, and investment profits.[9] As Peter Harris points out, local Communists have been so actively engrossed in Hong Kong's commercial life that they have become just another (albeit more highly politicized) interest group within the vast interest group spectrum that makes up the colony's political substructure.[10] In a self-contradictory manner, the Chinese regime has little patience for Trotskyist zealots perceived to disrupt Hong Kong's political order.[11]

The omnipresent China factor has set a severe limit on what Hong Kong can do in the way of colonial politics. Hong Kong must always contemplate China's possible reactions when making critical policy decisions, to ensure that China has no reasonable grounds for complaint. China is free to set up schools, organize trade unions, publish newspapers, and distribute propaganda in the colony; so long as these activities are kept within the law, the authorities have no objection. This privilege is, however, more guardedly allowed the Nationalists; Taiwan's officials are regularly denied entry to the colony and Taiwanese films that may cause offense to China are banned. Likewise, fearful of inflaming China, the British have turned down Soviet requests to establish airline offices, newspaper bureaus, television offices, a news agency, official shipping offices, a consular mission, and a cultural exchange office.[12]

POLITICAL COMMUNICATION

Just as China is too big, Hong Kong is too small. The only sure route to absorb the pressure of the China factor is to *depoliticize* Hong Kong. Hong Kong must stay above, or at least stay neutral in, the feud between the Chinese Communist Party (CCP) and the Kuomintang (KMT), as Sir Alexander Gratham said:

> We cannot permit Hong Kong to be the battleground for contending political parties or ideologies. We are just simple traders who want to get on well with our daily round and common task. This may not be very noble, but at any rate it does not disturb others.[13]

Early on, the British pronounced that Hong Kong's political order depends on "the tripod of consents" of China, Britain, and the people of Hong Kong.[14] Representative of this view was a statement made by D.C. Bray, former commissioner of the New Territories:

> Fundamental changes in the nature of the central government seem to me to be ruled out because they would destroy the stability of Hong Kong. In

most territories a government will stay in power so long, but only so long, as it retains the consent of the people. Hong Kong's stability rests not on one leg but on a tripod of consents, each one of which is essential for continuation of anything like the present way of life. The three consents are the consent of Hong Kong people, the consent of China and the consent of Britain. The withdrawal of any one of these three consents will endanger the whole structure.[15]

The impact of China's politics on Hong Kong is too pervasive to be eradicated. Therefore the British have been content with setting the rules of the game and seeking to absorb exogenous political forces into Hong Kong's legal framework. The British often have to delicately balance one element against the other in order to gain some room to maneuver, and usually respond to change in a highly paternalistic and defensive way. Sympathizers of mainland China and Taiwan are permitted to set up their propaganda organs as long as they stay within the confines of the law and do not threaten the legitimacy of British rule.[16]

Hong Kong has no grass-roots democracy. It is an "administrative state," with a proliferated machinery of government effectively built on a traditional colonial administration. As one observer noted, Hong Kong's pattern of representation has hardly progressed beyond the nineteenth century as far as franchise extension is concerned. What has flourished is a "bureaucratic phenomenon," with the government bureaucracy as the sole repository of power.[17] In adroitly exercising what Ambrose Yeo-chi King calls the "administrative absorption of politics," the colonial government coopts the political forces, often represented by industrial–commercial elite groups, into an administrative decision-making body, thus achieving some level of elite integration.[18] The key to achieving the goal of political stability, according to King, is the "administerization" of politics—the antithesis of politicization.

The China factor has conditioned the role and function of Hong Kong's public opinion and mass media. Along with its economic non-interventionism, the British bureaucratic polity is careful not to intrude upon the social domain of Chinese life.[19] Although the Hong Kong government cannot be voted out of office, it must maximize popular consent for its policies or, at a minimum, find the compromise that gives least offense. The government is therefore painfully attentive to public opinion, claiming itself to be a government "for the people," if not "by the people."[20] Since the 1970s, the mass media have performed the crucial role of airing the grievances of increasingly assertive pressure groups. The government has set up a vast apparatus to manage the flow of information to the press and to monitor public opinion through the press, interpersonal, and bureaucratic channels.

But public opinion is merely a safety valve. The government has little interest in true democracy; public opinion is used only to fine tune the administrative machinery and forestall popular discontent. Public opinion, thus, is largely a negative check on the government: it can sometimes restrain the government from taking certain action, but it is often unsuccessful in persuading the government to initiate change.[21] This is manifested in the paradox of active information management by the government, coupled with the attempt by most of the partisan press to construct selective political and social realities.

PRESS FREEDOM

By the same token, press freedom in Hong Kong, the level of which is second only in Asia to Japan, is more an absence of explicit government censorship than a right to participate in democratic politics. Moreover, this freedom is extended primarily with reference to the contending Chinese parties, not toward the colonial government itself. The Hong Kong press has always had considerable freedom to attack Chinese rulers—from the Manchurian Qing emperors of imperial China to the current Nationalist and Communist leaders—but it has never been allowed to jeopardize the vital interests of British rule. And historically the British have been very sensitive to any press attacks on imperialism and colonialism.[22] Fortunately for the British, the dissident Chinese intellectuals who take refuge in Hong Kong are oriented toward China and do not seek to overthrow the colonial regime. Likewise, the ordinary populace are ingrained with traditional Chinese devotion to benevolent paternalism, and abhor political activities that might "rock the boat." Press freedom, it can be argued, has served the British well by letting off the steam and by enhancing the legitimacy of British rule in Hong Kong against the larger backdrop of postwar yearnings for national liberation and self-determination. Insofar as partisan rifts between mainland China and Taiwan can be absorbed into Hong Kong's legal framework, their potential threats can be readily exposed and tackled.

Internally, Lau Siu-Kai characterizes Hong Kong as a "minimally-integrated social–political system."[23] That is, an efficient, paternalistic, British-bureaucratic polity is superimposed on a Chinese society. The Chinese society is primarily self-sustained through its enduring family units, which have limited linkages and exchanges with the polity. While the elite is coopted into the administrative machine, the masses are deprived of political participation. It is at the boundary between the polity and the civic society that the media perform the crucial role of aggregating popular interests and channeling public opinion.

Before 1970 the Hong Kong press was primarily concerned with Chinese politics but exhibited considerable indifference to indigenous local affairs. In a study of newspapers between 1951 and 1966, Robert E. Mitchell found that editorials critical of the Hong Kong government were rare indeed.[24] Rapid industrialization and demographic changes have, however, contributed to the rise of local autonomy and the transformation of the political landscape. The indigenous born now outnumber immigrants from mainland China. The politics they crave for is "here and now." They are less obsessed with their parents' China dream and yet more assertive about their legitimate rights in Hong Kong. Therefore the 1970s and 1980s saw an outburst of civil protests that sought to harness the media to reformist causes.

Legal Control

What is the source of Hong Kong's press freedom? Popular myth attributes it to the magnanimity of the liberal–democratic tradition in Britain. This explanation, while partially valid, does not square with the record of struggle for press freedom in other former British colonies. Nor does it take into account the mixed bag of anti-liberal, arbitrary, and rigid legislation against press freedom that the British have enacted in Hong Kong since 1949. Hong Kong's ordinances run into the hundreds, of which over 30 bear direct relevance to the media. Had these all been faithfully executed, Hong Kong would have written a very dark page in the history of press freedom.

Historically, exiled intellectuals in Hong Kong were allowed to advocate reformist or revolutionary political doctrines against Chinese rulers so long as they did not provoke diplomatic confrontations with China. But the British showed little patience for any threat to their authority, and these ordinances represented serious attempts to minimize, contain, or nip any such menace in the bud.

The Communists cooperated with the British in Hong Kong during the Second World War and helped rescue British prisoners of war from the hands of the Japanese army. After the war, the British regained control of the colony and asked the Communist-controlled East River Column Army to help maintain public order. The British did not bar the Communists from developing their organizations and fringe leftist groups (such as labor and teacher associations) in the territory. But after the Communists crossed the Yangtze River and defeated the KMT army in 1949, the British took abrupt measures to outlaw more than 38 leftist organizations and later expelled their activist leaders from Hong Kong.[25] Considered an outpost of the "free world" during the cold war of the 1950s, Hong Kong deeply feared the formidable threat that Mao's Communist revolution might pose.

Emergency regulations were summarily declared, empowering the colonial authorities with the right to suspend without explanation any agitating publications. The passage of the Control of Publications Ordinance in 1951 authorized the government to punish any newspaper that publishes matters "prejudicial to the security of the Colony" or "likely to alarm public opinion or to disturb public order." Obliquely referring to the Communist–Nationalist feud, the ordinance also makes it an offense to become a member of "a political group established outside the Colony."

Under the Treasonable Offenses Ordinance, any person who intends to "deprive or depose the Queen of the United Kingdom" or to "levy war against her Majesty" can be sentenced to life imprisonment. The Sedition Ordinance outlaws "an intention to bring into hatred or excite disaffection against the Hong Kong government, to raise racial or class discontent, or to incite violence." The Public Order Ordinance, which was passed after the 1967 riot, stipulates that the press shall not print any news about an unlawful assembly, defined as "a gathering of 10 or more persons in a public place without a police permit."[26] Many of these vague and arbitrary ordinances have been repealed since 1985 partly out of the fear that they might fall into the unrestrained hands of Communist China after 1997.[27]

The British sought to put Communist forces under legal control, while warily tolerating pro-Taiwan forces that they hoped would countervail the Communists. The restrictive ordinances were not rigidly pursued, but not for lack of attempts. The British tried to legally subjugate the Communist press in as early as 1952, but Beijing vehemently repudiated such attempts. On this occasion, minor conflicts broke out when the police denied entry to a Guangdong delegation that wanted to visit the victims of a Hong Kong fire. Three Communist papers reprinted an editorial from the *People's Daily* that called for strong protests. The Hong Kong government brought agitation charges against the three papers and ordered them suspended under the Control of Publications Ordinance. The charges were dropped after Beijing protested that Hong Kong had "trampled on the Chinese citizens' basic freedom and rights." Not until the 1967 riot did the colonial government again invoke the publications ordinance, this time against three fringe leftist papers. The government, however, avoided confrontation with major Communist organs.[28]

In sum, these ordinances were initially enacted to stem the influence of Communist propaganda immediately after the People's Republic was established. After a failed attempt to test China's might, the colonial regime has not strictly enforced them—for fear of seriously offending the giant northern neighbor on whose good will only can Hong Kong survive. In addition, since Hong Kong has no indigenous political parties and only weak labor unions at best, and since the media are not structurally integrated with these institutions to present any formidable challenge to the colonial power, there is even less need to subject the media to overt control.

PARTY–PRESS PARALLELISM

Many observers have proclaimed "the end of ideology" in post-industrial Western democracies.[29] Historical changes in the United States can be more aptly characterized as the decline of partisanship. The two major American parties, battling for the political center, are by no means ideologically free. Media professionalism—defined as commitment to the canons of objectivity and neutrality, with facts rigidly segregated from values—developed historically in response to the rise of market democracy, and caused the gradual demise of the party press since the 1830s.[30] Media professionalism is, ideologically, premised on an uncritical and generally unarticulated commitment to the established order. Political consensus and middle-class liberalism are taken for granted and within these contexts there is a technical concern with how well things are done.[31] Protest movements and "new politics" are, for example, often branded as deviant.

In other societies, ideologically polarized political parties have persisted. For example, although the various French parties may not offer radically different solutions to everyday problems, they symbolize the revived socioeconomic cleavages. The French press is accordingly characterized by partisan commitments and interests.[32] Thus, a middle-of-the-road, market-guided, "professional" press coexists alongside the candidly partisan press. This results in what Colin Seymour-Ure calls "party–press parallelism": the press is linked closely to party organization, identifies with party goals, and caters to partisan audiences.[33]

Party–press parallelism is as weak in the United States as it is strong in France. As in France, this parallelism is an outstanding characteristic of the Hong Kong press. Unlike France, however, Hong Kong's party–press parallelism is not rooted in local politics but is a residual microcosm of modern Chinese party conflicts. Politics in Hong Kong is sharply divided on the line between the Communist Party and the Nationalist Party (or KMT).[34] The British, controlling the rules of the game, have tolerated the relentless CCP–KMT propaganda wars fought in the colony. These fights may have had the latent consequence of restraining antagonism from bursting into violence, and may, as mentioned earlier, have given the British room to play one side against the other.

A Growing Hong Kong Identity

Hong Kong has weathered five major waves of immigration, all closely related to the vicissitudes of China. The first came in 1911, when Chinese Nationalists overthrew the Qing Dynasty and established the Republic of China. The second wave was set off in 1937 by the Japanese invasion of China. The third wave was triggered in 1949 when the Communists took control of China, and the fourth wave occurred in 1962 when China was threatened with widespread starvation. The fifth wave came when the post-Mao bureaucracy, lax in discipline, opened the floodgate of immigrants (both legal and illegal) to Hong Kong. Hong Kong has always been a refuge for Chinese trying to stay away from the turmoil in China.[35]

Anti-Communist refugees who swarmed into Hong Kong in the 1950s and the 1960s nourished the illusion of someday returning to the Chinese homeland. To them, Hong Kong was the lifeboat; China was the sea. While those who have climbed into the lifeboat don't want to rock it, their ultimate concern is with the tranquility of the sea.[36] The press, naturally, was preoccupied with the CCP–KMT struggle, and only peripherally interested in the stuff of life that went on in what was thought to be the temporary sanctuary of Hong Kong.

But this infatuation with China has changed over time. As Table 1–2 indicates, the proportion of local born has grown steadily, almost equalling those born in China by 1961, and overtaking them a decade later. By 1986, six out of ten citizens of Hong Kong were native born. Had it not been for a large inflow of immigrants from China at the turn of last decade, the proportions of native born would have been even more dramatic. Unlike the preceding generations, native-born have put their roots in Hong Kong; China signifies to them a geographical, cultural, and political entity about which they feel intensely ambivalent but under which most of them have not lived. A Hong Kong Observer poll taken in the early 1980s showed that 65% of the Hong Kong people considered their roots to be in Hong Kong, only 24% (mostly the elderly) in China.[37]

This demographic change has reshaped the ideological panorama

TABLE 1–2. Population by Place of Birth (in Percent)

Birth place	1911	1921	1931ᵃ	1961	1971	1981	1986
Hong Kong	31.5	26.7	32.5	47.7	56.4	57.2	59.4
China	62.2	70.1	64.3	50.5	41.6	39.6	37.0
Population (in millions)	.46	.63	.85	3.13	3.94	4.99	5.40

Source: The Census Reports of Hong Kong, various years. Partly based on Fan Shuh Ching, *The Population of Hong Kong* (Hong Kong: Swindon, 1974).

ᵃNo reliable figures could be ascertained for 1941 (due to World War II) or 1951 (due to the political turmoil in China).

of the Hong Kong press. A pristine Hong Kong identity began to form in the early 1970s as the epitome of the growing local autonomy vis-à-vis China. Local and immediate concerns took precedence over the distant and perennial KMT–CCP fights. As a natural consequence, the market-oriented newspapers cropped up and prospered. They owe no binding partisan allegiance to either the CCP or the KMT. Benefitting from Hong Kong's thriving economy and its formidable advertising industry, they focus on local coverage that inspires the immediate concerns of their readers. The result has been a weakened relevance of the partisan or party press, and its peaceful coexistence with the increasingly robust commercial, "professional" press.

Press Structure and Press Ideology

Hong Kong has a daily consumption rate of 350 newspapers per 1,000 population, second in Asia to Japan (497) and ahead of the United States. Of the 485 publications registered with the government, 57 are newspapers and half of these, appearing irregularly, are devoted to horse-racing tips and entertainment gossip. Less than 20 are serious enough to warrant government monitoring. Ideologically, these papers span the full ultraleftist–centrist–rightist–ultrarightist continuum. Papers on the extreme left account for 6% of the total readership while those on the extreme right account for 2%; but because these extremes reflect the CCP's and the KMT's motives and policies, they define the ideological boundaries in Hong Kong. The bulk of the circulation and advertising revenues are claimed by the market-oriented centrist and rightist papers. Since Hong Kong's main political landscape is to the right of center, there is no leftist counterpart to the rightist press.[38]

The nine newspapers, as outlined in Table 1–3, are most representative of the whole ideological/partisan spectrum of the Hong Kong press.

TABLE 1–3. Political Ideology of Major Newspapers

Press ideology	Year founded	Ownership	Circulation	Readership (percent with high school education or higher)
Ultraleftist				
Wen Wei Pao	1948	Shanghai's *Wenhui Pao* holds 31% of the shares, with the rest owned by 11 other PRC-related individuals & organizations.	40,000	57,000 (44%)
Ta Kung Pao	1948	Fei Yimin held 51% of the shares, with the remainder owned by 9 PRC-related individuals.[a]	50,000	57,000[a] (NA)[b]
Centrist				
Ming Pao	1959	Louis Cha owns 80% of the shares.	110,000	399,000 (50%)
Sing Pao	1939	Ho Man-fat	300,000	808,000 (39%)
Oriental Daily News	1969	The Ma family	400,000	1,480,000 (33%)
Rightist				
Sing Tao Jih Pao	1939	Sing Tao Group (Sally Aw: chief stockholder)	50,000	131,000 (50%)
Wah Kiu Yat Pao	1925	The Shum family	50,000	54,000 (47%)
Ultrarightist				
Hong Kong Times	1949	Hua Hsia Investment (the KMT)	15,000	35,000[a] (NA)
Kung Sheung Yat Pao	1925	The Ho family	NA[c]	NA

Source: The ownership information is based in part on Emily Lau, "A Media Melting Pot of All Political Stripes," *Far Eastern Economic Review,* 13 February 1986, p. 27. The 1989 readership figures were provided by Survey Research Hong Kong. Percentages of high school education or above among the readers were computed from *SRH Media Index 1989* (Hong Kong: Survey Research Hong Kong, 1989), Table New1B, General Report. The circulation estimates, which were not subject to standardized auditing in Hong Kong, are based on Emily Lau, "The Press Gang," *Far Eastern Economic Review,* 27 September 1990, p. 26.

[a] Estimated.
[b] NA = Not available.
[c] Closed in 1984.

Inclusion of additional newspapers would not make this analysis more general. Specifically, these nine papers represent four types of press ideology:

1. *Ultraleftist*. As China's propaganda mouthpieces under Xinhua News Agency's supervision, *Ta Kung Pao* and *Wen Wei Pao* refer to mainland China as "the motherland," "China," "the People's Republic of China," or "our country;" Taiwan as "Taiwan," "the Taiwan authorities," "the Taiwan province," or "the Chiang clique;" and honor the PRC's national day on October 1. As China's propaganda organs, they have frequently contradicted themselves because of mainland China's relentless power tumults and policy reversals. Hostile to British colonialism and American imperialism, they were partly responsible for organizing the 1967 riot in Hong Kong as a spinoff of China's Cultural Revolution. The circulation of *Wen Wei Pao* hit an all-time low of 3,000 copies during the Cultural Revolution; *Ta Kung Pao* did not fare any better.[39] Both papers are closely scrutinized by the colonial regime to identify China's policies.

Fei Yimin, publisher of *Ta Kung Pao*, was a member of China's National People's Congress Standing Committee and a vice-chairman of Hong Kong's Basic Law Drafting Committee before he died in 1987. Fei was succeeded by Yang Qi, formerly a secretary general of Xinhua in Hong Kong. Shanghai's *Wenhui Pao* "theoretically" holds a controlling interest in Hong Kong's *Wen Wei Pao*, but it is an integral part of China's propaganda apparatus under Xinhua's supervision. (The concept of stockholding is irrelevant as all of China's media are state-controlled.) Lee Tse-chung, a member of the Standing Committee of the Chinese People's Political Consultative Committee, was *Wen Wei Pao*'s publisher before being ousted by Xinhua in 1989 for having supported the pro-democracy movement.[40]

2. *Centrist*. These papers are market-directed and not linked to either China or Taiwan. The centrist category represents an assortment of papers stratified by the tastes of the elite and mass cultures, but the centrist newspapers all share a primary Hong Kong identity. While *Ming Pao* is read by a relatively high-brow public (22% college educated, 29% high school graduated), *Sing Pao* appeals to the less sophisticated (13% college educated, 26% high school graduated), as does the even more mass-oriented *Oriental Daily News* (10% college educated, 23% high school graduated).[41] Despite this variation, they all refer to mainland China as "China," "Communist China," "the Mainland," and Taiwan as "Taiwan," or "the KMT government."

Though *Ming Pao*'s rise as a leading intellectual paper was attributed to its internationally acclaimed expertise on China watching, it professed in editorials its primary commitment to Hong Kong's stability and prosperity. Louis Cha, the publisher, writes the majority of the paper's most important editorials. Widely regarded as a loyal ally of the colonial regime, Cha became an enthusiastic supporter of Deng Xiaoping's reform policy in the 1980s and an active participant of the Xinhua-led Basic Law Drafting Committee. But he was very upset with Beijing's suppression of the democracy movement in 1989.

The most significant mass-circulated newspapers are the *Oriental Daily News* and *Sing Pao,* owned by the Ma family and the Ho family, respectively. Making little pretense about political high-mindedness, they focus on local coverage, soft pornography, violence, and horse-racing tips—always written in simple, vulgar, but lively Cantonese vernacular. Positioning themselves as champions of the underdog, many of whom were victims of Communist rule, these papers are at times quite critical of China.

3. *Rightist.* Sing Tao Jih Pao (founded in 1938) and *Wah Kiu Yat Po* (founded in 1925), two of Hong Kong's oldest newspapers, tilt toward Taiwan because of historical ties with the KMT, each bearing the "Republic of China" on its masthead and honoring Taiwan's national day on October 10. In fact, they were born long before the Communists took hold of China. They refer to mainland China as "Communist China," "the Mainland," or "the Communist Party," and Taiwan as "the Republic of China," "Nationalist China," "Taiwan," and "Free China."

Both the centrist and the rightist papers constitute the centrifugal forces in Hong Kong. They owe their success in circulation and advertising to the vibrant Hong Kong economy that ultimately depends on political stability. Many of their publishers have been honored by the British with medals or prestigious titles and are regularly briefed by the colonial regime on major policies. A special government commission praised *Sing Tao Jih Pao* and *Wah Kiu Yat Pao* for being a stabilizing force in helping the government combat Communist propaganda during the 1967 riot.[42] Their eminent position in the market has since been overshadowed, if not overtaken, by the high-brow *Ming Pao* or by the low-brow *Oriental Daily News* and *Sing Pao.*

4. *Ultrarightist.* The *Hong Kong Times* is owned by the Hua Hsia Investment Company, a front agency of the KMT's propaganda arm in Taiwan. The paper was established in 1949 as a propaganda outpost after the KMT withdrew to Taiwan, following their defeat by the Communists on the mainland. The *Times,* as a symbol of the KMT, commanded the allegiance of refugees in Hong Kong aspiring to return to

the mainland. With most of the older KMT followers now dead, aged, or gone and the younger generation born in Hong Kong turning apathetic to the KMT–CCP rift, Taiwan's traditional anti-Communist enthusiasm has lost much of its appeal. The colonial regime has excluded the paper from briefings and activities but has closely monitored its content. Capable of limited maneuvering, the *Times* has largely toed the colonial government line in an effort to counterbalance or frustrate the Communists.

Kung Sheung Yat Pao had very close ties with the KMT, drawing public attention, as early as 1925 in its inaugural editorial, to the "disaster of Communism." While loyal to the colonial regime, it is as fervently anti-Communist as the *Times*. Once ranking itself with *Sing Tao Jih Pao* and *Wah Kiu Yat Pao* as Hong Kong's most significant papers before the 1970s, this paper has since then found its influence and circulation in steady decline because its bitter anti-Communism had little appeal to the younger generation. The paper's demise in 1984 was hastened by the political transition.

FORMING A DUALISTIC POWER STRUCTURE

Although Britain was one of the first countries to officially recognize the People's Republic, Britain rejected China's requests to establish an official mission in Hong Kong because, as Governor Gratham was quoted as saying, "There is no room for two governors." [43] As a U.S. ally in the cold war era, Britain was fiercely anti-Communist, not allowing China any opportunity to challenge the colonial power. On the other hand, China refused the British proposal to set up a consulate because this would have meant a tacit recognition of the unequal treaty that ceded Hong Kong to Britain as a colony.

Since its founding at the peak of the KMT–CCP civil war in 1948, Xinhua's Hong Kong branch has acted as China's de facto official representative. Its sensitive political role took on added significance after 1949, given that China was barred from official representation in Hong Kong and isolated from the international community. But the role of Xinhua rose and fell in tandem with Sino-British relations and the changing international political economy. The colonial regime had long subjugated Xinhua to the status of a foreign agency whose operation was a public mystery. The relaxation of Sino-British tensions has enhanced the status of Xinhua in Hong Kong considerably. [44]

Xinhua has a double role to play, primarily as a political institution and secondarily as a news agency. Xinhua's Hong Kong branch, assuming a ministerial-level status, is under the direct jurisdiction of the State Council in Beijing. In his capacity as the director of the Hong Kong and Macao Work Committee of the CCP, Xinhua's director in Hong Kong is ultimately responsible for coordinating and supervising all of the Chinese interlocking interests and organizations (including banks, department stores, labor unions, trading and investment companies, schools, and the press). Of the 500 staff members in Xinhua's Hong Kong branch, only 30 people work in the news department.[45] It is an anti-KMT command post and Beijing's intelligence center in Southeast Asia. More recently, Xinhua even negotiated in Hong Kong with countries (such as South Korea) with which China has no diplomatic ties.

Since 1984, Xinhua has moved to the political forefront. Xinhua, representing China, has risen in influence to be the second power center in Hong Kong, challenging the dominance of the colonial government. Under the directorship of Xu Jiatun, Xinhua has been reorganized to comprise elaborate departments, closely paralleling the colonial government structure (see Chapter 3). Regarded as Hong Kong's "shadow government," Xinhua has actively recruited local talents (now about half of the 500 staff) to cope with the political transition and to fill the British vacuum in 1997.[46] More importantly, Xinhua takes charge of the ongoing processes of political transition. The momentous political transformation of reverting a British colony to Communist China is under way.

Chapter 2

Power, Mass Media, and Journalistic Paradigms: Continuity and Change

In Manila, the Philippines, at 9:30 A.M., on February 24, 1986, Ferdinand Marcos emerged on the state-run Channel 4 television to dispel the rumor that the first family had deserted the presidential palace. Twenty minutes later, the live broadcast was abruptly interrupted by the pro-Aquino forces, which were gaining control of the broadcasting complex. Hours later came the anchor's greeting: "Channel 4 is on the air again *to serve the people*." Marcos was toppled.[1]

In South Korea in 1980, General Chun Doo Hwan seized power after a coup. In the name of a "purification movement," Chun banned 800 politicians from politics and purged 900 journalists from the profession. Forty-one publishers were taken to the Martial Law Command, where they pledged "voluntary will" to shut down their newspapers. The 23 survivors thrived on government favoritism. Seven years later, the yearning for press freedom was crystallized into a rallying cry for an anti-Chun popular revolt that paved the way for democratization.[2]

In China, mass media are inextricably both an instrument and a battlefield of political struggle. In 1957 Chairman Mao wrote editorials to launch the Anti-Rightist Campaign; in 1967, to spearhead the Cultural Revolution, he authorized editorial assaults by radical leftists on party regulars and intellectuals. The ensuing decade saw every newspaper in China, large and small, do nothing but copy editorials from the *People's Daily*—verbatim from the headline, typeface, down to its size and placement. After Mao's death, the *People's Daily* was criticized as a manufacturer of falsehood. History was repeated in 1989 with a bloody crackdown on journalists and the students in Tiananmen Square who made the demand, among others, for press freedom.

These are dramatic, but hardly isolated, examples of the close affinity between media and power. The scenario we face in this book is the equally profound transfer of power from a colonial regime to a Communist regime. We aim to study, specifically, how the Hong Kong press—in China's orbit—dances to the tune of this pivotal change in power. What changes have taken place, over time and in various contexts, in the Hong Kong press? What changes have been brought about by the political transition in terms of the press's external ties to the newly constituted power structure as well as internal news policies within the press? What are the conditions and limits of the media's relative autonomy in political transition?

To establish our cognitive orientation, we shall articulate the theoretical tie between mass media and power, explicate the concept of "journalistic paradigms" central to this project, and identify the *conditions, processes,* and *consequences* of journalistic paradigm shifts. It should be noted that given an almost total absence of the theoretical and empirical studies directly pertinent to Hong Kong, we shall have to resort to the general literature from which to extrapolate implications.

MEDIA AND POWER

News is an active production of meanings. It is not a crude and mechanical mimic of "objective" reality, but a dialectic of social construction mediated by interests, power, and ideology. Different objects present themselves to media consciousness and constitute multiple realities. Among the multiple realities, the one defined, or assigned a particular prominence, by the power structure stands out as the dominant reality. The dominant reality simply dominates rather than monopolizes; it is not fixed but continually contested by alternative or sometimes oppositional realities. If the power structure holds unchallenged authority, then the media uphold the dominant reality and weaken alternative or oppositional realities by incorporating, marginalizing, or directly opposing them.[3] But if there should be a collapse of elite consensus or if the power structure should face a legitimacy crisis, then conflicting definitions might battle one another until the political dust is settled.

Power is generally defined as the ability to get what one wants and the ability to influence others in ways that further one's own interests.[4] The sources of power include personality of leadership (charisma), property, and organization, with organization as most vital in a modern society. The instruments of power consist of condign power (punishment), compensatory power (reward), and conditioned belief, which is the ability to manufacture ideological consent so that the fact of submission would not be recognized.[5]

Mass media, as a constituent part of a social system, interact with other subsystems and draw on one another's resources to function effectively. Social subsystems do not exert equal influences over the media: Herbert Gans likens news to be a "tug of war," the resolution of which depends on power.[6] News is an exercise of power over the interpretation of reality, and thus favors the power centers that hold a dominant position in the authority relations. In tracing the structure of media control and ownership, Marxist political economists regard the media as an instrument to propagate the dominant ideology of the capitalists or the capitalist class who own them.[7] Louis Althusser argues that mass communication constitutes a "state ideological apparatus" which reproduces the conditions of social production.[8] The primacy of the infrastructure, Raymond Williams opines, is manifested in its ability to "set limits for," "exert pressure on" and "exclude alternatives to" the media consent, but the infrastructural–superstructural complex should be regarded as an active process of social praxis.[9] Todd Gitlin views mass media as part of the culture industry that produces and transmits hegemonic ideology.[10]

We maintain, theoretically, that mass media reflect unevenly the perspectives of the *power structure* and thus react unevenly to the changing *power relations* in society. Journalistic perspectives are embedded in, and elaborated by, the underpinning processes of social formations and the larger structure of power and authority. We define social formations as interpenetration between state and society as well as formations and coalitions among the dominant groups. Therefore, the media construct realities to make sense of the changing power dynamics. They are neither totally autonomous from, nor totally subservient to, the established power.[11]

Traditional pluralists put undue emphasis on media autonomy by maintaining that power is decentralized in democratic polities in which the media serve as a "fourth estate" or a "watchdog" to check and balance the established authority.[12] For the "truth" to emerge, they argue, the media should compete in the "free marketplace of ideas" and journalists should apply professional canons of objectivity, impartiality, and balanced reporting.[13] The very concepts of "fourth estate" and media professionalism, in fact, evolved as an ideological construction to enhance the occupational and political status of journalists as well as to legitimate opposition to state control of the press.[14]

Even in democratic pluralism, empirically speaking, the more powerful the social groups, the readier access they have to media resources.[15] Gaye Tuchman and Mark Fishman argue that the rhythm of news work is in tandem with the cycle of legitimated institutions, where "objective facts" can be discovered.[16] Structural dependence of news media on official sources predisposes journalists to empathize the official perspective. According to Leon Sigal, almost eight out of ten domestic and foreign front-page stories carried by the *New York Times* and the *Washington Post* originated from public officials.[17] David Paletz, Peggey Reichert, and Barbara McIntyre concluded that press coverage of a city council in North Carolina consistently supported the local government authority despite challenges from citizens groups.[18] Harvey Molotch and Marilyn Lester showed that press coverage of an oil spill focused on information about powerful oil companies and federal agencies, as compared with information about local groups.[19] Clarice Olien, Phillip Tichenor, and George Donohue discovered that established groups overwhelmingly evaluate the media as "helpful" while less established groups tend to see them as "harmful."[20] While the media may not abstain from covering deviant groups, the farther the groups are perceived to be from the status quo, the less favorable the coverage.[21]

Media professionalism and canons of objectivity are, in fact, predicated on a generally unarticulated commitment to the established order. Like any positivist discipline, journalism must have concepts with which facts can be grasped, and the concepts themselves incorporate a set of unspoken assumptions about the external reality. Gans contends that American journalists ground their facts in an array of enduring values such as ethnocentrism, altruistic democracy, responsible capitalism, small-town pastoralism, individualism, and moderation.[22] Philip Schlesinger shows that the British Broadcasting Corporation (BBC), noted for balance and fairness, had no qualms about labeling the Northern Irish Republican Army (IRA) "rebels" threatening to undermine the consensual basis of British parliamentary democracy.[23] Correspondingly, antiwar protesters, the women's movement leaders, and other radical political groups were framed by mainstream American media as "deviants."

Internationally, Edward Said maintains that U.S. media are apt to reduce the rich complexity and contradictions of foreign countries and cultures to "us against them" in a cold war context.[24] Despite their bickering about domestic issues, U.S. mainstream media are often enthusiastic celebrants of a bipartisan foreign policy. They "domesticate" international news as a domestic extension without the benefit of the indigenous third world perspective.[25] Furthermore, Edward S. Herman and Noam Chomsky argue that the U.S. media portray people abused in enemy states as "worthy victims" but downplay the "unworthy victims" of human rights abuse in client states. The media may lash out with moral indignation at enemy leaders for tormenting "worthy victims" but show no such compassion toward "unworthy victims."[26]

Public opinion tends to rally around the flag. That is, the media and the public always surge to support the appeal of esteemed leaders; they give the president, national leaders, and their policies generous benefit of the doubt, particularly when these policies involve conflicts with foreign countries. President Reagan's popularity reached an all-time high after his invasion of Grenada, so did Prime Minister Margaret Thatcher's following a British victory in the Falkland Island war. Although criticized for the loss of U.S. marine lives in Lebanon, President Reagan was never challenged on grounds of the U.S. right to meddle in the region.

As far as China policy is concerned, the media have toed the official U.S. line, no matter which administration was in power. Chang writes of "concentric circles" of influence in which the foreign policy-making power is ultimately vested in the president, who may delegate some authority to his inner-circle advisers and cabinet members. Meanwhile, the U.S. Congress largely responds to the president's initiatives.[27] There is a presumption of hierarchy and authority: It is people at the top who know how to best protect the "American interest" in China or elsewhere. While the media set the agenda for the public, it is plain that Washington sets the China policy agenda for the media.

The media are, however, not innocent pawns of the capitalist power. Liberal media reflect the *configurations* of simultaneously cooperative and competitive social forces. The media are also a site of interclass struggle as well as intraclass struggle within the bourgeoisie.[28] They exhibit what Peter Dreier calls "corporate liberalism," that is, the attempt to coopt dissent by exposing government and business wrongdoing (such as the Watergate scandal).[29] The reformist liberal media do not undermine the fundamental power base of the system. They may play a role in the redistribution of political power, but always among the already powerful.[30] Rather than strictly being a "watch dog" (totally independent) or a "lap dog" (totally dependent), the media are what Donohue, Olien, and Tichenor call a "guard dog" (primarily dependent on) of the power structure.[31]

The dominant definition of reality by the media, as mentioned earlier, is challenged by alternative, even oppositional definitions. Since a high degree of indeterminacy is particularly embedded in political transition, the press is allowed a wider terrain of the ideological framework in which different definitions of social reality are possible. But alternative or oppositional definitions should not violate core hegemonic values or contribute too heavily to radical critique or social unrest. To scrutinize and compare the struggle among, and the shifts of, different definitions, we have developed a concept called "journalistic paradigms."

JOURNALISTIC PARADIGMS

We first proposed the concept of journalistic paradigms in an article published in 1984 titled "Journalistic Paradigms on Civil Protests: A Case Study in Hong Kong."[32] We borrow the concept of a paradigm from Thomas Kuhn, who uses it to explain the growth of science.[33] Margaret Masterman identifies three major uses of the term "paradigm." The first, in a metaphysical sense, refers to a total worldview, gestalt, or weltanschauung within a given science; a paradigm is thus a way of "seeing," a general principle governing perception, and a "map" that describes which entities exist and how they behave. The second use of a paradigm is as a concrete "exemplar" (such as a math formula) that can be learned step by step. The third meaning is as a specific tool and instrument.[34] Although Kuhn originally defined paradigm in the metaphysical sense, he seems to have retreated to the constituent parts of that concept (as an exemplar, or an instrument) in the face of criticisms on the concept's inexactitude.[35] George Ritzer claims, however, that the gestalt view of the concept is most inspiring for his attempt to structure sociological theory.[36]

It is the first meaning of the Kuhnian paradigm that we borrow to refer to the holistic core assumptions that the press makes about reality. As Gans argues, journalism is akin to empirical disciplines that must rely on untested or even untestable concepts with which to grasp facts.[37] While not all information-producing fields are organized around paradigms, journalism possesses many characteristics of paradigm-based fields. These characteristics include control over the training of practitioners, standardization of methods for gathering and representing information, and authoritative internal review of new claims and contributions.[38]

We define a "journalistic paradigm" as a set of taken-for-granted and unspoken assumptions, cognitive maps, or gestalt world views that inform the media as to what "social facts" to report (and what not to report) and how to interpret them. A journalistic paradigm thus is a way of "seeing" that defines the entities of journalistic concern and results in patterns of selective coverage, interpretation, emphasis, and exclusion. From an organizational perspective, a journalistic paradigm is imperative to the mapping of time and space and to the organizing of a glut of occurrences into news events. This paradigm also enables media organizations to reduce environmental uncertainty by routinizing their recurring task activities, enforcing organizational norms and values, and exercising social control in the newsroom.[39] Other writers have used "news frames," "news perspectives," or "news logic" to connote a similar idea.[40]

Once a perspective achieves the status of a paradigm, especially that which is deeply entrenched in political ideology, the perspective is bound to acquire enduring qualities. Journalistic paradigms thus have an inertia, tending to continue in the same direction and resist change unless they are acted upon by significant external or internal forces.[41] Fundamental paradigm shifts rarely occur unless there is a collapse of elite consensus, an internal division, or a reconstitution of the power structure and the like.[42]

The Golden Jubilee School Case

The function of political ideology in structuring journalistic paradigms can be observed most clearly in ambiguous social situations whose nature is open to conjectures. As Herbert Fensterheim and M. E. Tresselt argue, the less well defined the stimulus, the greater the contribution of the perceiver.[43] Analogously, Stuart Hall pointed out that the role of the media in the labeling process is at its maximum in situations that are unfamiliar or ambiguous.[44] The mass media, in Hall's words,

> . . . do have an integrative, clarifying, and legitimating power to shape and define political reality, especially in those situations which are unfamiliar, problematic, or threatening: where no "traditional wisdom," no firm networks of personal influence, no cohesive culture, no precedents for relevant action or response, and no first-hand way of testing or validating the propositions are at our disposal with which to confront or modify their innovatory power.[45]

The media may in this case safely fall back on their journalistic paradigms rooted in ideologies. To test this, we studied the Golden Jubilee School case, an ambiguous situation.

The Golden Jubilee School is a traditional, conservative, and obedient Catholic high school in Hong Kong. In 1973, protests erupted among teachers and students against the school principal suspected of defrauding public funds. The principal responded to the protests by dismissing some teachers, while suspending students who had protested against her. The protesters petitioned the bishop to no avail and then appealed to the governor, but the government abruptly closed the school on suspicion of external instigation. The angry teachers and students staged sit-ins, sleep-ins, demonstrations, petition drives, and press conferences, which drew the support of various pressure groups and led to a mass rally of 10,000 people. The protest was so well organized and disciplined that some people suspected it to be Communist-planned, while others surmised that the protesters seemed too serious about their goals to be externally instigated. For want of concrete information, the newspapers consciously or unconsciously tried to illuminate the situation through their own ideological paradigms.

In our 1984 article we related the concept of journalistic paradigms to press ideology:

> Journalistic "paradigms," as determined by political ideologies, make newspapers attribute different cause-and-effect relationships to civil protests and assign varying degrees of support to protesters. As a rule, the leftist journalistic "paradigm," although endorsing social stability in Hong Kong, tends to lend a more sympathetic ear to civil protests even if these are nonpolitical in nature. Conversely, the rightist journalistic "paradigm" is constantly antagonistic to civil protests, fearing that these activities are conspiratorial and Communist initiated. The centrist "paradigm," standing somewhere in between, displays a less consistent pattern and can be for and against civil protests, with each case being weighed on its own merits.[46]

We concluded:

> The rightists, characterized by a political suspicion of radical civil protests, read [mainland China vs. Taiwan] party politics into the Jubilee Affair. They politicized, stereotyped, and attributed the cause of the protest to ulterior motives and external Communist conspiracies. Their high propensity to advocate suppressive measures to end the protest was correlated with a strong support for the government's policies and harsh criticisms of the protesters. Their tolerance of social conflict was relatively low, while the concern for social order was high. In contrast, the leftists were more supportive of the protesters. Condemning the Hong Kong government's suppressive policies, they tended to attribute the occurrence of a protest to internal social–structural deficiencies. The centrist papers, on the other hand, appeared to be more moderate and diversified in their outlook.[47]

Since the publication of this article in 1984, we have used the concept of journalistic paradigms to study other critical events. For instance, Lee discovered that the partisan press assigned diverse ideological interpretations to what presumably was "neutral" government information.[48] Lee and Lee show that during a radical riot in Hong Kong in 1967 the ultraleftist press attacked British colonialism, the rightist and centrist press endorsed the Hong Kong government's efforts to maintain law and order, and the ultrarightist press echoed Taiwan's official anti-Communist stance.[49] In addition, we have used this concept to analyze the relationship between Hong Kong's press and political transition.[50]

DETERMINANTS OF JOURNALISTIC PARADIGMS

We identify three major determinants that jointly and interactively shape the formation of journalistic paradigms. The first is the larger pattern of power distribution. The second, on an industrial–organizational level, is the market forces. The third is press ideology. The market-oriented press is privately owned, profit-motivated, and inclined to adhere to mainstream ideology and canons of media professionalism. The partisan press is, on the other hand, marked by its close organizational, financial, and ideological ties to political parties.

Journalistic paradigms are a joint product of the cross-level interactions among these three determinants. There is no single, universal journalistic paradigm shared by all journalists; rather, they construct a plurality of paradigms contingent on the combinations of these determinants. Of these determinants, distribution of social power is most encompassing and sets the overall shape of journalistic paradigms. The degree of centralized power is inversely associated with the importance of the market determinant; in that case, ideological and organizational ties of the media to the power centers become a very potent factor of the journalistic paradigm. On the other hand, a decentralized power is positively associated with the market operation that encourages media professionalism.

The commercial press tends to be oriented toward the market logic and to abide by professional practices, whereas the partisan press is more prone to bow to political and ideological pressure. This contrast is most visible in the coverage of political matters; both the professional and partisan press, however ideologically divergent, may still have certain common values with regard to nonpolitical news issues.

Distribution of Social Power

The scope of the media's "relative autonomy," as argued earlier, is broadly related to the distribution of social power. If social power is concen-

TABLE 2–1. A Typology of the State–Press Relationship

	Inducements	
Constraints	Low	High
Low	Laissez-faire	Cooptation
High	Repression	Incorporation

trated in the hands of a few, the press is subjected to direct, centralized control. When social power is distributed among a multiplicity of holders, then state control of the press is less direct and less intrusive.[51] Journalistic paradigms reflect the dominant social assumptions as well as the emergent sociopolitical formations. Based on the distinctions made by William Gamson's "inducements–constraints," Antonio Gramsci's "consent–coercion," John Kenneth Galbraith's "condign–compensatory power," or the "carrot–stick" metaphor, four types of press control can be identified, as in Table 2–1.[52]

The first type, laissez faire, is characterized by a low level of state inducements and a low level of constraints, as commonly found in liberal democracies. As in the United States, with the market being the primary governing force, the state takes a minimalist and passive approach to the control of press ownership and content. Even in the sphere of broadcasting, it was only after airwave interference in the United States had become chaotic did the state reluctantly assume regulatory responsibility to keep the channel of market competition open.[53] The privately owned media nonetheless reproduce the existing order, by cultivating value consensus rather than resorting to state coercion. Within the boundaries of capitalism and liberal democracy, the press amplifies diverse voices, especially those of the legitimated elite dissent. But the intensified capital concentration and conglomeration may stifle market competition and exclude a range of alternative and nonprofitable ideas.

Opposite to laissez faire is repression. In a totalitarian system, the state intrudes into every domain of the civil society and levies strict constraints on the press without delivering a corresponding level of inducements. Outright press control is imposed. Mass media, such as in China during the Cultural Revolution, are used by the state to create a "total institution" and impose ideological hegemony on the civil society. They provide ex post facto policy justifications by selectively interpreting official dogma; they also initiate policy shifts that often come after intense power struggles.[54]

The third type of press control is incorporation, a mixed type involving a simultaneous or intermittent interplay of repression (high constraints) and cooptation (high inducements). The press is politically kept as a weak, auxiliary, and dependent organ of the state but not strictly as its mouthpiece. Press lords amass huge amounts of wealth before—but, in some cases, because—they are incorporated. But press owners are invariably too imbued with vested interests and dominant ideology to challenge the established power.

To compare, if China epitomizes state repression of the press, then Taiwan and South Korea until recent democratization constituted prime examples of state incorporation. A *repressed* press tends to exist on state subsidy and have little autonomy whether in political or nonpolitical spheres. An *incorporated* press, on the other hand, often garners huge profits from crass commercialism or state favoritism; while politically subservient to the state, the press has a substantial room to maneuver in *nonpolitical* areas. Those who willingly accede to state inducements relish vast economic benefits and political status, but those who contest the power structure would undoubtedly suffer from coercion or suppression.

Hong Kong is characteristic of yet another type of press control: state cooptation. A high level of inducements is accompanied by a low level of constraints. Neither power center in Hong Kong has a monopoly of power; each has its own challenges and stands in need of press support to bolster partial legitimacy. Coercion alone is infeasible. The colonial regime possesses little condign power to coerce the press, none of which survives on state subsidy. Therefore, the regime reckons with the coexistence of the indigenous commercial press and the externally controlled partisan-ideological press. Little muscle can be flexed against the Communist press that has perennially defied colonial authority. While the press is a strict mouthpiece of the Party on the mainland, neither can China coerce the Hong Kong press without incurring vast costs. The only viable approach for either power center is through the method of cooptation, providing the press with a variety of symbolic and financial inducements. The pace of cooptation has accelerated in the wake of the Joint Declaration (see Chapter 3). We shall return to elaborate cooptation as a process causing shifts in journalistic paradigms.

When a "hard" authoritarianism is transformed into a "soft" authoritarianism marked by growing political participation or democratization, the state may shift its press control from *incorporation* to *cooptation*. This process is actively under way in South Korea and Taiwan, where opposition parties and grass-roots groups have gained solid legitimacy to challenge the ruling regime's monopoly. Vibrancy of market competition has also served to reduce press reliance on the state and to loosen state coercion of the press.

Market Forces and Media Professionalism

In the United States, the partisan press has given way to media professionalism since the 1830s as a response to the rise of a market democracy.[55] Western journalists pride themselves on being professional, adhering to canons of objectivity and neutrality with facts rigidly segregated from opinion. But we have argued that media professionalism is ultimately committed to the market logic. Even the apparently simple commandment questions of journalism (i.e., the five Ws and one H) presuppose a platform for inquiry, a framework for interpreting answers, a set of rules about who to ask what about what. These frameworks, platforms, and rules can be traced to political and economic structures, occupational codes and organizational routines of daily journalism, and literary forms that journalists work with.[56] The professional journalistic paradigm presumes the authority as the official reference point for any news event, thus objectifying the status quo. This news value is transmitted through formal education and internalized through informal socialization in the newsroom.[57]

Moreover, market forces shape news production. All news organizations have to minimize the cost of news production while maximizing the market value of their news products. They seek scoops on the one hand and take pains not to miss stories on the other. While commercial television competes for the largest share of the audience, newspapers tend to be stratified into the elite press and the popular press.[58] The market-oriented press is more likely to favor socioeconomic stability. By contrast, the party or partisan press that survives on political subsidies tends to appeal to a much smaller core of readers, although this does not preclude any attempts to reach a better market penetration.

Modern press in most third world countries was inaugurated with the awakening of national consciousness when the people came into contact with the previously unknown European powers. The primary function of this press was to advocate enlightenment, reform, and national independence. Antithetical to this advocacy tradition, Western norms of professionalism in the third world were largely transferred from without, through such mechanisms as colonial history, institutional cooperation, education, and career socialization. In a society like Hong Kong, even if the "professional" press (such as *Ming Pao*) has obvious traces of Western influence, the moralist Confucian legacy remains strong. At times, however, even the partisan press has had to pay lip service to, or hide its reportage in the disguise of, objectivity.[59]

Political Ideology

The literature in the media studies, mostly originated from the United States, tends to be focused on media professionalism. This media professionalism is consonant with the dominant ideology, which is most apparent in the coverage of foreign nations. In many European and most third world nations, however, the press makes no secret about its ideological stance and organizational ties with political parties. In what Colin Seymour-Ure refers to as a "party–press parallelism," the press is linked closely to party organization, identifies with party goals, and caters to partisan audiences.[60] The Hong Kong press, as shown in Chapter 1, spans the full ideological spectrum.

Political ideology determines journalistic paradigms and media–institution control. Organizational control is exercised through recruitment, policy guidance, and other reinforcement mechanisms.[61] Hong Kong's ideologically stratified press, as our study shows, exercises organizational control primarily through entry recruitment. Reporters are ideologically so congruent with their newspapers that the majority of them do not feel they are subjected to specific or explicit guidelines in the news work. As a practical matter, they need not be told specifically what to write. Social control in the newsroom is a structural and subtle process, with reporters tending to absorb the institutional definitions of the situation and news norms.[62] The most effective institutional control occurs at the level of the "conditioned belief," that is, the control exercised by conditioning the journalist's belief so that the fact of submission to organizational norms is not recognized.[63] This is achieved through recruitment to ensure ideological conformity, and reinforced through socialization as embodied in job descriptions and task prescriptions.

JOURNALISTIC PARADIGMS: CONDITIONS FOR CHANGE

Journalistic paradigms acquire stability. But if the dominant power structure is fundamentally upset, the emergent sociopolitical configurations may engender important, even vital, shifts of journalistic paradigms. Kuhn argues that a scientific paradigm undergoes changes only after it fails consistently to reconcile newly discovered phenomena.[64] This is a moment of "paradigm breakdown" or "hegemonic crisis." The media, likewise, tend to "normalize" or assimilate anomalies into the existing journalistic paradigm. They persist to the end until the paradigm cannot be repaired.

Gitlin's rich account on how the U.S. media made and unmade the New Left of the 1960s is instructive. He writes,

> When political crises erupt in the real world, they call into question whether the hegemonic routines, left to themselves, can go on contributing to social stability. Now some of the opposition movement's claims about reality seem to be verified by what mainstream reporters and editors discover about the world. Then the hegemonic frame begins to shift.[65]

As Gitlin argues, the political crisis was not confined to a back-and-forth process between sealed-off elites; the elites experienced political crisis precisely because of the upswelling of opposition—both radical-militant and liberal-moderate—throughout the society.[66]

In a similar vein, Daniel Hallin observes that before the Tet Offensive, the American media had been a celebrant of the officially sanctioned policy on Vietnam. The media did not question the official war policy on Vietnam until after the issue moved from the "sphere of consensus" into the "sphere of legitimate controversy," meaning that the issue had become a focus of rancorous dissent in the Congress and the two-party politics.[67] This suggests that the media may experience a "paradigm breakdown," and hence cognitive shifts, when elite consensus collapses.

Gans discusses hypothetically the odds of journalistic paradigm shifts:

> If in a political crisis, a significant proportion of the audience moved to the left, it is conceivable that journalists would follow, both in their opinions and in the kinds of stories they judged to be important. Still, if a leftward swing damaged their own interests or the economic interests of their firms, it is also conceivable that they would not follow. On the other hand, if a large segment of the audience moved to the right, if a crisis spawned a widespread demand for totalitarian leadership in Washington, journalists would be under strong pressure to relinquish their belief in altruistic democracy.[68]

Theoretically, change in journalistic paradigms follows changes in the three determinants, as previously mentioned: distribution of power, the market condition, and press ideology. But for the moment of "paradigm breakdown" or "hegemonic crisis" to arrive often requires a major power restructuring in particular. Otherwise, paradigm change may not be as visible or drastic. Transition from media partisanship to professionalism in the United States closely paralleled the century-long evolution of the market and other social conditions.[69] But once a market is in place, media professionalism is assured, and any shifts in journalistic paradigms, however drastic, cannot be total. The paradigm reversion is only partial and, at times, uncertain. In Hong Kong, for example, even the most rigid partisan press has to compete in the marketplace for credibility and influence, if not for profits, because the audience has access to a plurality of paradigms. The market, it can be argued, acts as a partial corrective to the gravity of political force, and the press thus exhibits continuity and discontinuity in journalistic paradigms.

Concurring with Peter L. Berger and Thomas Luckmann, we believe that journalistic paradigms and their shifts are an outcome of the dialectic *interaction* between subjective perception and objective occurrences that form the basis for news.[70] Neither subjective perception nor objective facts can exist in a social vacuum. Occurrences must be perceived to make news. This perception or reality-construction process is mediated, triggered, and shaped by critical events. Such events as the Tet Offensive (in Vietnam) and the Sino-British Joint Declaration (in Hong Kong) expose the lack of agreement between the prevailing paradigm and empirical facts, thus forcing news workers to reconstruct reality. After the Tet Offensive, for example, the news started to present war demonstrators as responding to moral disorder caused by the president and his hawkish advisers.[71] And the Joint Declaration impinges on the Hong Kong press to acquiesce to political change (see Chapter 5), but the Tiananmen crackdown provided for a press revolt against Beijing, at least temporarily (see Chapter 7).

On occasion, certain events may unexpectedly heighten the severity of a situation so that reality is construed anew. For example, the dormant antinuclear movement in the United States was revitalized by media publicity of the Three Mile Island incident, even though the "scientific proof" on nuclear safety remained the same. Likewise, protests against establishing a nuclear power plant on the border between Hong Kong and China were hushed by the loud acclamation of the plant's economic values. But media publicity of the Chernobyl nuclear disaster in the faraway Soviet Union suddenly gave Hong Kong's antinuclear movement a new life (see Chapter 6).

PROCESSES OF JOURNALISTIC PARADIGM SHIFTS: COOPTATION, ACCOMMODATION, AND REGRESSION

Social formations—that is, reconstitution of the power structure and sociopolitical forces—engender journalistic paradigm shifts. From an organizational perspective, political transition generates environmental uncertainty. Both the power structure and the press have to develop strategic interorganizational relations to cope with, and to reduce, this uncertainty.[72] Furthermore, internal resources of the press are not capable of self-maintenance; the press must enter into transactions and relations with the new political structure in the changing environment for further resources and services. This means that, in order to consolidate their legitimacy, power centers have to coopt the press with the delivery of considerable inducements without imposing concomitant constraints. The press in turn has to accommodate this pressure by according the power centers with legitimation.

Cooptation

China is an unwelcome master in Hong Kong. Opinion poll results and press commentaries in Hong Kong unequivocally opposed China's takeover.[73] The Sino-British Joint Declaration was thrust upon the Hong Kong people against their will. Even if China may legally wield domination in Hong Kong, this power lacks legitimacy, or what Max Weber calls "the subjective *belief* in the validity of an order which constitutes the valid order itself."[74] Therefore, Xinhua has taken great pains to coopt the Hong Kong press in the hope of helping to attain the consent of the governed and the legitimacy of the new order. For Xinhua, neither laissez faire nor outright repression nor incorporation is a viable strategy (see Table 2–1).

Cooptation is defined as the process of bringing outsiders (usually resource-poorer) inside (usually resource-richer) so that the outsiders' views can be in line with those of the central authority. In a seminal study of the Tennessee Valley Authority (TVA), Philip Selznick defines cooptation as "the process of absorbing new elements into the leadership or policy determining structure of an organization as a means of averting threats to the organization's stability or existence."[75] The TVA, according to Selznick, was established to implement grass-roots participation that neutralized opposition of local farmers to federal decisions on the use of the land in the area. He further argued that formal cooptation would occur either when the organization's legitimacy is questioned by outside elements, or when there is an administrative need for establishing formal communication with outside groups.

Both of these conditions for formal cooptation seem to be in evidence in Hong Kong. The colonial regime is besieged with questions about its ability to govern effectively as a lame duck—a gap likely to widen as time draws close to British exit. The regime thus has to retain press loyalty or stem its possible defection to China's intensified cooptation. On the other hand, public distrust of Communist China runs deep in Hong Kong; without proper management, the political transition can be stormy. It is therefore essential for China to placate public opinion, deflate press criticisms, and even win over the hearts and minds of the people.

Formal cooptation, as Selznick points out, does not imply transfer of power. The colonial regime and Xinhua continue to be, in Selznick's words, "the focus of significant decision making" in this cooptative game.[76] Xinhua dispenses vast resources including political enticements, economic benefits, bestowal of prestige and symbolism (such as nationalism), as well as news information that is the life blood of the press. The more the press is dependent on the power centers for such resources, the more likely it will view them as being influential and align with them. Central actors appear even more powerful.

Accommodation

While Selznick regards cooptation as a strategy to avert opposition, the more recent literature treats cooptation as a strategy that may bear positive benefits to both the coopting and the coopted parties. Jeffrey Pfeffer and Phillip Salancik note, for example, that cooptation is "a strategy for accessing resources, exchanging information, developing interfirm commitments, and establishing legitimacy."[77]

Both the coopter (the power centers) and the cooptee (the press) in Hong Kong seem to profit from the exchange. While the power centers bolster their legitimacy by building a better communication with the press, the press procures resources from the power centers in return. We describe this process as accommodation, in which press organizations maximize profits and minimize risks by reckoning with legitimacy and authority of the focal organizations (the power centers) in society.

In some respects the press is more vulnerable to cooptative pressure than most business enterprises in Hong Kong. If the worst happens after 1997, business enterprises may find it easier to move out of Hong Kong than the press, which is constrained by cultural and linguistic barriers.

Harold Lasswell notes that the press has three primary social functions to perform: surveillance of the environment, correlation of parts with the social whole, as well as transmission of cultural heritage.[78] As Howard E. Aldrich argues in an organizational framework, when a social environment becomes more turbulent the information-processing function of the boundary-spanning role (in our case, the press) should become central to the society's ability to effectively gather, analyze, and act on relevant information.[79] This means that the press stands sentry over the uncertain political environment on behalf of the apprehensive Hong Kong public by monitoring the change and defining its meaning. But the press depends on the power structure for news and results in accommodation.

The consequences of cooptation and accommodation vary widely with press ideology. Newspapers of diverse ideological commitment are bound to have different interests (or, in organizational terms, "resource dependencies") and establish various interorganizational relations with the power centers. Interorganizational relations further necessitate intraorganizational changes. With detailed elaborations reserved for the following chapters, a brief overview seems in order:

- Each newspaper seeks to strike an optimal balance between its political stakes and economic advantages. The mainstream press plays duplicity with the colonial regime and Xinhua (if possible, with Taiwan also) for maximum gains. The partisan press must assimilate political pressure in such a way as to perform its political function credibly yet without being completely marginalized out of the market existence. Examples include the ultrarightist press's moderated anti-Communist policy and the ultraleftist press's reduced anti-colonial overtone.
- Attempts have been made, with mixed results, by various press organizations to reorganize ownership structure through internationalization, diversification, and localization as part of the preemptive effort to forestall potential environmental turbulence.
- Press organizations have established a China beat, restructured internal routinization of what Tuchman calls "news net" in order to absorb external pressure.[80]
- Prominent media leaders have been coopted by Xinhua into the Hong Kong Basic Law Drafting Committee and its Consultative Committee. They have forged cordial personal and institutional ties with Xinhua and thus are more predisposed to empathize with its perspectives.

The amount of journalistic paradigm restructuring is determined by the amount of sociopolitical change. Returning to Kuhn, paradigm shift in a scientific revolution concentrates on radical shifts, which entail abandoning an old paradigm and adopting a new paradigm simultaneously. The new paradigm puts the old data in a new light by changing some of the field's most elementary theorems.[81] In the social world, if revolutions occur, journalistic paradigms may also be restructured in a dramatic fashion. As a result, the media yield their self-identity and autonomy in compliance—often out of fear rather than will—with the goals and practice of the authority structure. Examples can be drawn from the Iranian revolution and the Chinese Cultural Revolution that produced mass purges among journalists and large-scale change in media content.[82]

But in most cases paradigm shift in the social world is not radically revolutionary, but more likely to be an evolutionary growth that redefines reality incrementally. Hong Kong's political transition is characterized by a gradually phased-in process and provides for a calculated accommodation in journalistic paradigm shifts. The press tried to "fix" a small part of the paradigm, that is, to "normalize" or assimilate anomalies into the existing news framework.[83] These piecemeal, ad hoc shifts are made to save the paradigmatic structure and the core media assumptions about reality. But when small shifts cannot cope with huge external changes, the press then reaches a "paradigm breakdown" or a "hegemonic crisis." Under such circumstances, the press must, voluntarily or involuntarily, make major shifts in journalistic paradigms to acquiesce to the reconstituted power relations and social formations.[84]

Regression

Under certain conditions, paradigm shifts may also result in regression, in which the press settles its journalistic paradigm from the extremes to the ordinary course. Once a journalistic paradigm is redefined, it regains relative durability. Even if the press may on occasion exhibit significant departure from this terrain of redefined paradigm, the change is expected to be temporary and to be brought back within its boundary. In general, the extent and duration of this paradigm regression depend on the extent to which sociopolitical change is reversed, the firmness of control by the power structure, and the severity of the perceived threat of such change to the system as a whole or to the press in particular. If the power structure has the authority, legitimacy, or resources to reverse sociopolitical change, then paradigm regression of the press may not occur or, even if it does occur, may only be minor and brief. But if the power structure is incapable of conflict management, imposing changes against the will of the public and the press may run the risk of illegitimation.

In the case of Hong Kong, the press has oscillated between different positions in responding to occurrence of events, but always within the trajectory of the established perimeter. The opposition by the Hong Kong press to China's construction of a nuclear power plant on the border did not challenge China's sovereignty (see Chapter 6). Likewise, the outrage expressed by the Hong Kong press toward Beijing's brutal suppression of a democracy movement was framed in terms of China's failure to uphold its "one country, two systems" policy, but the press took no aim at the policy itself (see Chapter 7).

In conclusion, the politics and boundaries in Hong Kong are already enclosed by the political transition, but within these boundaries the press may fluctuate in its position. In other words, the general direction of journalistic paradigms have been determined, yet their content is not predetermined. This indeterminacy is particularly acute because the "one country, two systems" scheme is an unprecedented experimentation. This point will be made clear in the case studies that follow.

Chapter 3

Coopting the Press

China will be Hong Kong's master in the not too distant future. Britain's influence, though still vast, has sharply diminished and is continuing to slide downhill. The days of British colonial rule are numbered. The Sino-British Joint Declaration, thrust upon the Hong Kong people as a *fait accompli,* has set off a radical redistribution of social power, profoundly affecting the press's relationships with the political power centers. To wit, both the Chinese and the British colonial administration are confronted with a legitimacy crisis in Hong Kong: both are lacking subjective affirmation of *rightness* attached to their rule. The colonial regime is seen as a lame duck, whereas China's tumultuous record is a source of continuing unease for the Hong Kong people.

The press plays a vital role in the political transition by creating a legitimacy-enhancing climate of opinion. The Chinese and the colonial regime have been in a tug-of-war, each seeking to coopt the Hong Kong press: while China yearns to cultivate or repair press ties, the colonial regime strives to retain press loyalty. Within China itself, the state makes no apology for subjugating its press as a mere mouthpiece. And before recent democratic movements in Taiwan and South Korea, the states there used to incorporate the press, which was either handsomely rewarded if it complied to authority or otherwise severely punished. If, however, the powers in Hong Kong tried to mobilize coercive apparatuses to get their way with the press, their already low legitimacy would inevitably deteriorate even further. Hence, they have tried to coopt the Hong Kong press by providing "carrots" rather than applying "sticks."

Through cooptation, the power centers entice the press into an existing sociopolitical framework, a system of power, and a vision of the world, in an attempt to defuse the press's grievances and gain its support. The power centers may impose their superior (political, economic, or moral) authority and resources on the press, which may consent to the defined situation out of self-interest. Furthermore, since politics is always a give-and-take process and since cooptation is a game of providing baits to preserve advantages, the power centers are expected to concede part of their power and share it with the press. But by preserving a lion's share of the social power or resources, the power centers can continue to dictate the terms of exchange and even use power to spawn more power. Finally, the power centers may structure a specific worldview and define the rules of the game to convince the press that this is the way it has always been or the way it ought to be. Submission to authority is then taken for granted and unrecognized—a process akin to what Galbraith terms a "conditioned belief" or what Gramsci calls "hegemony." [1]

In this chapter, we shall begin by analyzing the colonial regime's cooptation: the bases of power; the practices, processes, and instruments of cooptation; as well as the effects of hegemony. Particular attention will be paid to the role of the Government Information Services (GIS). We shall then proceed to examine China's cooptation, focusing on the role of Xinhua News Agency, which is China's command post in Hong Kong and a new power center countering the colonial regime. It should be noted that both regimes bear a striking resemblance to each other in terms of their intent and strategy for consolidating elite support and coopting press sympathy in Hong Kong. At one level, both regimes are companions trying to weave a stable fabric that will enable the power transition to proceed smoothly; at another level they are opponents, each vying to gain a more solid foothold than the other.

COLONIAL COOPTATION AND HEGEMONY

Synarchial Rule

Through consent and coercion, the colonial regime was in virtual control of Hong Kong's political life until mid-1984. Attempts are still constantly made to instill in the press an ideology that values stability over change and stresses economic prosperity over political democracy. Although the Hong Kong press is often scathingly critical of mainland China and Taiwan, the legitimacy of British rule is beyond challenge. Press ordinances are exceedingly arbitrary and strict. To defuse political challenge, however, the colonial regime is painfully sensitive and responsive to public grievances, especially those that can be met through technical and administrative means.

As an alien authority, the colonial regime is extremely paranoid about threats to power equilibrium and inimical to parliamentary debate. Former Governor Sir Murray MacLehose said in 1975:

> It is indeed not the tradition that Hong Kong should be governed by debate, or that there should be debate and opposition for debate and opposition's sake. Denied as we are, for reasons well understood here, the pos-

sibility of an elected legislature, our tradition is rather to govern by consensus. We attempt to achieve this by many different ways. Representations to UMELCO [Executive and Legislative Councils], the wide use of advisory committees, green papers, the perception of City District Officers and their ever widening contact with mutual aid committees and area committees and of course the Kaifongs [neighborhood associations]. The role of the press and media is vital. So too is a willingness on the part of the Government to give time for considered reactions to new proposals to develop.[2]

This remark is indicative of the practice of *synarchial rule,* an effort to build consensus within a joint administration shared by the British rulers and a small circle of wealthy Chinese. This political arrangement is aimed to achieve a form of elite integration and to prevent the development of counter-elites.[3] For this reason, the colonial government aptly plays the politics of entitlement to incorporate social elites into the government, thus giving them an illusory aura of power, honor, and participation.

The Executive Council and the Legislative Council—nominally the highest ruling bodies—are not two houses of the Congress empowered to check and balance the governor; they are at best the governor's advisory bodies. All members of the Executive Council, plus 20 of the 57 members of the Legislative Council, are appointed by the governor; most of the remaining Legislative Councillors, though elected, are close to the government in their thinking. Nineteen district boards were established in 1982 under the District Administration to serve as statutory bodies to provide a forum for public consultation and participation.[4] Each board is composed of appointed members and elected members, in the ratio of about 1 to 2. Through these linkages, opinion at the local level can be mobilized to legitimize government policies.

Aside from these formal structures, the colonial government also invites elites to serve on numerous and diffuse advisory boards. Their opinions do not, however, have legally binding power on the government. Twice a year, about 180 distinguished citizens are awarded to the coveted Queen's New Year and Birthday honors lists.[5] All this entitlement derives honor from the authority of the colonial administration and serves to secure elite solidarity. With the colonial regime fading out of the scene, the significance of British-conferred entitlements will diminish, although China is expected to play more of the same game.[6]

Typically, when there is a dispute with China over an important issue, the Hong Kong government plays the "public opinion card" by activating the political linkages with the Executive and Legislative Councils and the District Administration, coupled with the publicity campaigns, to create a climate of opinion overwhelmingly pro-government. In some cases, the governor himself takes time to speak to a joint closed-door session of the Executive and Legislative Councils and stress the importance of social support for a policy. Members of both councils then rush to pledge their allegiance. The official line is loudly echoed at district board meetings. The seeming unanimity of support from these leaders is then communicated to the press.

Controlling Government News Flow

Where the press is concerned, the colonial regime exercises cooptative efforts primarily via its vital information arm, the Government Information Services. Riots erupted in 1966 and 1967, escalating from a minor conflict to embroilment in, as a spinoff of, the Chinese Cultural Revolution. The security of Hong Kong was endangered. While the police were trying to maintain law and order, the entire government information apparatus was suddenly faced with the arduous task of combating Communist propaganda and widespread rumors. As normalcy returned, a special commission appointed by the governor surmised that the communication gap between the government posed a source of danger. To ease the crisis of governing, the commission urged that the government develop "a greater consciousness of the need for public relations at all levels," with special attention paid to mass media.[7] As a result, the GIS was reorganized and broadly expanded to meet the situation.

The colonial regime cajoles, rewards, and sometimes punishes the press. Some tactics are blatant, others more subtle. Prominent publishers of influential pro-British papers are awarded with British medals of honor. A handful of mainstream papers are certified as having the power to carry legally valid advertisements while other papers are denied the same treatment. While coopting the mainstream press, the regime keeps the ultraleftist and the ultrarightist press, along with other activists, at bay and under surveillance.[8] The British Official Secrets Act of 1911, though modified by the British Parliament in 1971, remains in effect in Hong Kong, making press coverage of unauthorized official information illegal. Tough press ordinances, though seldom invoked, are at the government's disposal.

Barring unusual circumstances, however, the Hong Kong government need not coerce people or the press into accepting its views or recognizing its legitimacy. The most effective social control occurs when the fact of submission to authority or power is taken for granted or is unrecognized.[9] The perceptions and preferences of people and groups are shaped in such a way as to make them accept their role in the existing order.[10] This is a process of hegemonic cooptation. Borrowing the concept from Gramsci, Gitlin defines "hegemony" as:

> [a] ruling class's (or alliances') domination of subordinate classes and groups through the elaboration and presentation of ideology (ideas and assumptions) into their common sense and everyday practice; it is the systematic (but not necessarily or even usually deliberate) engineering of mass consent to the established order.[11]

In the case of Hong Kong, substitute "the colonial regime" for the "ruling class," and "the Chinese people" for "the subordinate classes and groups," then you have before you a vivid case of hegemony. This hegemonic process perpetuates the status quo by transforming the dominant ideology into everyday taken-for-granted practices. Alternative or oppositional ideologies are simultaneously absorbed and marginalized.[12]

The GIS performs this hegemonic function in relation to the press. The GIS comprises three interlinking divisions staffed by a huge corp of handsomely paid information officers.[13] The news division is in charge of diffusing government information to the press and answering public inquiries. The *Daily News Bulletin* furnished to the press at no cost has enabled the GIS to acquire a de facto monopoly on the flow of government information. The publicity division coordinates government campaign efforts, whereas the public relations division monitors press opinion. All 24 government departments are staffed with information units under the supervision of the GIS with a clear mission to deal with the press.

It comes within the purview of government department heads to release or withhold certain information. Until the commencement of the Sino-British negotiations the department heads had allegedly been arrogant and bureaucratic.[14] Government officials were advised to "say nothing" to reporters at cocktail parties or during business hours, and were discouraged from answering press inquiries without GIS participation. To interview an official, a journalist had to contact the GIS and submit questions in advance. The official could refuse to answer those questions not previously submitted on the original list. But the GIS would discuss major events with editors on regular Wednesday conferences to solicit their cooperation.[15]

On the other hand, the GIS is quick to respond to letters to the editor in the newspapers that, for the most part, make minor complaints about government services, especially in the areas of police, housing, transport, and education. In fact, government departments are requested to answer such letters within three weeks of their publication. These citizen complaints can be promptly tackled with appropriate attention and thus avail the GIS of the opportunity to score propaganda points. All news media are hooked up to the GIS wire which constantly feeds through the telex machine information ranging from hourly weather bulletins and traffic information to major government policy statements and details of official proposals. This service keeps the editors up to date about current or prescheduled events, aiding them to reserve news space or allocate appropriate staff. The identical news copy may be telexed several times a day to ensure that it is attended to. At the day's end, the GIS again deposits a full copy of the release in each of the mail boxes reserved for news clients at the GIS headquarters.

Put the Government's Best Foot Forward

The GIS therefore plays the double role of news producer and news distributor, or, in the words of a GIS director, it is the government's "news, advertising, public relations and printing agencies."[16] Monopolizing the flow of government information, the GIS distributes to the press ready-for-print news releases that are written by veteran journalists-turned-staff versed in the profession's language and knowledgeable about media needs. Most Hong Kong papers are so understaffed that they often find it convenient to duplicate GIS copies to fill space. Former GIS director Peter Tsao boasted: "On any given day, about half of the local spot news stories appearing on Hong Kong newspapers were either releases from the GIS or assisted by the GIS."[17] *Wah Kiu Yat Pao,* for example, reserves half a page daily to print GIS releases disguised as news.

All newspapers regardless of ideology have to "touch base" with GIS teleprinters regularly, if just to ensure that they do not miss significant stories. Worse yet, the Hong Kong Chinese papers seldom byline their stories lest a star system emerge and drive up journalists' salaries. GIS releases are often disguised as *Ben-bao-zhuan-xun* ("information exclusive to this paper"). GIS staff were also found to have written articles under pseudonyms for various leisure magazines or weekly supplements to hail government achievements or defend its policies.[18]

GIS press releases tend to follow the "objective news" format, unlike Xinhua's explicit commentaries and outright propaganda. A GIS official defends this practice:

> The GIS integrates government information and provides opinions, but it does not censor news. It is up to the media themselves to decide whether

to use the information we provide; the government does not centralize the control of information distribution.[19]

But his "objective" news is not value-free. It is predicated on explicit or implicit support for government policies: the bulk of GIS items focus on the smooth running of the administrative machinery. They are, in a nutshell, government bulletins.[20] Through careful selection of topics and information, the GIS sets the agenda for the press and defines the political situation from an official vantage point. Monopoly of government information allows the GIS to set limits on what the press can publish, exert pressure on what it should publish, and exclude an alternative range of news.[21]

If the main purpose of government public relations is "to put the government's best foot forward," then it is the GIS's job to provide positive government information, some of which borders on window dressing, even white washing. The GIS claims that an "oversupply of negative news" serves no useful purpose and erodes public confidence in the government.[22] Cheung Man-Yee, former GIS director, finds no fault with the GIS's boosterism role because GIS staff are "official reporters" who cover news inside the government.[23] She confessed:

> Yes, we report only the good news, not the bad. All that the government announces are things related to construction, government policy, and things that promote Hong Kong's development. Naturally, we should all look to the positive. There is no reason to publicize negative information or to suggest that the government is doing nothing.[24]

Briefing as News Control

The GIS frequently uses press briefings as a channel to release information to the public. These briefings are held at various levels. On the lowest level, heads of government departments or GIS officials host regular briefing sessions to chief reporters (assignment desk or city desk editors) and even frontline beat reporters. The GIS is not particularly discriminatory about who should be invited to these regular briefings. Occasionally reporters may request interviews with a specific official. If several reporters make the same request, the GIS will organize a briefing session or a press conference for them.

A somewhat more restrictive kind of briefing is only open to prominent journalists from a few influential media organizations, to whom the government provides background on specific issues. In some cases, the briefing is on a one-to-one basis. A number of criteria govern who should be invited, such as the subject matter to be discussed, the status of the news organizations, the seniority of the journalists, and their rapport with GIS personnel.

Even more restrictive is the "deep background briefing." The top journalists working for the most influential media who appear at these briefings describe them as "wind-blowing sessions." Through briefings senior government officials, sometimes including the governor, champion their lines of policy thought, especially on those involving Sino-British relations. The GIS never bothers to explain why some reporters get invited and others are excluded, creating a suspense among journalists as to how well they fare with the government. The ground rules strictly prohibit the press from quoting government officials directly; rather, reports are attributed vaguely to "a high ranking government official," "a reliable source close to the government," "an informed source," or simply "a source." According to a GIS director, very few journalists break this rule because they do not want to risk not being invited the next time. The GIS claims that such anonymity allows officials to be more candid and more inclined to criticize opponents of government policies.[25] But the occasion also enables the government to show favoritism to some journalists, to defend and trial-balloon its policies, and to subtly guide press orientations. Those criticized by officials on an off-the-record basis in these sessions are at a loss as to how to respond openly. Such briefings are the GIS's "trump cards," serving as mouthpieces for government officials who want to influence public opinion.

Two examples illustrate how this works. First, in 1979, the government decided to abrogate its "touch-base" policy, which had allowed illegal Chinese immigrants to remain in the colony once they crossed the boundary street that divided Kowloon (British concession) and the New Territories (on lease to Britain). Before it was made official, *Ming Pao* and others had come out to advocate and promote this idea, thus helping to legitimize policy change. For another example, several hours before the British scheme to grant the right of abode to selected Hong Kong people was announced in London (in late 1989), the Hong Kong governor had a "deep background briefing" with a few selected journalists. The governor used this occasion to emphasize that this scheme, limited as it might be, was the fruit of the Hong Kong government's persistent efforts in London and thus warranted press support.

The GIS prefers briefings to press conferences. Press conferences can sometimes be confrontational, and officials may make some statements that cannot be easily retracted later. Protected by anonymity or confidentiality, however, officials can get off the hook quickly in briefing situations and be absolved of any responsibility for the information reported. GIS briefings also serve to release sensitive information slowly and unofficially in order to divert the heat of public reaction. The GIS regards press briefing as "especially useful for focusing attention on lesser known aspects of the administration and for publicizing activities of which the media might not be fully aware."[26] At times the Hong Kong government also conveys certain intent and messages to China through press briefings, thus helping to manage conflicts that may arise. For example, facing a huge influx of Vietnamese refugees who entered into Hong Kong via China, the head of the Hong Kong government's security branch held a press briefing to hint that China should be responsible for helping stop the influx. After the June 4, 1989, massacre in Beijing, the chief secretary called a briefing to explain the Hong Kong government's orientation toward China.

The GIS does not have to ask the press for favorable coverage. The GIS just "feeds" the press information and hopes for the best, as most journalists do not fail to promote the official line. The most that journalists generally do is balance the story with reactions from other parties, but the government view always precedes other sources. Most journalists have no desire to burn their bridge to the GIS; many have developed a trustful bond with GIS officials; some of them, particularly the older colleagues, even aspire to be recruited by the GIS for better pay.

The GIS and the Political Transition

At the onset of the Sino-British negotiations the GIS was upgraded to shoulder additional responsibilities necessitated by the circumstances. Peter Tsao became the highest ranking official to head the GIS, and he moved swiftly to reorganize and streamline the agency in what some journalists referred to as part of the government's "decorrosion" or "revitalization" program.[27] Advocating that the GIS must launch "public relations offensives" to replace its typical defensive posture, Tsao elevated the status of the public relations unit by separating it from the news unit.[28] Urging high-ranking officials to come forward and explain their policies face to face with the media, Tsao ordered all government public relations units to answer press inquiries promptly. In an apparent effort to counter Xinhua's intensified united front campaign when the negotiations reached a deadlock in 1983, for example, the usually taciturn Hong Kong officials were suddenly seen eagerly mingling with journalists, even baiting media owners with medals of honor.[29]

Incapacitated by Britain's failure to gain more ground in the negotiations, the GIS could do little more than restore government credibility and repair public confidence.[30] Home Secretary David Acker-Jones vehemently denied that the colonial regime was a lame duck; Xinhua concurred by stating that the British would remain in charge until 1997.[31] But despite these disclaimers, Xinhua is undoubtedly viewed as an "underground government" or a "shadow government."[32] Excruciatingly aware of the Hong Kong government's image problems, a GIS director privately remarked: *

> What points can you score by arguing that the Government is not a lame-duck? The only way out is for us to show that the government is active. The government plans to build a new airport, to redevelop the metropolitan area and to construct other infrastructures . . .[33]

Another official put it even more bluntly:

> Politically, we are passive. No matter what we do, there is no way to change the fact that power will be transferred in 1997. It is difficult for us to take a persistently resolute stance. If we do that, we shall first hear Li Hou rebuking us, followed by [Premier] Li Peng, and finally by Deng Xiaoping himself. How can we stand the pressure?[34]

In each of the successive conflicts with China—whether Hong Kong should be returned to China, whether to introduce direct election to the Legislative Council in 1988, and so forth—the Hong Kong government mustered popular support, but China ended up the winner. And the Hong Kong government and the GIS have had to launch frustrating operations to induce the public to forget the past and look forward to the future.

To illustrate, the press had for the most part toed the GIS line throughout the Sino-British negotiations, only to discover that the "wishful" promises made by the British were broken one by one. The British could neither get the lease of Hong Kong extended nor bargain for the authority to administer Hong Kong. Feeling betrayed, the press swore not to embrace the GIS's words uncritically. Once reversion of the colony to China was settled, however, the press could only bolster the British plan to introduce major direct elections to the Legislative Council in 1988. Although democracy has eluded the colony for a century and a half, the British now suddenly saw wisdom in direct elections

---

* This and the majority of other interviews cited in the notes were conducted from January to April 1986 (see Appendix I), but they have been updated from time to time. The promise of anonymity in many cases prevents us from disclosing specific names or locations.

as a way to insulate Hong Kong from Beijing's explicit interference in
the future. This did not, of course, escape China's attention. In what
amounted to another slap in the face of the press, Britain, under China's
threat, has backed off from its original commitment in terms of the
speed and the scope of the direct elections.[35] The Basic Law Drafting
Committee rejected all the proposals (including one made by Hong Kong's
Executive and Legislative Councils) and released a finalized version of
Hong Kong's political model in February 1990, which was much more
restrictive than expected and allowed for very limited direct elections
beginning in 1991. At this point, the Hong Kong government could do
nothing but urge the people to reconcile conflicts with China and to
make the maiden direct election a success.

Overall, a major publicity problem facing the government during
the political transition is that the issues are getting more complex, more
political, and more international in nature. The government is also
growing in size. Therefore the government has doubled its publicity efforts to map out strategies, deciding on what, when, and how the policies are to be made public. In the past, a deputy secretary in the secretariat was responsible for coordinating government agencies; more
recently, an "information coordinator" post was created in 1989 under
the direct control of the chief secretariat. The duties of the information
coordinator, who can attend Executive Council meetings, include taking
charge of information policies, coordinating the government's publicity
overseas, and assessing public reactions to government policies. While
the GIS director has some input in making these publicity strategies, the
GIS remains basically an executive apparatus.

The GIS has tried to shift public attention away from the high drama
of Hong Kong's future to focus on the government's "openness" and
achievements. As a GIS director confessed, the citizens are now "more
prone to examine with a critical eye the working of the administration
and comment—either individually or through civic organizations, privately or through the media—on their findings." The Hong Kong government is thus held more accountable now than ever before and is
"under greater pressure to explain its policies and defend its decisions."[36] The GIS has therefore gone through a period of rapid expan-
sion, growth, and reorganization.

GIS services have been improved by technologically automating the
teleprinters and facsimile system linked to the media. The GIS staff give
high-ranking officials mock interviews to prepare them for regular
meetings with the press.[37] The formal, stern, arrogant, and bureau-
cratic-sounding style that once pervaded government correspondence has
given way to a more affable, colloquial style.[38] To sensitize senior offi-

cials, the GIS prepares reports of public opinion with more speed and more accuracy than ever before.[39] An emphasis is also placed on the GIS staff to develop "an instinct for the likely reaction to proposed policy changes still in the pipeline."[40] Even so, press reliance on the GIS seems to have lessened. Rather than reprinting GIS copies in total, the press either reproduces a portion, rewrites them, or covers the issues on its own. The GIS releases serve to "whet the appetite" of journalists who may follow up on the leads.

The GIS cannot communicate with Xinhua directly without the mediation of the political branch of the Hong Kong government, but more interaction between them is expected in the years ahead.[41] The twin primary tasks of the GIS before 1997 are to communicate with the Hong Kong people and to boost Hong Kong's image abroad so foreign investments will not ebb.[42] The GIS overseas public relations subdivision produces materials to present Hong Kong's "irrepressible economic performance" as a major world trading, manufacturing, and financial center.[43] The GIS overseas divisions work with Hong Kong offices in London, Brussels, New York, and San Francisco to plan public relations strategies, cultivate media relations, and organize campaigns.

Until 1997, the British will still hold the waning administrative and legislative machinery to effect cooptation. The Hong Kong government is toiling all the more arduously to retain press loyalty; officials have repeatedly urged the media not to censor themselves when criticizing China.[44] But, in actuality, the GIS is akin to other government departments plagued by "brain drain" and low morale. Taking a dim view of the civil service, many GIS workers have emigrated or left for the private sector. The Association of Government Information Officers wrote to Chief Secretary Sir David Ford in early 1990, pressing the government to treat the GIS as a "sensitive" department so that GIS workers could be qualified for the right of abode in the United Kingdom after 1997. GIS staffers privy to information are fearful of persecution by China after 1997.[45] No matter whether this fear is justified, the GIS will undoubtedly suffer from continuing demoralization as 1997 approaches.

XINHUA: COOPTATION THROUGH THE "UNITED FRONT"

Because Great Britain has refused to let the People's Republic set up an official mission in Hong Kong, the Hong Kong branch of Xinhua has acted as China's envoy there since 1949. Despite its vast influence as a news agency and a political institution, Xinhua kept a low profile until 1984. Having now emerged as Hong Kong's second power center and a "shadow government" vis-à-vis the colonial regime, Xinhua has taken charge of drafting the Basic Law as part of the transition into 1997.

Xinhua's cooptative web, woven in accordance with China's "United Front" policy, aims at the present stage to uphold its "one country, two systems" policy. Mao Zedong Thought dictates that primary contradictions be tackled by rallying the support of intermediate forces and temporarily shelving secondary targets. Once a contradiction is overcome, a new United Front then moves on to confront the next target.[46] Mao credited the Communist Party, the Liberation Army, and the United Front with being the three major *baos* (treasures) that led to his seizure of power and defeat of the KMT. This ideology also partly explains the underlying causes of China's relentless movements, purges, and external conflicts in the past forty years.[47]

Under the "open and reform" policy of the 1980s, China intensified the United Front drive in lieu of issuing harsh military threats against Taiwan. United Front units have been installed in the state, party, and military structures directed specifically at Taiwan, Hong Kong, and overseas Chinese communities. With national unification now defined as a top-priority contradiction, the drama of Xinhua's cooptation has been most vigorously played out in the open stage of a transitional Hong Kong. The press has been a conspicuous target of this cooptation due to its ability to manufacture consent about China's legitimacy in Hong Kong. Figure 3–1 depicts an organizational chart of Xinhua, in which both the United Front work and the Taiwan-related work figure very prominently in the leadership groups.

Xu Jiatun, the highest-ranking Chinese official to direct Xinhua's Hong Kong branch, arrived in July 1983 for the start of Sino-British negotiations. Xu was formerly party secretary of Jiangsu Province and a member of the Chinese Communist Party Central Committee, said to enjoy strong political backing of Deng Xiaoping and two successive Party general secretaries, Hu Yaobang and Zhao Ziyang, and hence able to bypass the State Council.[48] Xu's status imparted Xinhua with the elevated authority required to accomplish more effective cooptation.

Within days of his arrival in Hong Kong, Xu inspected *Ta Kung Pao* and *Wen Wei Pao*, two Communist organs, and visited China-controlled financial, commercial, and educational institutions.[49] Trying to shed his predecessors' secretive image, Xu actively mingled at banquets, sport events, concerts, and theatrical performances and received people from various walks of life. He hosted frequent banquets for social and opinion leaders, including anti-Communist writers and journalists, at

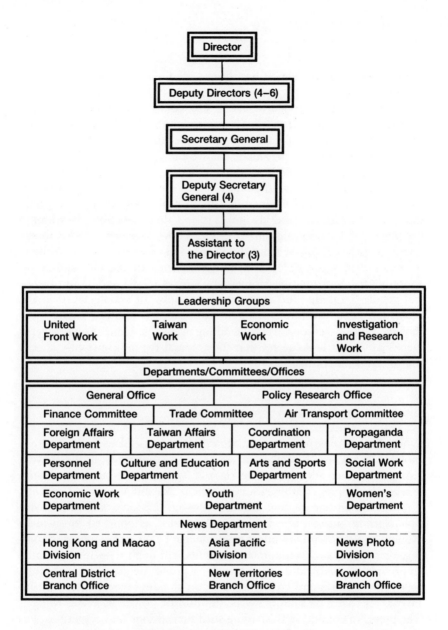

```
                    ┌─────────────┐
                    │  Director   │
                    └─────────────┘
                           │
              ┌────────────────────────┐
              │ Deputy Directors (4–6) │
              └────────────────────────┘
                           │
                ┌────────────────────┐
                │ Secretary General  │
                └────────────────────┘
                           │
                ┌────────────────────┐
                │ Deputy Secretary   │
                │ General (4)        │
                └────────────────────┘
                           │
                ┌────────────────────┐
                │ Assistant to       │
                │ the Director (3)   │
                └────────────────────┘
```

Leadership Groups			
United Front Work	Taiwan Work	Economic Work	Investigation and Research Work

Departments/Committees/Offices			

General Office		Policy Research Office	
Finance Committee	Trade Committee		Air Transport Committee
Foreign Affairs Department	Taiwan Affairs Department	Coordination Department	Propaganda Department
Personnel Department	Culture and Education Department	Arts and Sports Department	Social Work Department
Economic Work Department	Youth Department		Women's Department

News Department		
Hong Kong and Macao Division	Asia Pacific Division	News Photo Division
Central District Branch Office	New Territories Branch Office	Kowloon Branch Office

FIGURE 3-1 The organizational chart of Xinhua News Agency in Hong Kong. The organization of Xinhua corresponds to the bureaucracy of the Hong Kong and Macao Work Committee of the Chinese Communist Party, of which Xinhua's director is the head. Data adapted from *Contemporary Weekly*, 16 December 1989, p. 19; and John P. Burns, "The Structure of Communist Party Control in Kong Kong," *Asian Survey*, 30, 8 (1990), p. 754, Table 1.

Xinhua headquarters which had been "off limits" to outsiders before his arrival.[50]

Xinhua was expanded in 1985, now comprising elaborate departments, some of which were closely patterned after the Hong Kong Government structure (see Figure 3–1): foreign affairs, Taiwan affairs, coordination, propaganda, personnel, culture and education, arts and sports, social work, general administration, policy research, and personnel, in addition to three district offices and three committees. To avoid political sensitivity, Xinhua renamed its United Front Department the Coordination Department and assigned it the dual function of winning friendship and coalescing support. The News Department distributes news releases with input from the Propaganda Department and others. Xinhua's Propaganda Department corresponds to the GIS and is responsible for coordinating Hong Kong's news media and analyzing social trends.[51] Of the 500 staff members, only 30 people work in the news department while the rest are assigned to political tasks.[52] Although Xinhua refrains from meddling with the Hong Kong government's affairs, it is no secret that the colonial regime constantly checks things out with Xinhua.

Xinhua's Power Resources

While Xinhua has not attained what Anthony Giddens calls the "authorization power" to make citizens obey its commands, it does have a vast power over allocating tangible and intangible resources.[53] Firstly, it rewards the press with news, economic perks and advertising benefits, political appointments, and access to powerful people and status symbols (such as junkets and banquets). Secondly, as opposed to rewards, Xinhua could potentially inflict punishments by withdrawing, withholding, or denying such support and benefits, although it so far has opted to provide rewards rather than to deliver punishments. Thirdly, Xinhua sets news agendas and creates an opinion climate favorable (or less unfavorable) to China's ultimate assumption of power in Hong Kong.[54] The press, so conducive to shaping such perceptions and cognitions, has turned from its original opposition to China's "one country, two systems" policy to urge that the policy be faithfully executed.

Xu's term coincided with China's era of reform and openness, and he was intent on coopting rather than alienating the bourgeois classes in Hong Kong—even at the expense of the working classes. He expanded the United Front work by skillfully manipulating the strategy of simultaneously unifying and struggling with opposing forces. In an interview Xu was quoted in 1988, when China's political liberalization was at its maximum, as saying,

> During the past movements there were people who departed [from China] for Hong Kong. These people lack trust in the Communist Party, which is understandable. . . . We used to propose to arrive at similarities while preserving differences, which tended to be understood as arriving at big similarities and preserving small differences. Now we propose to arrive at big similarities while preserving big differences. To arrive at big similarities is to love China and love Hong Kong. To preserve big differences is to allow continued criticism of the Chinese Communist Party and socialism. . . . The principle I follow in Hong Kong is not to take a defensive posture toward criticisms that various circles level at our work on the mainland.[55]

Xu elevated the politics of cooptation to an artistic form. Relying on Xinhua to produce news, the media have securely established the "China beat" since 1985: News that was once buried on the less weighty "spot news" page now dominates the most significant "political news" page. Competitive pressure makes the media susceptible to manipulation by news sources. It is no secret that Xinhua has favored certain newspapers with scoops, exclusive interviews, and purposeful leaks in order to maximize its cooptative effect.[56] Access to Xinhua has become a symbol of status, as one writer described:

> The situation in Hong Kong has changed today. It is not merely a fashion to form ties with the leftists, especially with Xinhua, but it is one of the ways that the upper society can boast its social status.[57]

Xinhua has an important say in deciding with whom China trades. China's vast and complex networks of financial, economic, and cultural interests in Hong Kong fall under the Xinhua director's jurisdiction as head of the CCP's Hong Kong and Macao Work Committee. The director, in this Party capacity, is held ultimately responsible for coordinating and supervising the following Chinese interlocking interests and organizations:

- 265 branches of the 23 PRC-based banks (including the largest, Bank of China, Hong Kong Branch), which have a combined asset of approximately US$15 billion (or 7.5% of the total asset of the Hong Kong banking industry) and a combined deposit of approximately US$10 billion (or 15% of Hong Kong's total);
- The Hua Ren Group, which has tripled its trade volume from 1977 to approximately US$1 billion in 1985;

- 50 corporations;
- 90 leftist unions, with a total of 200,000 members, or 54% of Hong Kong's union members;
- in addition, there are leftist motion picture and book companies, schools, department stores, and investment companies—all under the command of Xinhua;
- Xinhua also controls the budget, personnel, and content of the Communist press in Hong Kong.[58]

Due to China's open-door policy, these interests have prominently advertised trade exhibitions, joint ventures, and products in the non-Communist press. Some publications have reportedly secured more ads despite (perhaps because of) their criticisms of China. Xinhua could potentially siphon off sizeable advertising income from them. Xu Jiatun preferred cooptation to coercion, unlike his predecessor who dealt an almost fatal blow in 1981 to several eminent leftist-leaning political magazines deemed to have gone too far astray from the approved line.[59] More importantly, Xu Jiatun was willing to reach out to—and to mend differences with—opponents and critics. To please Xinhua, a real-estate tycoon withdrew advertising from the *Hong Kong Economic Journal* because it continued to disparage China. But Xu did not encourage leftist concerns to follow suit and their ads continued to be prominently displayed on the pages of the *Journal*. Xu then invited Lam Shan-muk, the *Journal*'s publisher, to a banquet for a personal talk. Lam afterwards expressed respect for Xu as a person, if not for China's policy, and Mrs. Lam later accepted Xu's invitation to observe the People's Republic National Day in Beijing.[60] Similar examples have been frequently cited.

Reputation-enhancing inducements are to writers what economic profits are to the business community. For example, the Beijing-based China Friendship Publishing Company printed the collected works of overseas Chinese writers with the royalties, though meager, paid in foreign currencies. One writer who had been extremely critical of Beijing remarked, "That company promises to print 35,000 copies of my work. I've never had that many readers in my life!"[61]

The Politics of Entitlement

Since 1949 China has chosen delegates ostensibly to represent Hong Kong at the National People's Congress (NPC), nominally the highest legislative body, and at the Chinese People's Political Consultative Conference (CPPCC), both in Beijing. But since the British rule Hong Kong, the Guangdong Provincial People's Congress did the picking for the territory to signify that Hong Kong is an integral part of China. The 16 NPC delegates from Hong Kong were mostly prominent and trusted left-wing figures in major financial sectors. The CPPCC is a "patriotic United Front organization" aimed at making friends and winning influence to further the cause of reunification.[62] During the Sino-British negotiations in 1983, Beijing appointed 27 extra Hong Kong and Macao delegates to the original 20 CPPCC representatives, who were again mostly prominent businessmen, academics, and professionals. As events later proved, these delegates did their best to sell the Joint Declaration to the Hong Kong people.[63]

In the past, the titles conferred by China were never as weighty as the British honors (such as OBEs, MBEs, etc.). But now media elites, even members of the Executive and Legislative Councils who have pledged allegiance to the Queen, pride themselves on being conferred PRC titles as well as serving on the Basic Law Drafting Committee and the Basic Law Consultative Committee. There is little doubt that China has faithfully followed the British model of "elite politics": the constituent members of the Basic Law committees share with the colonial government the identical pool of upper-class British loyalists.[64] Few of these Chinese appointees, if any, come from the proletarian class, which the Communist Party purports to represent. China attempts to absorb political and economic elites with a view to preserving social stability.

The Basic Law Drafting Committee is the most important political body China has organized to chart the legal framework for post-1997 Hong Kong. Out of the 59 members of the Committee, 23 were appointed by Xinhua to represent Hong Kong while 36 were mainlanders appointed by Beijing to represent China. Typifying cross-cooptation by both the colonial and Chinese governments, Table 3–1 shows that 15 of these 23 Hong Kong members (or 66%) have either served as the colony's Legislative and Executive Councillors or received honors from the Queen of England. Only eight members of the Drafting Committee seem to have no significant ties with the colonial government; five of these eight members are coopted members of the National People's Congress or the Chinese People's Political Consultative Conference. But if we lower the threshold of the colonial ties to include service on the colonial government's advisory boards, then virtually all of the 23 people would eminently meet this qualification. It is clear that China has expanded its cooptative network from strictly pro-China figures to include those affiliated with the colonial government.

The Basic Law Consultative Committee was organized under Xinhua's direction to provide feedback on public opinion to the Drafting

TABLE 3–1. Coopting Hong Kong Elites by the Colonial Government and the Chinese Government: Hong Kong Members of the Basic Law Drafting Committee ($N=23$)

Name	Colonial affiliation[a]			Chinese affiliation[b]		
	LC	EC	Honors[c]	BLDC	NPC	CPPCC
Ann, Tse-kai	x	x	CBE, OBE, JP	x	x	
Cha, Chi-ming				x	x	x
Cha, Louis			OBE	x		
Cheng, Graham			JP	x		
Fei, Yimin				x	x	x
Fok, Ying Tong				x	x	x
Huang, Rayson	x		CBE	x		
Kok, Kwong				x		
Kwong, Peter				x		
Lau, Wong Fat	x		MBE, JP	x		
Lee, Martin	x		JP	x		
Li, David	x		JP	x		
Li, Ka Shing			JP	x		
Li, Simon				x		
Liu, Yiu Chu				x	x	
Ma, Lin			CBE, JP	x		
Pao, Yue Kong			Sir, CBE, JP	x		
Szeto, Wah	x			x		
Tam, Wai Chu	x	x		x		
Tam, Yu Chung	x			x		
Wong, Po Yan	x		OBE, CBE	x		
Wu, Raymond			JP	x		
Yung, Sanford				x	x	

Source: Based on Kelvin Sinclair, ed., *Who's Who in Hong Kong*, 4th ed. (Hong Kong: Asianet Information Services, 1988).

[a]LC = member of the Legislative Council; EC = member of the Executive Council.

[b]BDLC = Member of the Basic Law Drafting Committee; NPC = Member of the National People's Congress; CPPCC = Member of the Chinese People's Political Consultative Committee.

[c]CBE = Commander of the Order of the British Empire; OBE = Officer of the Order of the British Empire; MBE = Member of the Order of the British Empire; JP = Justice of Peace.

Committee, with all of the 176 members appointed locally in Hong Kong. The Consultative Committee is slightly more widely representative than the Drafting Committee, though still overwhelmingly skewed towards the socioeconomic elites. Despite its revolutionary rhetoric to the contrary, China has not made any serious effort to embody working class members on either committee.

More specifically, Table 3–2 lists 21 prominent *media* proprietors and senior journalists who have been coopted by the colonial government, the Chinese government, or both. The Hong Kong government prefers to shower media owners (such as Sally Aw, Louis Cha, Run Run Shaw, and Shum Choi-sang) with British orders of honor or knighthood, although most of them concurrently take part in China's Basic Law committees. Other media proprietors have sent their personal representatives (such as Poon Chun-leung) to serve on the two Basic Law committees. A total of 13 publishers, editors, and station managers represent the media to the 176–member Basic Law Consultative Committee. To create an image of fair representation, the Committee also includes such members as Nick Griffin, former head of the Hong Kong Journalists Association, and Hu Chu-jen, editor of the rightist *Pai Hsing Semimonthly* magazine. Membership in the National People's Congress and China's Political Consultative Conference is, however, strictly restricted to trusted leftist media owners or journalists, such as Fei Yimin of *Ta Kung Pao,* Lee Tse-chung of *Wen Wei Pao,* Tsui Sze-man of the *Mirror Monthly,* Ho Sai-Chu of the *Tin Tin Daily News,* and Chiu Deacon of Asian Television.

Weaving a Cooptative Fabric

Contrary to his conservative predecessors, Xu Jiatun openly courted capitalists. He published an article on *Qiu Shi,* the CCP's key theoretical organ formerly know as *Red Flag,* in which he profusely praised the vigor of Hong Kong's capitalists and urged people not to view modern capitalism with orthodox stereotypes.[65] In fact, he wooed capitalists at the expense of laborers, whose leaders complained about having little communication with Xu and about having insignificant representation (only 9 out of 176 members) in the Basic Law Consultative Committee.[66] As a *Wen Wei Pao* reporter complained, "Xu never touches us on the shoulder as he sometimes does with other nonleftist reporters. He must have thought that we are already his boys. There is no need to smile at us to get us to work for him."[67]

Xinhua has woven a cooptative fabric stretching from institutional absorption to friendship ties and focusing on media owners, publishers,

TABLE 3–2. Cooptation of Media Owners and Senior Journalists by the Colonial Government and the Chinese Government (*N*=21)

Name	Title	Colonial ties[a]	Chinese ties[b]
Aw, Sally	Publisher, *Sing Tao Jih Pao*	OBE, JP	
Cha, Louis	Publisher, *Ming Pao*	OBE	BLDC, BLCC
Chang, Wan Fung	Deputy editor-in-chief, *Wen Wei Pao*	JP	BLCC
Chiu, Deacon	Director, Asia Television	JP	CPCCC
Fei, Yimin	Publisher, *Ta Kung Pao*		BLDC, NPC, CPPCC
Griffin, Nick	Principal reporter, TV Broadcasts Ltd.		BLCC
Ho, George	Director, Commercial Radio	OBE, JP	
Ho, Man Fat	Publisher, *Sing Pao*		BLCC
Ho, Robert	Publisher, *Kung Sheung Daily News*	JP	
Ho, Sai-chu	Director, *Tin Tin Daily News*	MBE, JP	CPPCC
Ho, Ting Kwan	Assistant general manager, TV Broadcasts Ltd.		BLCC
Hu, Chu-jen	Editor-in-chief, *Pai Hsing Semimonthly*		BLCC
Lee, Tse-chung	Publisher, *Wen Wei Pao*		CPPCC
Li, Chuwen	Deputy director, *Ta Kung Pao*		CPPCC
Poon, Chun-Leung	Editor-in-chief, *Sing Tao Man (Evening) Pao*		BLCC
Pun, Chiu-yin	Assistant general manager, Commercial Radio		BLCC

(cont.)

TABLE 3–2 (Cont.)

Name	Title	Colonial ties[a]	Chinese ties[b]
Shaw, Run Run	Director, TV Broadcasts Ltd.	CBE, KT	
Shum, Choi-sang	Manager, *Wah Kiu Yat Pao*	OBE, JP	BLCC
Tsui, Sze-man	Publisher, *Mirror Monthly*		CPPCC, BLCC
Wong, Wai-sing	Secretary, Asia Television		BLCC
Wong, Yat-huen	Program officer, Radio & TV Hong Kong		BLCC

[a] CBE = Commander of the Order of the British Empire; OBE = Officer of the Order of the British Empire; MBE = Member of the Order of the British Empire; JP = Justice of Peace; KT = Knight of the Order of the Thistle.
[b] BLCC = Basic Law Consultative Committee; BLDC = Basic Law Drafting Committee; NPC = National People's Congress; CPPCC = The Chinese People's Political Consultative Conference. (Note that because of personnel turnover, the present media representatives in the BLCC may be different from those when the committee was first set up [as shown].)

and senior journalists. Hong Kong Television (TVB), reaching 80% of the audience, can easily request interviews with Xinhua's department heads; press conferences are not convened until TVB's camera crew arrives.[68] Likewise, the mainstream (centrist and rightist) press, which accounts for 75% of the readership, has a privileged access to Xinhua's information and interviews. But a special olive branch has been extended to pro-Taiwan papers as part of the United Front strategy. Xu proclaimed: "I fully intend to work on the arch-rightists."[69]

Xinhua holds a list of "good" journalists and "bad" media and its propaganda department has been routinely keeping files on journalists, but Xinhua prefers subtle cooptation to overt coercion. Typifying Chinese negotiating styles, Xinhua pursued its objectives "through a variety of stratagems designed to manipulate feelings of friendship, obligation, guilt or dependence."[70] One of Xinhua's most conventional and effective strategies is to throw lavish banquets and send gifts—Xu reportedly spent an upward of US$800,000 on banquets and gifts per year.[71] To his critics, Xu sent baskets of seasonal fruits (such as Cantonese lichees and Xinjiang honey dew melons) with handwritten notes that breathed not a word of politics. Many of the recipients pleaded discomfort in returning inexpensive perishable gifts, but then found it harder to decline Xinhua's subsequent banquet invitations, especially when the invitation was extended by Xu himself or by one of his top lieutenants. The high frequency of such invitations, averaging several times per year for some people, made guests wary of uttering things that might embarrass the host and, in turn, themselves.[72] Xu's personal touches radiated warmth and compelled his recipients to reciprocate kindness. As one writer commented:

> As a Chinese proverb says, "Those who attend others' banquets have their mouths hushed, and those who take gifts have their hands tightened." Whatever grudges [journalists might have held] have been dissolved into their stomachs by the fine wine and good food served . . . some recipients said that next time they write about China they will be more reserved. The wine cup works like magic . . . in dissolving "temperamental" anti-Communist figures. At a certain point during the Sino-British talks, it was reported that not a day went by without the leftists hosting a banquet. Sure, not every banquet goer pleased the host, but . . .[73]

Friendship in the Chinese context goes beyond cordiality to imply a set of cultural obligations to repay interpersonal debts, which has served to chip away at the critical posture of some journalists. Xu not only professed to peruse articles critical of China, Xinhua, and even Xu himself, but also repeatedly invited his critics to dinner banquets. During those encounters Xu paid close attention to the opinions of his critics but refrained from arguing with them.[74] Har Kung, a satirist, said that Xu was discreet enough not to bring up his anti-Communist writings at the dinner table, but the occasion spoke for itself.[75] Others conceded that it would be "difficult to be very critical of Xu if you know him, particularly if you are to meet with him periodically for news information."[76] A publisher who frequented Xinhua's banquets observed, "The message is implicit: China is maintaining a dialogue with you. China has changed for the better. Give us 'face' and write less about the dreadful past [of the Cultural Revolution]."[77] Anti-Communist columnist Wang Ting-zhi argued that the people and journalists of Hong Kong will be better off if they take advantage of China's United Front and to establish communication with Xinhua rather than resist it.[78] Having said that, Wang later emigrated to Hawaii.

It was over these exquisite meals and fine wines that Xu would disclose certain nuggets of information to his guests, who often reported them without directly quoting the source. Xu killed two birds with one stone: while exposing his guests to China's stance, he also made a lot of friends.[79] As a practical matter, an observer said,

> You get invited, so you have some "inside tips" to write about. But if you *jingjiu bu chi chi fajiu* [refuse a toast only to drink a forfeit, meaning being ungrateful and having to submit oneself to someone's pressure after first turning down his request] and keep writing negatively about Xinhua, you burn the bridge, and then you don't get invited—how long can you keep the well from being dry? How long can you rehash the old stuff?[80]

Patriotism is a favorite appeal and a nice excuse for refusing tough questions. Deng Xiaoping said that as a matter of national pride, he is confident that the "Hong Kong people can run Hong Kong well."[81] Other Chinese leaders have used patriotism to dodge journalists' queries.[82] Chairman Peng Zhen of the People's Congress told Hong Kong reporters in a "heart-to-heart chat" that he treated them ("Chinese deep down in hearts") as "members of the family," rather than as reporters.[83] The unspoken assumption is simple: Since only outsiders would be rude and tough, once accepted as insiders, journalists are not supposed to embarrass the head of the family, or the Chinese authorities. Patriotism dictates that national interests be put head and shoulder above journalistic duties, thus barring reportage that might rock the boat.

Besides, Chinese officials treat journalists preferentially. Deng declared that Hong Kong's future leaders would comprise journalists, business people, professionals, and students. Needless to say, Chinese officials ingratiated themselves with Hong Kong journalists through banquets and praises. When covering the National People's Congress and the Political Consultative Conference in April 1985, Hong Kong journalists received "the highest accolade" of being invited to what was described as the "leadership pantheon," while the rest of the world's correspondents could only stare at Xinhua's teleprinters.[84] The best press seats were saved for those Hong Kong reporters unfriendly to the Communists, who were further told by Xinhua that if they wished they could request a line of children welcoming their "homecoming," but they did not take up that offer.[85] (This preferential treatment is not consistently applied, depending on how China's political wind blows. After the Tiananmen crackdown in 1989, Hong Kong journalists became persona non grata in Beijing.)

Reporters have also traveled on Xinhua's junkets to China. Despite their claims that no professional integrity was sacrificed, reporters typically wrote one or two positive stories about China at the close of each tour. They felt obliged to repay Xinhua's courtesy, admitting that the

Xinhua press officers who escorted them on these trips have triumphed in forging cordial links. The reporters were deprived of excuses for turning their backs on Xinhua officials who called to tip or invite them to presumably major events.[86]

Xinhua as an institution remains secretive, manipulative, and rigid. Excepting that which Xu Jiatun himself divulged over the dinner table, Xinhua officials, unless hard pressed, are tight-lipped about even the most commonplace events. When Lu Ping from China's Office for Hong Kong and Macao paid a visit to Hong Kong in January 1986, reporters from more than 20 news organizations sent a joint letter demanding that Xinhua release Lu's itineraries.[87] On visits to Beijing, in contrast, British Foreign Secretary Howe had his spokesman brief the press regularly on his activities, which put China at a publicity disadvantage. Learning from these mistakes, Xinhua seems to have gradually sharpened its public relations skills in dealing with a "free press" and competing with the colonial regime for media attention. At present Xinhua is particularly interested in learning how the Hong Kong government's information service operates, and has followed its suit to provide frequent informal contacts with highly placed editors.[88]

CONCLUSION

In this chapter we have analyzed the strategies of cooptation by the Hong Kong government and Xinhua News Agency. It is worthy to note that before the Joint Declaration, the British were in virtual control of the production and distribution of government information, and succeeded in inculcating a set of worldviews that insulated Hong Kong from the perennial struggle between mainland China and Taiwan. The Government Information Services has become highly responsive to public complaints. The press has been coopted to create an image that although the colonial government is neither "by the people" nor "of the people," it is nonetheless "for the people."

The government's advantage seems to have been shrunk by the Joint Declaration. Xinhua, which previously kept a low profile, has emerged as a "shadow government" in the political transition. With the dust over Hong Kong's future settled, Xinhua has reversed its traditional anticolonial stance in an effort to sustain a business-as-usual image, which is a psychological imperative to sustaining Hong Kong's stability and prosperity. Likewise, while the colonial regime is pitted against Xinhua in some areas, it seems determined not to obstruct the process of political transition. Press cooptation by both sides should be seen in this context. Cooptation derives from the power center's ability to reward, punish, and persuade. In this process, the press must try to align itself with the new power reality—a process that we call accommodation.

Chapter 4

Accommodating the Power Structure

Hong Kong's political transition has progressed in full swing. The freshly constituted power structure has marshaled resources (rewards, punishments, and persuasive beliefs) to coopt either compliance or consent of the main groups in society. Failing to mobilize counter-resources to withstand such pressure, many of these groups, including the press, have had to submit to the power authority and to the rules of the game it has defined. This process of accommodation is not uniform but expressed in different forms. The weaker parties would resist submission if they found more attractive options than the one charted for them; however, refusal to accommodate the power structure puts them at risk of being further marginalized or even forcefully attacked. Under these circumstances, a partial accommodation is more likely to result—be it out of love, fear, or conversion of beliefs—with strategic decisions between and within press organizations readjusted accordingly.

The Sino-British Joint Declaration has fundamentally reshaped Hong Kong's political landscape. Legitimacy of British rule in Hong Kong had been upheld at China's expense or vice versa, but now politics has been broken loose by the Joint Declaration. Politics is no longer a zero-sum game; areas of mutual interests have evolved to the extent that the media can play duplicity with Britain and China, who in turn share overlapping—if also competing—loyalty of the Hong Kong press. Because both powers perceive the peaceful and smooth transition of Hong Kong as their overriding priority and neither has the desire to "rock the boat," the majority of Hong Kong's newspapers have developed cordial, though uneven, working relations with both powers. The restructuring of institutional ties between the power centers and the press has led to corresponding changes in the internal processes of press organizations as well. This chapter will draw on extensive interviews and intensive study of documents and reports (see Appendix I) to explore the way in which Hong Kong newspapers accommodate Xinhua as a power center while maintaining their ties with the colonial government.

Table 4–1 summarizes the tripartite links among the press, the colonial government, and Xinhua before and after the Joint Declaration.[1]

TABLE 4-1. The Changing Structural Relationship between the Press and the Power Centers (1979–1990)

Press type/ Relationship	Hong Kong Government		Xinhua	
	Pre-accord	Post-accord	Pre-accord	Post-accord
Ultraleftist press				
Power centers toward press	Exclusion (1949–1979) & partial inclusion (1979–1990)	Uneasy cooptation	Strict control	Somewhat more relaxed control
Press toward power centers	Suspicion and criticism	Moderation	Submission	Submission but with more autonomy due to market concern and localization
Centrist press				
Power centers toward press	Cooptation	Cooptation	Little relationship	Cooptation
Press toward power centers	Cooperation and support	Cooperation	Criticism, opposition, or apathy	Cooperation
Rightist press				
Power centers toward press	Cooptation	Cooptation	Little relationship	Cooptation
Press toward power centers	Cooperation and support	Cooperation	Opposition	Cooperation
Ultrarightist press				
Power centers toward press	Exclusion	Exclusion	Hostility	Cooptation and ostracization
Press toward power centers	Cooperation	Cooperation	Hostility	Hostile and defensive accommodation

This table indicates the structural linkages from the perspectives of (a) the power centers (the first row for each type of the press) and (b) the press (the second row). It is clear that Xinhua has put an all-out effort to coopt the press of various ideological persuasions, but the press has responded in different fashions. Faced with Xinhua's aggressive initiatives, the colonial regime has also tried strenuously to retain loyalty of the press. The mainstream (centrist and rightist) press is a most favored target in this cooptative game and thus most liable to pressure toward change. Consequently, this press not only remains loyal to the colonial regime, but also is ideologically and organizationally flexible enough to show a visible shift in their journalistic paradigms to accommodate Xinhua. The ultrarightist press, because of its ideological extremity, has less latitude for change and displays less accommodation toward Xinhua than does the mainstream press. In fact, the ultrarightist press has such limited maneuverability that it can only echo the colonial regime's rhetoric. For the sake of a smooth transition of power, the ultraleftist press moves away from its traditional anticolonial stance to court a more cordial link with the colonial regime, while continuing to follow Xinhua's established line.

Media organizations face the external and internal constraints that shape their editorial policy and journalistic paradigms. They develop interorganizational relations—through such strategies as forestalling, forecasting, or absorbing—to cope with environmental uncertainty.[2] Interorganizational relations necessitate intraorganizational adaptation. The fundamental dilemma of mass media is one of freedom versus constraint in an institution whose professional ideology places a premium on originality and freedom, yet whose organizational setting requires quite strict control.[3] Through routinization, an organization reduces uncertainty about the wider environment by establishing programs, standard operating procedures, and prior prescriptions for recurring task activities. Tuchman shows that media organizations establish a "news net," distributed in time and space, to maximize the chance of capturing news events when and where they are likely to occur. Journalists use what she terms "strategic rituals" that emphasize verifiable facts and involve the attribution of news to authoritative sources.[4] Sigelman argues that news organizations exercise controls over selective recruitment, policy guidance, and socialization.[5] These processes of professional socialization and social control in the newsroom are widely found among U.S. and British media.[6] In Hong Kong, however, journalists are ideologically so consonant with their employing organizations that many of them do not feel subjected to newsroom control.[7]

THE MAINSTREAM PRESS

The mainstream (centrist and rightist) press is aversive to Communist ideology and committed to upholding Hong Kong's stability, on which the "free market" depends. Therefore this press had found it more attractive to throw in its lot with the colonial regime and to distance itself from China and its surrogate, Xinhua. During the 1967 riot the mainstream press firmly backed up the Hong Kong government in combating Communist propaganda. For many years after, while the mainstream press dodged Xinhua as a nest of dogmatic revolutionaries, Xinhua was determined to conquer this anti-Communist stronghold. Not until Beijing's official denunciation in the late 1970s of the leftist riot in Hong Kong (in 1967) and the Chinese Cultural Revolution (1966–1976) did the tension between Xinhua and Hong Kong's mainstream press begin to thaw. By the time Hong Kong's future surfaced as an issue in the early 1980s, this press had gradually lessened its belligerence toward China but remained quite skeptical about the direction it was taking.

When Sino-British negotiations formally commenced in 1982 and then trod on a rough road of bluffs, threats, and counter-threats throughout 1983 and 1984, the mainstream press unequivocally sided with the British—at the price of being branded by China as traitors. The outcome of the negotiations was, however, not in Britain's favor. As will be shown in Chapter 5, the mainstream press could barely conceal their anger at feeling betrayed by Britain's ultimate decision to relinquish Hong Kong, vowing that the Hong Kong people must look after their own self-interests rather than count on Britain's illusory protection. Since 1984, Xinhua has stepped up its United Front campaign in Hong Kong, making the mainstream press one of its prime targets of cooptation. This press has thus staked out double loyalties by ingratiating Xinhua without having to sever rapport with the colonial government.

The Rightist Press: *Sing Tao Jih Pao* and *Wah Kiu Yat Pao*

The rightist press has, notably, developed two sets of duplicitous ties. Congenial to both the colonial government and China on the one hand, this press has managed to nurture China's cooptative overtures while conserving traditionally good ties with Taiwan on the other. At times, the press has to guard local interests against Beijing's encroachments, as illustrated by the unified opposition to the establishment of the Daya Bay nuclear plant, located in China but close enough to Hong Kong to pose a potential safety hazard (see Chapter 6). A hasty and radical swing to embrace China has not been forthcoming, for nothing is to be gained by jeopardizing relations with Taiwan. Furthermore, taking such an "opportunistic" move may offend the reader's sensibility and, paradoxically, diminish its own leverage as a target of Xinhua's cooptation. China has allowed this duplicity to exist, partly to send a reassuring message to the Hong Kong people that business was proceeding as usual and no radical change would be in the offing. Taiwan meanwhile was acquiescent to old friends flirting with China because a hard-line reaction might backfire.[8] Indicative of their duplicity in this chaotic time, both *Wah Kiu Yat Pao* and *Sing Tao Jih Pao* have published copies of stories produced by Taiwan's Central News Agency as well as those by Xinhua.

As a public corporation, *Sing Tao Jih Pao* can afford to have a greater latitude than *Wah Kiu Yat Pao* in coping with uncertainties of the power transformation. No sooner had the Joint Declaration been reached did *Sing Tao Jih Pao* launch active operations to have its capital investments internationalized and diversified. The paper's parent company was relocated to Sydney, Australia in May 1985 in the hope that China would be more prudent in dealing with foreign investors than with national capitalists. *Sing Tao Jih Pao* has also invested more heavily in its international (North American) editions, presuming that China must think twice before interfering with a supposedly "foreign" company, especially at a time when the mainland is vigorously courting overseas support. Finally, *Sing Tao Jih Pao* has taken additional measures to spread out its risks through diversified investments into real estate, again on the assumption that real estate values are bound to grow whereas the press is more vulnerable to periods of political instability.

As the paper caters primarily to real estate and business circles, Sally Aw, publisher of *Sing Tao Jih Pao,* reportedly instructed her staff "to talk more about economics and less about politics," which was interpreted to mean pursuit of a more neutral, balanced, and "less polemical" stance.[9] Despite its limited circulation in Taiwan, *Sing Tao Jih Pao* has maintained a strong emotional affinity with the Kuomintang dating back to the pre-1949 days. When the KMT ruled on the mainland it paid such an enormous tribute to the founder of *Sing Tao Jih Pao,* Aw Boon Haw, that his daughter Sally has vowed not to abandon Taiwan. Besides, Sally Aw treasures her status as a Founding Chair of the World

Chinese Press Association, of which about half of the members are affiliated with Taiwan.[10] *Sing Tao Jih Pao* (daily) continues to bear the KMT's "Republic of China" title on its masthead.[11] Aw further declined an invitation from Xinhua to serve on the Basic Law Consultative Committee but sent her Taiwan-educated editor of *Sing Tao Wan Pao* (evening), Poon Chun-leung, as her personal representative instead.[12] (When Poon and publisher Shum Choi-sang of *Wah Kiu Yat Pao*, both members of the Consultative Committee, attended an annual conference of the World Chinese Press Association conference in Taiwan in December 1985, they complied to Taipei's request that they pay tribute to the late President Chiang Kai-shek's memorial and broadcast anti-Communist messages from the outpost island of Quemoy.[13])

In contrast to Aw, Shum Choi-sang of *Wah Kiu Yat Pao* has been seen actively mixing with Xinhua officials and appeared to be deeply involved in the Basic Law Consultative Committee. This family-owned paper has fewer cards to play in weathering the political storm. Shum admitted that the paper may not survive if moved outside Hong Kong, which partly explains why *Wah Kiu Yat Pao* is more vulnerable to Xinhua's pressure than *Sing Tao Jih Pao*. Adopting a "wait and see" attitude, Shum will not decide on the paper's future until 1991 when China unveils the Basic Law and its five-year plan.[14]

Wah Kiu Yat Pao has long been regarded as a sure mouthpiece of the Hong Kong government; a GIS official boasted that such papers as *Wah Kiu Yat Pao* might not have survived without the free daily supply of government releases.[15] After 1984, although the paper continued to print the GIS staple, it shortened the releases and discarded the leftovers that had previously been saved for publication in the ensuing days. As one editor puts it, "It is trendy for the press to be tougher on the (Hong Kong) government. We want to be in tune with public sentiment."[16]

The Centrist Papers: *Ming Pao*, *Sing Pao*, and the *Oriental Daily News*

All of the centrist papers are privately owned. Several of them responded to the power change with efforts to shelter themselves as public corporations. The *Oriental Daily News* managed to go public before the stock crash in October 1987; its stock issues were greeted with enthusiasm, reducing the financial risk associated with political uncertainty. But *Ming Pao* and *Sing Pao* were not as fortunate in their attempts to go public. *Ming Pao* had envisioned a stock exchange program with the British-owned *South China Morning Post* in order to infuse "international" capital as a protective cushion against radical change.

This effort was stymied when Rupert Murdoch wrested control of the *Post* from British interests in 1987 and teamed up with the now Australia-headquartered *Sing Tao Jih Pao.*

Ming Pao has pledged to remain in Hong Kong after 1997, adding that it will close down its operation in the very unlikely event that press freedom does not exist there any longer.[17] Dissension arose from within the paper around 1985, with some reporters inveighing against *Ming Pao* for having moved "too left" of the political center.[18] Editors who took part in the paper's strategic planning were apprised of *Ming Pao*'s intent to establish itself as the most authoritative newspaper in the future Chinese-run administration, a status held by the English-language *South China Morning Post* under British rule.[19] Building on its reputation in China watching, *Ming Pao* has hired mainland stringers and commissioned the official China News Agency (*Zhongguo Xinwenshe*) for exclusive reports.

Ming Pao's publisher, Louis Cha, is a popular novelist, shrewd businessman, and eminent editorialist. He composes many of the daily editorials for *Ming Pao* and his insights as a China watcher are internationally acclaimed. Frank about his editorial policy, Cha said,

> I keep interference with my staff's work to the minimum so that they can develop their potential. But when they deviate from our policies, I tell them. As a matter of course, they will understand our positions after working together for some time. The new recruits usually do not occupy important positions; after working for a period of time, they naturally will keep in step with us.[20]

Cha said that his journalists are allowed to hold opposing views but if a writer persistently contradicts editorial stands, the problem would be solved "through consultation."[21]

The paper owes much of its success to its virulent attacks on China's radical-leftist policy during the Cultural Revolution in the 1970s. But when Deng Xiaoping led his post-Mao reformist protégés to return to the power stage, *Ming Pao* turned out to be one of the first and foremost Hong Kong newspapers China sought to befriend. Granting Cha an exclusive interview as early as 1981, Deng intimated that he was "a faithful reader" of Cha's editorials in *Ming Pao.* Cha seems to take pride in Deng's personal recognition, having alluded to this unusual encounter. Through much of the decade that followed, the paper has done almost everything it could to bolster the position of the reformist wing of the Chinese leadership against the periodic onslaughts of the more rigid wing.

Ming Pao is the only non-Communist paper to which an estimated

10,000 readers in China, including cadres in government and state enterprises, intellectuals, and newspaper editors, could subscribe. According to one of his aides, Cha values *Ming Pao's* important influence in China and has no desire to undermine this trust by antagonizing Chinese leaders.[22] Cha acknowledged that *Ming Pao* had softened its sharp criticisms of China since the start of the 1980s not because of self-censorship, but because he considered Deng's reform policies to be rational and worthy of support.[23] Cha pledged that *Ming Pao* would fully endorse China's scheme of "one country, two systems" and "earnestly report about and participate in" activities of the Basic Law Drafting and Consultative Committees.[24] And he drafted what was generally regarded as an orthodox "mainstream resolution" for these committees, advocating a slow approach to the question of direct elections in Hong Kong. Cha was severely criticized by promoters of a rapid democratic reform in Hong Kong before 1997.

To impart an "impartial" image to its readers, however, *Ming Pao* has also highlighted outspoken critics of Xinhua in a presumably "objective" manner.[25] Editorially cautious and reluctant to attack the powers that be, the paper nonetheless allows popular free-lance writers to launch point-blank criticisms of China in their assigned columns. This results in a curious yet effective juxtaposition of a reserved editorial stance on the front page that represents Cha himself, with critical commentaries made by free-lance writers on inside pages. With one stroke, *Ming Pao* thus preserves its rapport with Beijing and meanwhile satisfies its readers' interests. Even Xinhua officials have conceded that it is easier to coopt publishers than these "free-spirited" columnists.[26]

Cha forbade personal attacks on Deng, while permitting criticisms of the Communist Party and its policy. In a revealing episode, Cha once ordered that several articles by popular satirist Har Kung that assaulted Deng by name be taken off the press. Har Kung angrily quit writing for *Ming Pao,* sparking speculation that Xinhua had applied its big stick—a rumor that Cha was forced to dispel in an editorial. While several other papers tried to lure Har Kung away, *Ming Pao* reinstated his column six months later and gave him a much freer rein. This episode vividly demonstrates that market interests exert a countervailing pressure to political judgment in the capitalist system of Hong Kong. Therefore, it is not as meaningful to ask whether Hong Kong's press freedom will be won or lost *in toto* after 1997 as to pore over the extent and conditions that press freedom can survive political threats.

Sing Pao, with a mass circulation second only to the *Oriental Daily News,* caters to lowbrow readers through its vulgar and sensational crime stories, scandal, and soft pornography written in lively Cantonese vernacular. *Sing Pao* was too apolitical to even bother carrying daily editorial; columns called "Short comments" and "News talks" were nothing more than news briefs. Publisher Ho Man-fat has reportedly never traveled to either Taiwan or China. As Sino-British negotiations proceeded, however, *Sing Pao* suddenly instituted a daily editorial and solicited articles from pro-China columnists. Meanwhile, the paper moved into a new tower building replete with advanced technologies and facilities. Given this investment, few reporters anticipate that *Sing Pao* will move out of Hong Kong.[27] Now a member of the Basic Law Drafting Committee, Ho has often been seen entertaining Xinhua and visiting Chinese officials in the paper's new offices.

The *Oriental Daily News*, the most widely circulated mass paper, has a tarnished image because its publisher Ma Sik-chun jumped bail on charges of drug trafficking and fled to Taiwan, where he has continued to direct the paper by phone since the early 1980s. Although protected by the absence of an extradition treaty between Taiwan and Hong Kong, Ma is virtually Taiwan's hostage since he cannot take refuge elsewhere. The paper steers clear of political controversy partly because of Ma's personal plight, but more importantly because the less-educated mass readers to whom the paper caters are not interested in politics. In the absence of formal editorials, the short "Miu Yu Column" written by a deputy editor-in-chief served briefly as a quasi editorial. Miu Yu, a self-styled spokesman for the underdog who harbored few illusions about the Communists, was scathingly critical of China for many years. But he abruptly changed gears, heaping profuse praises on Xinhua and China as soon as the Sino-British accord was concluded.[28] The column was soon canceled, presumably under Taiwan's pressure.

Wedged between the cross-pressure from the rightists and the leftists, the *Oriental Daily News* appears to have opted for a course of neutrality, deliberately avoiding political commentary. Anti-China columns have been canceled; the remaining "short editorial" column eschews polemics. The paper also plays a game of duplicity, at times dispatching reporters to cover events on both sides of the Taiwan Straits and subscribing to stories produced by Xinhua and Taiwan's Central News Agency.

A large number of the *Oriental Daily News*'s staff, having received their college educations in Taiwan, remain ideologically and emotionally attached to Taiwan. While acquiescing to the Joint Declaration, they seem to distance themselves from Xinhua and, unlike their peers, seldom accept Xinhua's offers of junkets and favors. Rewriting Xinhua's news, the paper often juxtaposes China's policy announcements with reactions from local critics. The paper has indefinitely shelved a plan to publish a weekly and a monthly, but is heavily reinvesting in its present operation to protect its lead in circulation.

THE ULTRARIGHTIST PRESS

Kung Sheung Yat Pao was closely allied to the KMT from its founding in 1925 by Sir Ho Tung. Sir Ho was a member of Hong Kong's established gentry class, and his heir General Ho Shih-li once served as Chiang Kai-shek's deputy defense minister after the Second World War. Regarded as a staunch defender of Taiwan's anti-Communist policy, *Kung Sheung Yat Pao*'s influence peaked in the 1950s and 1960s and declined from then on. Both *Kung Sheung Yat Pao* and the *Hong Kong Times,* a KMT organ, dismissed China's "one country, two systems" policy as nothing but a Communist United Front trick and "sugar-coated poison."[29] Both papers employed quotation marks liberally to cast doubt on the legitimacy of the Joint Declaration and the Basic Law Drafting and Consultative Committees. *Kung Sheung Yat Pao* was closed down in late 1984 after futile attempts to adjust to the new political situation.[30]

The colonial regime has kept the KMT forces at arm's length, putting the *Hong Kong Times* under minute scrutiny for its editorials, activities, and personnel. Former Governor Edward Youde, an old China hand, once disclosed that his daily reading included five Chinese newspapers: *Ming Pao,* the *Hong Kong Economic Journal, Wen Wei Pao, Ta Kung Pao,* and the *Hong Kong Times.*[31] Of these publications, *Ming Pao* establishes Hong Kong's centrifugal political opinion, and the *Economic Journal* provides penetrating economic analysis and serious political commentaries. The Communist and KMT journals made themselves into Governor Youde's reading list—and the GIS's daily monitoring—not due to their high influence or credibility, but because close surveillance of extreme opinions and activities served to protect British interests in the colony. While the colonial regime has warmed its ties with the Communist press, it continues to give the *Hong Kong Times* a cold shoulder.

The hierarchy of the *Hong Kong Times* has long been dominated by a complacent old guard that is increasingly out of touch with the changing political reality in Taiwan and the younger generations in Hong Kong. The KMT has made numerous attempts to replace these people with younger, abler, and trusted professionals from Taipei, only to run into stiff visa barriers from the Hong Kong government. The paper has thus had to draw its staff from a small pool of KMT-sponsored Chu Hai College graduates and other Hong Kong residents educated in Taiwan. Low status and low pay further compound the paper's impotence to recruit talents. Moreover, to avoid provoking China, the colonial regime has regularly banned anti-Communist films produced in Taiwan from public exhibition, even if their sarcastic tone is less biting than some of those produced in China or Hong Kong. Lest Xinhua raise eyebrows, many Taiwanese officials, journalists, and scholars have been matter-of-factly denied entry visas to Hong Kong.[32]

Wearing the smiling faces of the United Front, Xinhua has taken a two-pronged policy toward the *Hong Kong Times.* While Xinhua has refrained from launching a frontal attack on the *Hong Kong Times,* the Communist press does not hesitate to berate the KMT paper from time to time. Nonetheless, Xinhua and the Communist press have repeatedly echoed Deng Xiaoping in urging the KMT institutions to stay in Hong Kong.[33] Deng said,

> After 1997, Taiwan's institutions in Hong Kong can remain. They can . . . swear at the Communist Party; we are not afraid of being cursed; we cannot be cursed down. But in action, take note that [they] cannot create chaos, cannot play the trick of "two Chinas." "Two Chinas" is no longer a problem between the mainland and Taiwan; it is an international problem. We believe that they [those on Taiwan] all are Chinese, that they will stand on the side of our nation to defend our national situation and national dignity.[34]

But the boundary between legitimate criticisms and illegitimate troubles has never been articulated.

Xu Jiatun, Xinhua's director in Hong Kong (1983–1989), singled out three local KMT leaders at a press conference and invited them to serve on the Basic Law Consultative Committee. Xu's aggressive gesture put those KMT leaders in an awkward position because either response would give rise to various speculations. Of the three, Eddie Tseng (publisher of the *Hong Kong Times*) and Chen Zihuei (head of the KMT in Hong Kong) decided to turn a deaf ear to Xu's overture so as to avoid acknowledging Xinhua's supremacy. But the third member, Pok Shaofu, publisher of the pro-Taiwan *Newsdom Weekly* and a former member of Taiwan's Legislative Yuan (national legislature), believed that Taiwan should face up to China's challenge by initiating propaganda counteroffensives and that this would be a good opportunity to do so. He published an open letter, first politely thanking Xu Jiatun for inviting him and then expressing serious doubt about China's ability to carry out the proclaimed "one country, two systems" policy, given its own dreadful record of the past. Xu did not grace Pok with a response. Taiwan, however, rebuked Pok for having fallen victim to the Communist trap in the first place, and Pok had to publish a long follow-up article testifying his own loyalty to the KMT.[35]

Taiwan has much at stake in Hong Kong.[36] After initial hesitation Taiwan has decided not only to remain, but even to continue building an ever stronger economic base in Hong Kong. Despite rhetoric not to recognize the Joint Declaration, Taiwan has conducted indirect trade with the mainland via Hong Kong, the volume of which has been soaring, especially since Taiwan lifted martial law in mid-1987. Against this backdrop, the *Hong Kong Times,* which vowed not to retreat from Hong Kong,[37] has been far more restricted in its political maneuverability since 1984, obliging it to count passively on the colonial regime and the nascent local democratic movement as a counter-weight to Beijing's growing encroachments. The *Hong Kong Times* has enthusiastically endorsed such critics as Martin Lee, who often have harsh things to say about China for applying heavy-handed measures to nip Hong Kong's democratic formation in the bud.[38]

For years, instead of heeding the tastes of the Hong Kong public, the *Hong Kong Times* bowed to the pleasure of party bureaucrats in Taipei who furnished the money and appreciated its uncompromising anti-Communist rhetoric. While paying scant attention to local news, the paper published pages of materials that read as if Taipei's briefing sheets, rigidly boasting Taiwan's economic "miracle." Although Taiwan's economy is far ahead of China, the picture of Taiwan painted by the *Hong Kong Times* is not very persuasive to people in Hong Kong, where economic growth is equally, if not more, impressive. Moreover, while critical of China's human rights violations, the *Hong Kong Times* was reluctant to find fault with Taiwan's suppression of the democracy movement at least until 1987. Likewise, as a reverse mirror, the Communist papers feigned sympathy for anti-KMT forces in Taiwan but supported Beijing's crackdown on dissidents (except during the Tiananmen event in 1989). Both the ultraleftist and ultrarightist papers suffer from serious credibility gaps.

Now, affected by political changes, an adjustment in editorial line for the *Hong Kong Times* seemed overdue. A power struggle erupted within the paper in 1984, resulting in the resignation of six hard-line columnists in protest over what they perceived to be the paper's weakened anti-Communist vigor.[39] The space vacated by them is deliberately filled up with entertainment fare and nonpolitical content. Local news gradually replaces the pages previously reserved for parroting Taipei's official propaganda line. As a sign of growing flexibility, the *Hong Kong Times* has advertised itself regularly in such publications as the *Nineties Monthly* and *Cheng Ming Monthly*—magazines historically critical of Taiwan but now falling foul of Beijing—as "a newspaper by the Hong Kong people, of the Hong Kong people, and for the Hong Kong people." Editorially, the *Hong Kong Times* encourages Hong Kong to struggle for a more democratic system as a deterrent to Beijing's impending rule.[40]

Even with these changes, structurally speaking, what the *Hong Kong Times* can accomplish is fairly restricted. The paper cannot disregard Xinhua's status as a master player in the current game of political transition. Even if the *Hong Kong Times* is to report the political transition with skepticism or to interpret it with utter contempt, the paper has already lost its agenda-setting initiative and must now respond to Xinhua's agendas.[41] The *Hong Kong Times* has thus taken a defensive posture. For ideological reasons, the *Hong Kong Times* can neither establish a Xinhua beat nor print copy with a Xinhua byline. Reporters from the *Hong Kong Times* shun Xinhua-sponsored events and occasions unless Hong Kong officials and local critics of China are expected to attend. These reporters have also been seen at press conferences arranged by the GIS for visiting officials from China. Given its limited access to Xinhua, the *Hong Kong Times* has had to rewrite stories from the electronic media and the evening papers about Xinhua's activities and operation. The *Hong Kong Times* staff also telephones colleagues at friendly papers daily to ask for details about their stories involving Xinhua and, where necessary, for a copy of Xinhua's released documents.[42] This is hardly the most efficient way to cover news.

While clinging to its fundamental policy of anti-Communism, the *Hong Kong Times* has had to make some concessions. Taiwan's decision to let the *Hong Kong Times* stay put in Hong Kong amounted, in effect, to a tacit and de facto acknowledgment of the legitimacy of China's "one country, two systems" policy. For example, skeptical about its Communist rival, the *Hong Kong Times* covered a resolution passed by the pro-KMT Chung Ching General Association that challenged "the [Sino-British] authorities to carry out the Joint Declaration to its letter" rather than simply paying lip service to it.[43] Even though the *Hong Kong Times* can curse the Joint Declaration as a pack of beautiful but untrustworthy lies, it cannot pretend that Hong Kong will not be rebonded with China. This dilemma frequently makes the paper inconsistent in its rhetoric.

THE ULTRALEFTIST PRESS

There has never been any love lost between the colonial regime and the ultraleftist *Wen Wei Pao* and *Ta Kung Pao*. Besieged by Communist propaganda, the colonial regime attempted as early as 1952 (three years after the Communist takeover of China) to suspend *Ta Kung Pao* and prosecute the publishers of *Wen Wei Pao*, but these actions were quickly rescinded after China lodged mighty protests. Their mutual hostility culminated during the 1967 riots when the colonial regime closed three small fringe Communist papers, presumably to warn *Ta Kung Pao* and *Wen Wei Pao*, and jailed several Communist journalists and publishers, who were subsequently released in exchange for British diplomats held hostage in Beijing. Following this, the Communist press became even more stridently antagonistic to the colonial regime. Government reforms were invariably distrusted and endowed with ulterior motives; for example, welfare and housing programs were "tactics to prolong colonial rule," whereas the nine-year compulsory education was "aimed to provide the capitalists with cheap labor."

But these relations have vastly ameliorated since the early 1980s, first as part of Sino-British rapprochement and later as necessitated by the common interest to effect a smooth political transition. Reversing its antagonistic policy, the colonial regime has invited high-level editors of the Communist papers (but not the KMT paper) to the GIS's news briefing sessions and has granted *Wen Wei Pao* the privilege to carry legally valid advertisements.[44] Xinhua has been careful not to overshadow the "lame-duck" government, and the Communist press has moderated its anticolonial overtone.[45] "Whatever the Hong Kong government is doing will be inherited by us," a leading Communist journalist put it. "Nitpicking every [Hong Kong] government policy will make it difficult for us to shift gears in 1997."[46]

The Communist press is China's major cultural and propaganda arm in Hong Kong. Xinhua has until recently dispatched political commissars to preside over the political study sessions of the Editorial Affairs Committee of the Hong Kong Communist press, where specific political directives were given. Having now canceled full-scale political sessions, Xinhua still confers with high-ranking Communist editors at regular intervals to steer a common editorial policy in line with the political situation.[47] Nevertheless, Xinhua under Xu Jiatun encouraged the Communist press to lessen its ideological rigidity. In an internal review, Xinhua reportedly leveled criticisms at the Communist press for (1) preaching without convincing the reader; (2) failing to produce more exclusive stories about China and hence to establish authority in this area; and (3) carrying "high-sounding, one-sided and empty" editorials.[48]

Ta Kung Pao and *Wen Wei Pao* could no longer claim to speak with supreme authority for the Chinese Communist Party after the *People's Daily* published its Hong Kong edition in 1985. Both Hong Kong Communist papers are grudgingly losing their monopolistic advantage on China reporting, as many other papers have moved in swiftly to develop China expertise. Competition has been intensified by a number of non-Communist papers that have stationed reporters in Beijing. The official China News Agency (CNA), an organization targeted specifically at overseas Chinese communities, has also embarked on a new service that accepts commissions from Hong Kong papers for preparing custom-made "special features."[49] *Ming Pao, Pai Hsing Semimonthly,* and the English-language *Hong Kong Standard* are known to have used the CNA service without proper source attribution.

Antithetical to its past hostility towards capitalism, the Communist press has come to acknowledge its own weak market position and to admit that the press must first survive and prosper in the Hong Kong market if it is to achieve any political objectives.[50] Since the Joint Declaration guarantees that Hong Kong's capitalism be maintained after 1997, the Communist press chants a new slogan that it will henceforth "rely on the motherland, put root in Hong Kong, and face overseas." This slogan implies that Hong Kong's Communist papers should be run according to Hong Kong's capitalistic way, rather than as Beijing's appendage living off financial handouts.[51] Although *Wen Wei Pao* continues to be an official voice of the Chinese Communist Party, as a top official explained, "we shall try to get as close to the Hong Kong people as possible." This change in focus has resulted in policies that favor content diversification, localization, and some commercialization.[52]

As a result of these new policies, the formerly unthinkable has occurred: Instead of indiscriminately repudiating advertisement as a tool of bourgeois control or corrupt influence, *Wen Wei Pao* is advertising itself on prime-time television and unashamedly pursuing advertising revenues. Political loyalty being a prerequisite to employment, top-level positions in the Communist press have been staffed primarily by mainland appointees, whereas local employees have traditionally been recruited through political recommendation from the rank and file of pro-China radical student movements and leftist high schools.[53] Departing from that practice, *Wen Wei Pao* has recruited more than 30 local college graduates through open competition, now comprising one-third of its editorial staff. Their salary has been upgraded to a level competitive with the commercial press; they were also promised opportunities for study abroad, swift promotion, and foreign correspondence assignments. New recruits need not be ideological adherents.[54] Several local recruits from student movements of the 1970s have been promoted to such executive positions as deputy manager, head of the business section, news editor, and editorial committee chairman. Many recent recruits, however, have quit out of frustration with what they perceive to be the paper's rigidity despite its efforts at liberalization. *Wen Wei Pao* has thus increasingly had to recruit from among China-educated Hong Kong residents who are ideologically trustworthy and familiar with local needs.[55] *Ta Kung Pao's* pace of localization is slower as the older mainland appointees remain dominant.[56]

Both *Ta Kung Pao* and *Wen Wei Pao* are battling each other to broaden their respective readership among a homogeneous pool of managers, traders, and office workers. They have chipped away at some of their ideological inhibitions and resorted to what used to be castigated as capitalistic promotional gimmicks such as horse-racing tips, vivid accounts of sexy court cases, and exposés on celebrity scandals.[57] Column articles by credible nonleftist writers, professionals, and academics have been solicited to water down their straitjacket image. Although official mainland Chinese activities continue to command significant attention, both papers have become more sensitive to the coverage of marketplace, local issues, and Hong Kong government affairs. One editor put it bluntly: "Who is going to read your paper if you black out issues that affect daily life?"[58]

DISCUSSION AND IMPLICATION

We start with the theoretical position that mass media reflect the dominant power structure in society and that if the power structure is transformed, then a shift in journalistic paradigms will result. As previously argued, structural change dictates that journalists change their perceptions and attitudes, and cooptation serves to smooth this process out. Cooptation serves to bring outsiders (usually resource-poorer) inside (usually resource-richer) so as to align the outsiders' views with those of the central authority, and thus avert opposition or threat to the system's stability and of legitimacy.[59] Cooptation is a catalyst for change, but is itself not a sufficient condition for causing journalistic paradigm shifts.

China lacks legitimacy in Hong Kong. Opinion polls and press commentaries have shown an unequivocal opposition to China's takeover of Hong Kong. For example, in a March 1982 survey, 76% regarded maintenance of Hong Kong's status quo or Hong Kong's becoming a British trust territory to be probable outcomes; 85% expressed these options vis-à-vis a takeover by China as their preferred outcomes.[60] The Sino-British Joint Declaration was thrust upon the Hong Kong people against their will. Although China may legally wield domination, it lacks in what Weber calls "the subjective *belief* in the validity of an order which constitutes the valid order itself."[61] To attain the consent of the governed and to establish a subjective feeling of *rightness* toward the new political order, Xinhua has labored diligently to coopt the Hong Kong press.

We show that politics has been transformed from a zero-sum game to a non-zero-sum game. Through the offer of banquets, prestige, and status, Xinhua has disarmed skeptical journalists by showing China's good intentions and even opened a formal communication with them. Many anti-Communist writers professed their desire to have a dialogue with Xinhua—as one of them put it, "The odds are in their favor, if one cannot fight them, then join them, and talk with them; at least they mean well."[62] Banquets radiate human warmth and breed *guan-xi* (relations), which bind the recipient to repay personal and emotional debts.[63] Consequently journalists are brought, often unconsciously, closer to Xinhua's views and write more sympathetically about China and its policy.

This chapter has shown that cooptation has further resulted in uneven shifts of press norms and news policy at the institutional level. The more flexible mainstream press generally accommodates the new power with greater readiness. The KMT's *Hong Kong Times,* while resistant to Xinhua's cooptation, must face up to the inescapable implication of a reconstituted political reality, making its accommodation process painfully slow and reluctant. Meanwhile, the Communist press is allowed to pursue a localization policy as China implements United Front strategies.

Xinhua's cooptation has limits too. If Galbraith and Lukes are correct, it stands to reason that this domination might be challenged by those people, groups, or organizations who begin to imagine alternatives to the situation or do not value it as divinely ordained and beneficial.[64] The implication is clear: China must deliver its promises as laid out in the Joint Declaration, otherwise the partial "conditioned belief" it has achieved in Hong Kong will be lost. Beijing's suppression of the democracy movement in 1989 has seriously damaged Xinhua's credibility and aborted its cooptative efforts (see Chapter 7). Not only did Louis Cha of *Ming Pao* resign in protest from the Basic Law committees, but the Communist paper briefly—before Xinhua tightened its rein—revolted against Beijing. But the Joint Declaration has set an irreversible foundation. Instead of denouncing the Joint Declaration, the press urged China not to behave contrary to its spirit. To what extent Xinhua can repair the fabric of relations that it has so painstakingly woven with the Hong Kong press and journalists remain to be seen.

Chapter 5

Weathering the Storm, 1982–1986: Sino-British Joint Declaration

We view mass media as a social subsystem conditioned by the configuration of social forces. The previous chapters discussed how the change in Hong Kong's power structure forced a concomitant change in the journalistic paradigms of the Hong Kong press. This chapter analyzes specifically the direction and extent of paradigm shifts toward the twin power centers (the colonial regime and Xinhua) both before and after the Sino-British accord. We hypothesize that the magnitude of such shifts is inversely related to the ideological extremity of the press.

We shall begin with an account of the history of Sino-British negotiations. We shall then examine shifts in editorial stance before, during, and after the announcement of the Joint Declaration. Finally, we shall use quantitative content analysis to study news coverage.

THE CASE

Hong Kong's colonial status remained intact through the dark age of the Chinese Cultural Revolution in which anti-imperial and anti-foreign pitches ran rampant (see Chapter 1). Having emerged from the ruins of the Cultural revolution, China made great strides in improving ties with the United States and Britain, and embarked on an ambitious economic modernization program. Pragmatic post-Mao leaders led by Deng Xiaoping were not expected to steer a different policy as far as Hong Kong was concerned. The popular belief was that Hong Kong, providing for 40% of China's foreign exchange, was too important to the success of China's economic modernization to be messed around with. Therefore, both the British government and the Hong Kong people were quite convinced that they could get around the thorny issue of sovereignty when the lease expired. But that hope was misplaced, as Louis Cha, publisher of *Ming Pao*, observed in a post-hoc manner:

China has made it abundantly clear over the past year [1982] that sovereignty over Hong Kong must be recovered, although no definite date has been named. This has made quite a few Hong Kong people hope that China might still think the time is not appropriate yet by 1997 and the matter would be deferred for several more years. Other people entertain the wish that China would probably agree to Britain's returning the sovereignty over the whole of Hong Kong in exchange for allowing Britain to administer the territory for several years, or allowing Hong Kong to be jointly administered by China and Britain.[1]

In retrospect, Deng Xiaoping did not base his Hong Kong policy on any simple economic calculations; instead, he approached it from a macroscopically geopolitical framework. Hong Kong was not regarded as an isolated case; it became linked as a part of what Deng later envisioned to be a "one country, two systems" policy, in which Hong Kong, Macao, and Taiwan would be comprehensively reabsorbed into China as autonomous "special administrative regions." But at that time the Hong Kong people did not know of China's genuine intent, and the press threw in its lot with Britain in the sovereignty fight that ensued.

Sino-British Negotiations

In 1979, with the year 1997 seemingly faraway, China was in no hurry to enter into negotiations with Britain over the status of Hong Kong. But Britain could wait no longer. Unless China made its intent known in time, the Hong Kong business sector found itself increasingly at a loss to plan for the future; many transactions, loans, and investment and development projects were conducted on 20-year or longer terms and thus hinged on political predictability. Under such circumstances, Sir Murray MacLehose in 1979 became the first governor of Hong Kong ever to visit China; he tried to press for a clear answer on the question of Hong Kong but got a vague reply from Deng at best. Deng said that, since China never recognized the unequal treaties anyway, it might reclaim Hong Kong before, in, or after 1997—adding that investors should be advised to "put their hearts at ease" in any case.[2] The Hong Kong press, in a classical case of selective perception, immediately jumped to conclusions, rationalizing Deng's alleged assurance to investors as a "pro status quo" position, thus confirming the predisposition of the press itself.

Then for months that went by, there were small ripples of rumors and counter-rumors but nothing substantial enough to make a political wave. The first serious signs of massive change were detected in 1981.

On September 30, 1981, Premier Zhao Ziyang informed a visiting British cabinet member Humphrey Atkins that China would reclaim Hong Kong but respect its status as a free port and an international financial center. An uproar ensued when the British Parliament passed a resolution at the end of 1981 that effectively denied Hong Kong people the right of abode in Britain. Although London disavowed any linkage between the change in statute and the ambiguities over the status of Hong Kong, it is difficult to dissociate Governor MacLehose's China trip and Britain's preemptive legislative measures. On a parallel front, China made a new peace overture to Taiwan in September 1981, urging Taiwan to unify with the mainland as an autonomous Special Administrative Region (SAR) entitled to maintain its existing economic and political system. The status and right of Taiwan as a SAR, according to Beijing, would be fully protected under Article 31 of the Constitution of the People's Republic effective as of December 4, 1982. (This very model of SAR, as an integral part of the evolving "one country, two systems" policy, was later proposed to Britain as a formula for the settling of the Hong Kong question. It became clear that Beijing was intent on achieving the ultimate mission of national reunification with Hong Kong, Macao, and Taiwan under this formula.[3])

Britain decided it was time to negotiate with China. Prime Minister Margaret Thatcher visited Beijing on September 22, 1982; her proposal to use the treaties that ceded Hong Kong to Britain as a base line for negotiations was adamantly repulsed by Deng Xiaoping, who made it clear that China would not recognize those unequal treaties under any circumstances. Both sides nonetheless agreed to convene negotiations. To calm the tempest developing in Hong Kong, Thatcher pledged allegiance to protecting the security and interests of the people in the territory. Britain proposed that participants in the negotiations should include the tripod of delegations from Britain, Hong Kong, and China. China vehemently disallowed a separate Hong Kong delegation to be formed, insisting that the Chinese government solely represent the majority of the Chinese population living in a piece of Chinese territory called Hong Kong while the British officials who rule the colony, including Governor Edward Youde, could only be incorporated as members of the British delegation.

With both sides diverging sharply on the delegation issue, talks were off to a rugged start. Britain's first priority was to secure a Chinese concession on lease extension to cover the New Territories. But as soon as this subject was broached, China flatly rebuked British attempts as imperialistic. Britain tried different tacks, all to no avail. Between September 1982 and June 1983, Britain proposed several options, including one that would require return of Hong Kong's sovereignty to China provided that China let Britain continue to administer the territory after 1997. But China refused to budge, insisting that sovereignty and administrative right cannot be decoupled. The negotiation reached a deadlock, causing panic and capital flight. Both sides mobilized media support and used public opinion polls to blame on each other.

When talks resumed in July 1983, Britain, in what appeared to be a last attempt, claimed that Hong Kong's stability and prosperity hinged on continued British commitment and public confidence in the Hong Kong government. This implied threat caught China's ire. General Secretary Hu Yaobang of the Chinese Communist Party summarily announced on August 15, 1983, that China would claim Hong Kong on schedule—July 1, 1989—which was the first time such a date was disclosed. The leftist forces in Hong Kong immediately launched an assault on Britain, whereas Hong Kong dollars plummeted from $5 to $8 then to $9.5 for every U.S. dollar. China served an ultimatum that it would divulge a unilateral plan should an agreement not be reached before September 1984.

"One Country, Two Systems"

Having exhausted wits at this point, Britain had no alternative other than to announce a decision to relinquish the colony when the lease expires. Once that decision was made, the rest of the negotiations came to a rapid conclusion. Both sides finally initiated the Sino-British Joint Declaration on September 26, 1984, which contained the following key points:

> First, Hong Kong will become a Special Administrative Region (SAR) under the direct jurisdiction of the Central government in Beijing. To govern the future Hong Kong, a Basic Law will be drafted and approved by the National People's Congress in accordance with Article 31 of the Constitution of the People's Republic. Under the Basic Law, the SAR legislature will have the authority to enact laws subject to approval of the National People's Congress Standing Committee. The SAR executive officers will be appointed by Beijing from among the Hong Kong citizens through an electoral process or through "democratic consultation."
>
> Second, Hong Kong, as a SAR, will have a highly autonomous local government governed by the Hong Kong people. Hong Kong will be financially independent from Beijing and will be empowered to formulate separate policies applicable to local economy, trade, culture and education, although matters of foreign policy and national defense are domains of Beijing's prerogatives. The SAR administration will only involve the local people.

Third, Hong Kong's existing laws, its social and economic systems, as well as its way of life (i.e., capitalism, and private property) will remain unchanged for 50 years after 1997. Hong Kong will stay as a free port with its own tariff system, and as an international financial center.

Fourth, economic interests of Britain and other countries in Hong Kong will be protected.[4]

What is left for the British to do is complete the terms and prepare to exit honorably and graciously from the colony that it has ruled for a century and a half. Hong Kong's fate is irreversible; nothing will put it back under British rule. The Hong Kong people have meanwhile undergone the various cycles of initial shock, anxiety, and resignation—first rejecting, then cynically accepting the "one country, two systems" policy, and finally settling into the last hope that China will faithfully carry out that policy. China has reiterated the principle of that policy. But after the heavy involvement of the Hong Kong people in China's democracy movement (see Chapter 7), Ji Pengfei, director of the Hong Kong and Macao Office under the State Council, delivered a stern warning:

China and Hong Kong are to implement different systems. The central People's Government will not change the capitalist system in Hong Kong. Nor will it bring the socialist system into Hong Kong. Hong Kong and Macao should not seek to interfere with or change the mainland socialist system.[5]

SHIFTING EDITORIAL STANCE

The "Hong Kong issue" has dominated the news since 1982. The nature of the issue has taken on many zig-zags. Journalistic paradigm shifts, depending on the political/ideological commitment of individual papers, closely followed the life cycle of the issue in stages. When China indicated in 1982–1983, via informal channels, that it intended to regain Hong Kong, all but the Communist press greeted the news with distrust—on the grounds that Hong Kong's prosperity would be untenable under Chinese rule. Most editorials firmly supported British efforts to gain a concession from China for a continued British presence beyond 1997. This editorial chain of considerable unanimity began to break when Hu Yaobang, then General Secretary of the CCP, confirmed the long-circulated rumor of China's intention to retake Hong Kong. Shifts in centrist and rightist journalistic paradigms became particularly discernible and were further precipitated in 1984 by the British decision to forfeit

Hong Kong and by the Sino-British Joint Declaration. As expected, some papers shifted their stance more drastically, others reservedly. In what follows, we shall show that the nature and extent of change is principally contingent on where each newspaper stands in the political/ideological spectrum.

Rightist Journalistic Paradigm

Sing Tao Jih Pao

This newspaper supported a continued British rule with greater persistence than *Wah Kiu Yat Pao*. When the sovereignty issue was first broached, a typical editorial would read,

> There is no place for the British in Communist China's blueprint on Hong Kong. Under this circumstance, will the British remain to take up some administrative responsibilities? Definitely not. But whether the British have the full administrative power or not is the deciding factor of confidence and capital movement. Beijing leaders have missed this point.[6]

Like many nonleftist newspapers, *Sing Tao Jih Pao* was confident that the British commitment could fend off China's advances. In 1982, for example, immediately after Britain had agreed to enter into negotiation, *Sing Tao Jih Pao* wrote:

> Mrs. Thatcher, in the first hours of her first day in Hong Kong, has twice pledged that Britain would be responsible to the Hong Kong people and would express their interests during the negotiations with mainland China. . . . Because she has correctly grasped the "reality" of the Hong Kong people and their desire to maintain the status quo, she is uniquely qualified to perform the promised responsibility and to express Hong Kong people's interests.[7]

Sing Tao Jih Pao's support remained unfailing throughout the entire negotiations.[8]

Again, like many others, *Sing Tao Jih Pao* had faith in Britain's commitment to the status quo. It also overestimated the role of China's economic dependence on Hong Kong while underestimating its political motive of using Hong Kong as a showcase for reunification with Taiwan. Thus, *Sing Tao Jih Pao* concluded that there were "absolute reasons" to believe that Hong Kong would have a "bright future" (i.e. maintaining the status quo).[9]

As soon as the Sino-British Joint Declaration was initialed, *Sing*

Tao Jih Pao showed signs of acquiescing to the newly defined political "reality." For example, it argued,

> The five million people of Hong Kong have no choice but to have confidence in the "Sino-British Agreement" which determines Hong Kong's future. It is superfluous to doubt whether the Hong Kong people have confidence or not. Moreover, there is no reason why the Chinese majority of the local population who have created prosperity during British rule cannot maintain Hong Kong's prosperity when it is returned to China. It is clear that the rise and fall of Hong Kong, from now on, depends not only on the Hong Kong people but primarily on Beijing. If Beijing has confidence in implementing the "Sino-British Agreement" and the scheme of "one country, two systems," Hong Kong's future prosperity will certainly be greater than it is now.[10]

Dating from late 1984 *Sing Tao Jih Pao* seemed to have changed its tone to one of consistently supporting the Sino-British accord. Past worries seemed to have been replaced by a growing confidence. In late 1984, for example, it noted:

> Businessmen and government economic agencies from all the world have revived their confidence in investing in Hong Kong in the past ten months. The speed and magnitude of investment growth is unparalleled. This is very important for it at least erases people's worries about Hong Kong's future and the gloomy atmosphere, encouraging Hong Kong citizens to strive for further economic prosperity and social stability.

The very first precondition for the growth of confidence in Hong Kong, according to the same editorial, is the implementation of the "Sino-British Agreement."[11]

In an annual review editorial, *Sing Tao Jih Pao* even appealed to national pride:

> The dust aroused by the two-year-long negotiation over Hong Kong's future is now settled by the formal signing of the "Sino-British Agreement." The wounds and tears caused by the Opium War on the sons and daughters of China will soon fade into history. The life-style valued by the Hong Kong people is guaranteed for 50 years in black and white terms. At the same time, both mainland China and Taiwan have scored notable achievements in developing their economies and living standards. They, together with the steadily progressing Hong Kong, each with their own merits, form a tripartite system which constitutes an economic force able to compete with Japan.[12]

Such an optimistic vision was unthinkable just one year ago. One of its more recent editorials concluded:

> First, we must have confidence in mainland China in implementing the "Sino-British Joint Declaration" [which the paper formerly called the "Sino-British Agreement" after the British fashion]. Secondly, we should consciously and voluntarily work for a stable transition. Lastly, we should be proud to be Chinese and to return a perfect Hong Kong to China [which the paper formerly referred to as "Communist China" or "mainland China"]. Every citizen should work for this from now on.[13]

Wah Kiu Yat Pao

Sharing two propositions with Sing Tao Jih Pao, Wah Kiu Yat Pao initially argued (1) that mainland China was unlikely to retake Hong Kong for economic and strategic reasons;[14] (2) that the British prime minister and other British officials were trustworthy negotiators on behalf of the Hong Kong people.[15]

Wah Kiu Yat Pao, nonetheless, differed from Sing Tao Jih Pao in some key respects. First, Wah Kiu Yat Pao quoted some social leaders to discredit such policies as "letting Hong Kong people administer Hong Kong," while Sing Tao Jih Pao did not.[16] Secondly, it explicitly argued against the urge by Sing Tao Jih Pao and ultrarightist papers to internationalize the Hong Kong issue.[17] Thirdly, Wah Kiu Yat Pao's acquiescence was in greater haste than Sing Tao Jih Pao's. Wah Kiu Yat Pao had quoted Chinese officials more often and at greater length even before Britain made public its intention to withdraw from Hong Kong. In the heat of negotiations in 1983, for example, Wah Kiu Yat Pao referred to Hu Yaobang: "Now Hu Yaobang has once and for all stated the [takeover] date, we no longer need to guess and speculate. Given a definite period, we had better prepare in our own social positions for the new reality that is emerging."[18] Typifying its sharpened journalistic paradigm shift, the paper proclaimed in January 1984:

> For China [formerly referred to as "Communist China" or "mainland China"] to retake Hong Kong's sovereignty as well as jurisdictive power is absolutely right because Hong Kong is part of Chinese territories and its inhabitants are Chinese. If China, which owns the land and the people, is not entitled to Hong Kong's sovereignty, then what kind of ridiculous world would it be?[19]

Shortly before the Joint Declaration was initialed, Wah Kiu Yat Pao asserted that Hong Kong people "had no reasons to feel uneasy or lack of confidence in the future of Hong Kong."[20]

Centrist Journalistic Paradigm

Oriental Daily News

Deliberately "apolitical" and noncontroversial, this newspaper's short, daily editorial does not touch on Hong Kong's future except on a few very important occasions (e.g., the signing of the Sino-British accord). Instead, the politically sharp Miu Yu Column, signed and written by a deputy editor-in-chief, is generally regarded as the paper's "surrogate editorial."

At the outset, in 1982, Miu Yu deemed nationalism an "abstract" principle which must not be used to dictate the return of Hong Kong to China. He said:

> From hundreds of readers' letters sent to me, not a single one agrees to an immediate retaking of Hong Kong. Does this indicate that the *Daily's* readers do not care about the righteousness of nationalism? When righteousness contradicts interests, we need to keep cool in the analysis of costs and benefits. This is not to say that the righteousness of nationalism can be done away with. But in the last analysis, nationalism is mental, conceptual, theoretical and abstract in nature, while interests are concrete and personal. At this juncture labeling other people as "traitors to Chinese nationalism" is no proof of the labelers' righteousness but of their craziness.[21]

He often reiterated the concern for China's "inevitable" interference should Hong Kong become China's special administrative region. He commented, for example,

> Although the Chinese constitution may be drawn upon to protect "one country, two systems" or "one country, two sets of law" . . . it is inevitable that the law makers will include some mainland Chinese other than British and Hong Kong citizens and that the present Supreme Court of Appeal in London will be relocated in Beijing—by then the spirit of the rule of law in the British tradition will be all scraped.[22]

In short, in Miu Yu's estimation, "one country, two systems" is infeasible in practice.

Signs of a journalistic paradigm shift were visible as early as December 8, 1983. Miu Yu concluded in one of his columns, as follows:

> Beijing has sufficiently understood the importance of Hong Kong's prosperity. What the Hong Kong people fear is that Communist China may fail

to recognize this and may "irrationally" act it out in Hong Kong. But all indicators seem to point out that this fear is unnecessary.[23]

Miu Yu increased his favorable portrayal of Xinhua, saying,

> It [the New Year speech] is the first speech ever made by the head of Xinhua's Hong Kong Branch. In the past, no media organizations had invited the highest Chinese representative in Hong Kong to make such a speech. This event indicates that Xinhua's increasingly significant role in Hong Kong's affairs begins to command greater attention from the mass media . . . Director Xu Jiatun's speech is not a "super-governor's" act to overwhelm Hong Kong. On the contrary, only a rejection [of an invitation to speak] will pose himself as a "super-governor."[24]

In marked contrast to his repeated assertions of the past regarding the CCP's untrustworthiness on account of historical record, Miu Yu seemed to have developed a very different perspective by April 1984. He said:

> The present leaders of the CCP have repeatedly self-criticized [their past radical lines] in their public speeches. In light of their ideals and interests, the sincerity of their self-criticism is not to be doubted. This new consciousness has induced the birth of the concept of "one country, two systems" which is different in nature from the CCP's deceptive policies on nationalist bourgeoisie in the fifties.[25] . . . If we analyze Communist China's policies in Hong Kong merely in light of its past record and neglect all its present changes, we may be far from truth.[26]

Furthermore, Miu Yu began to exemplify "one country, two systems" as a solution for international conflicts. He said:

> In fact, the "one country, two systems" concept innovated by China is receiving increasing international attention and is generally considered to be a very honest and solid formulation that may be applicable in numerous international conflicts such as those between the Germanies and the Koreas.[27]

From then on, Miu Yu continued to expound China's Hong Kong policies, quoting economic figures to support his optimistic evaluation of the future, and sometimes to explain away what he saw as a misunderstanding between Chinese leaders and the local press.[28]

Sing Pao

Taking a position that was generally mild and somewhat obscure during the early stage of the negotiation, this paper did not carry editorials
until mid-1983. Quite revealing was its editorial on September 23, 1983:

> China always says that it will reclaim Hong Kong when the time is right.
> Is the expiration of the lease of the New Territories the right moment?
> Following the major goal set by China, let us use modernization as the
> criterion of judgment: leaving Hong Kong as it is would facilitate China's
> modernization. Taking modernization as the criterion is a flexible way of
> doing things while over-emphasizing the lease expiration is an indication
> of rigidity. Not only rigidity, it also damages a friendship [between Hong
> Kong and the People's Republic] that has lasted for more than 30 years.[29]

Sing Pao's support of the status quo was precipitated by the relocation of Jardine Company—a leading British corporation historically
tied to Hong Kong—to Bermuda. With a sense of urgency, it declared:

> Communist China should renew its understanding of Hong Kong, do away
> with the "emotional part" and revise the plans concerning Hong Kong's
> future. Within the principle of retaking Hong Kong's sovereignty, [China
> should] base its policies on the concrete situation in order to preserve Hong
> Kong's stability and prosperity and to facilitate the modernization of our
> mother country [i.e., China] and its whole unification. . . . In fact, the
> assumption of sovereignty itself is sufficient [to fulfill nationalism]—after
> that, Hong Kong should be left alone to become a sufficiently autonomous,
> free, democratic, prosperous and stable international city.[30]

Sing Pao, however, became quite favorably disposed to the final
outcome of the negotiation. When the date of initialing the Joint Declaration was drawing near, *Sing Pao* began to emphasize the legal binding power of the Declaration and to portray it as "the brainchild of
'far-sighted politicians.' "[31] *Sing Pao* wrote a series of editorials prais-
ing the scheme of "one country, two systems" after the initialization,
one of which said:

> The general reaction to the Joint Declaration just released is good because
> it is unexpectedly detailed and specific. It is better than expected. Overall,
> the majority of the Hong Kong people have accepted it; what differs is the
> extent of acceptance.[32]

In another, it argued, "We thought the most significant thing implied
by the initialization of the Joint Declaration is that Hong Kong people

will gradually be the master of Hong Kong, holding their fate and future in their own hands."[33] *Sing Pao's* positive assessment of China's policies in Hong Kong seems to increase with time. On January 7, 1986, for example, it said:

> In 1985 which just ended, the greatest achievement of Hong Kong is its enhanced political stability. One year after the signing of the Sino-British Joint Declaration, the feasibility of "one country, two systems" has become more and more deeply rooted in people's hearts.[34]

To sum up, *Sing Pao* provides a clear demonstration of an editorial shift that follows the larger structural power change in the system. From a status quo mind-set, it became one of the first supporters of Chinese policies on Hong Kong. This is a paper heavily identified with the *existing* power rather than with consistent ideology.

Ming Pao

Positioning itself as a leading intellectual paper, *Ming Pao* has made various proposals to mediate the positions of the China, Britain, and the "Hong Kong people." The process of its editorial paradigm shift was at first subtle, gradual, and smooth, but the pace was quickened once Britain announced that it would give up Hong Kong's sovereignty.

Based on the economic logic, *Ming Pao* was confident that China would not claim Hong Kong in 1997. It observed in 1981:

> Thorough studies on the historical, legal, economic, political, diplomatic and strategic aspects of the issue have been made. The consensus is that it is quite unlikely that China will take back Hong Kong or the New Territories in 1997 when the New Territories lease expires.[35]

Ming Pao often made its point through the use of metaphors or parables. For example, it said:

> Some people hold the view that following the takeover by China and the introduction of limited changes to the system here prosperity may still survive. This is from an idealistic rather than a pragmatic point of view and is not founded on facts. . . . Hong Kong is a strange goose laying golden eggs. It is not beautiful at all, offensive to the eyes of many others. However, if it is stripped of its ugly feathers and dressed in phoenix or peacock feathers, it will cease to lay golden eggs.[36]

Although *Ming Pao's* trust in Britain's commitment to Hong Kong was not as strong as that of the rightist papers, it nevertheless defended Mrs. Thatcher's promise of moral responsibility toward Hong Kong when she was under attack by leftist newspapers.[37] It reasoned that the British, albeit on the weaker side of the negotiation table, had three cards in their favor. One is the "public opinion card": The majority of Hong Kong's citizens favor the status quo. The second is the "prosperity and stability card," that is, China's economic self-interest to preserve Hong Kong's status quo. The third is the "international treaty card," referring to China's obligation to observe the Nanking Treaty by which Hong Kong was ceded to Britain. With these three cards in hand, *Ming Pao* predicted that the British "would have more to bargain for than a simple abrogation of Hong Kong's sovereignty."[38]

Ming Pao doubted that the Chinese policies being disclosed would be feasible. In particular, it raised the concern that once their current leaders had died, policies toward Hong Kong might have a problem of continuity.[39] Meanwhile, *Ming Pao* did not think that Chinese leaders would be willing to state their promises in black and white.[40]

After Hu Yaobang announced that China would regain Hong Kong on July 1, 1997, *Ming Pao* began to show signs of growing accommodation to Beijing's plans. Commenting on Ji Pengfei's (head of China's Hong Kong and Macao Office) promises of a high degree of autonomous rule by the Hong Kong people, the rule of law and the free flow of capital, *Ming Pao* said:

> For fairness' sake, we would say the measures enumerated by Ji Pengfei are liberal enough to make the people here feel satisfied. There are still some issues to be touched upon. . . . But these can hardly be described as key issues.[41]

Since then *Ming Pao* has published long editorials to provide economic, political, and strategic rationales for China's policies, saying that they might not be untrustworthy after all.[42] When Premier Zhao Ziyang reiterated China's Hong Kong policies in his address to the Canadian parliament in June 1983, *Ming Pao* was quick to point out that it represented an "official pledge and guarantee to the people throughout the world" and reflected China's "sincerity" in implementing its pledge.[43]

Ming Pao's shift of journalistic paradigm appeared to take a quantum leap as the Joint Declaration was about to be initialed. From thence editorials used lengthy quotes from Xinhua and other Chinese officials in an effort to clear up what it perceived to be public misunderstandings of China's policies.[44] This process culminated in a series of editorials heaping praises on the concept of "one country, two systems" and the Declaration. In an article especially written for the *People's Daily* (the CCP's official organ), Louis Cha, publisher and principal editorial writer of *Ming Pao,* reiterated the idea that the concept of "one country, two systems," being "far-sighted and grand in scope," serves as a model of conflict resolution for the whole world. Cha concluded that it is "a dictum that can teach a hundred generations."[45]

Ming Pao urged the Hong Kong people to have confidence in the "one country, two systems" plan because it is born out of a concrete situation rather than ideological orthodoxy and is linked to China's primary national goals. Evaluating the Joint Declaration, *Ming Pao* said:

> After a detailed reading of the agreement, we discovered the demands that we have raised in the past two years have all been incorporated. We may say that both China and Britain have accepted all—not just the basic ones but 100%—of the requests made by the majority of the Hong Kong people. We cannot really think of what else to add to such an agreement. The Hong Kong people have got what they wished, what else can they ask for?[46]

Cha, as a prominent member of both the Basic Law Drafting Committee and its Consultative Committee, has professed to participate actively to effect a smooth political transition.

Ultrarightist Journalistic Paradigm

The ultrarightist newspapers, *Kung Sheung Yat Pao* and the *Hong Kong Times,* have opposed China's policies in their respective editorials. Their editorial paradigm largely remained unscathed in spite of the structural change in power. But subtle signs of accommodation can be detected. During the Sino-British negotiation, the ultrarightist newspapers strongly supported the British pursuit of continued rule over Hong Kong. Welcoming Margaret Thatcher's visit to Hong Kong, for example, the *Hong Kong Times* said:

> In an interview with the BBC, Mrs. Thatcher repeatedly stated that Britain is responsible to the five million people of Hong Kong. She also mentioned that Hong Kong's prosperity is attributable to British rule over the years. Hong Kong's citizens have faith in Britain which is responsible to them. The British prime minister has also restated that Britain will keep the three Sino-British treaties which cannot be repealed at will. . . . Our previous quotations from Mrs. Thatchers prove that this British prime minister pays

considerable attention to the interest and wishes of the Hong Kong people.[47]

Both *Kung Sheung Yat Pao* and the *Hong Kong Times* argued that "the nature of the Hong Kong problem" could not be encapsulated in such terms as "national interest" or "nationalism" but must rest in the "livelihood of the Hong Kong people." *Kung Sheung Yat Pao* argued that Hong Kong's "autonomy and independence" was an appropriate realization of "nationalism."[48] The *Hong Kong Times,* claiming that Beijing is not a legitimate negotiator with Britain over Hong Kong's sovereignty, denied the validity of the Joint Declaration thus produced.[49] As a recurring theme before and after the Joint Declaration, they pictured "one country, two systems" as nothing but a "united front gimmick" designed to deceive the Hong Kong people.[50] The *Hong Kong Times'* editorials, pointing to China's tumultuous 30-year history, described the new policies as "sugar-coated poison."[51] Similarly, *Kung Sheung Yat Pao* cast doubt on China's promise of autonomous rule in Hong Kong. It said:

> The slogan of "Hong Kong people administering Hong Kong" and the idea of turning Hong Kong into a "special administrative region" have dangerous ulterior motives. They are sugar-coated poison designed to kill two birds with one stone. On the one hand, they soften Hong Kong people's determination to maintain Hong Kong as it is. On the other, nationalism, as they seemingly implied, disarms Hong Kong people's resistance.[52]

Now that the political dust has settled, the integrity of the editorial agenda of the ultrarightist press is being put to a severe test. Overall, both papers showed little sign of editorial paradigm shift, insisting that they could not acknowledge the legitimacy of the Declaration. But as newspapers, they could not totally shy away from editorial responsibility to cover such major political developments as the Joint Declaration, the Basic Law Drafting Committee and its Consultative Committee, Xinhua's activities, and China's elaborations of the idea of "one country, two systems."[53] In late 1984 the uncertain political future dealt a death blow to *Kung Sheung Yat Pao,* which had been suffering from chronic losses and low morale.

As a KMT organ, the *Hong Kong Times* has taken a tactical turn from hard-line to milder anticommunism, demonstrated by the ouster of six staunch anti-Communist columnists,[54] the cancellation of a page devoted exclusively to anti-Communist themes, and the softening of its overall rhetoric. The *Hong Kong Times* has supported, in news and editorials, local rightist and centrist groups calling on Beijing to let Hong Kong have parliamentary democracy. Voicing such as proposal represents the paper's subtle acquiescence to eventual rule from Beijing.

Ultraleftist Journalistic Paradigm

The ultraleftist newspapers, similar in their editorial paradigm, have considerably moderated their stance toward the Hong Kong government after the Sino-British accord. They have toned down anti-colonial rhetoric and have "rehabilitated" the colonial institutions and policies they once so harshly criticized. As recently as mid-1983 Governor Youde was seen by *Wen Wei Pao* as a local agent of the British Empire, whose interest was incongruent with that of the Hong Kong community.[55] In the heat of the "public opinion war" amidst negotiation deadlocks, both papers published several editorials tending to delegitimize colonial rule. One of them posed a series of rhetorical questions:

> What is the Hong Kong Government? A fair coordinator and distributor of interest or a partial ruler in favor of corporate interest at the sacrifice of public welfare? Does the government really listen to public opinion? Or does it merely act from its self-interest and the opinions of a few? We have often heard of boasts about how much the government respects public opinion and how perfect its political system is, but on the issue of price raises, where is this respect for public opinion?[56]

No sooner had the Joint Declaration been initialed in 1984 than both papers switched their editorial stance to legitimize the Hong Kong governor as a ruler serving the public good. Commenting on the governor's annual report, *Wen Wei Pao* said, "At the conclusion of the Sino-British negotiation, people doubted whether Hong Kong's prosperity could be preserved; Governor Youde's third report has given positive answers."[57]

Moreover, both papers have moderated their traditionally critical evaluations of the colonial regime's performance. *Wen Wei Pao's* 1985 annual review said:

> In spite of the general slackening of the world's economy and the rise of trade protectionism, Hong Kong's economy remains stable and has secured some growth. . . . In light of the neighboring areas' zero or negative growth, we can only conclude that Hong Kong's economic achievement is not easily attained.[58]

The Hong Kong Government's Independent Commission Against Corruption (ICAC) was once labeled by the Communist press as an organization designed to rectify corruption inherent in colonial capitalism in order to prolong British rule. In very different terms, *Ta Kung Pao* now had this to say:

> The suspects charged by the ICAC will certainly be tried according to strict legal procedures. Hong Kong remains as a society ruled by law and citizens still have confidence in legal justice. People need not speculate about what is behind the scene. What we want to point out is this: The establishment of ICAC is no doubt a positive factor for the Hong Kong society.[59]

Likewise, *Wen Wei Pao* has also enthusiastically endorsed the Hong Kong government's decision to go on with a construction project. The paper seized this project as a "proof" that despite, even because of, political transition, Hong Kong continued to be a stable and prosperous entity—something that had previously been described as "deceptive" or "distorted."[60]

Seldom had the Communist press commented on elections sponsored by the colonial regime. When they did, the comments were largely derogatory. When the colonial regime tried in the early 1970s to promote a sense of "Hong Kong belongingness" among citizens, the Communist press regarded it as an attempt to check the growth of nationalism among the students. With reference to district council elections in early 1985, however, *Wen Wei Pao* argued that "an active participation in public affairs" is "essential."[61] Urging the Hong Kong government to use civil education to ensure that the voters knew what they were doing, it concluded: "Hopefully, this district council election can enhance the citizens' sense of social participation."[62]

It should be noted that moderating its anticolonialism does not imply that the ultraleftist press refrain from criticizing the Hong Kong government in toto. But these criticisms are now framed as "constructive" suggestions, unlike past characterizations of colonial rule as fundamentally immoral. At times, especially after the Tiananmen incident in 1989 when relations between China and Hong Kong were sour, the ultraleftist press could strongly attack British policies (such as that which granted Hong Kong people the right to abode in Britain). But such criticisms were leveled on an issue basis only.

WHO MAKES THE NEWS?

As we have argued, when the dominant order is firmly in place, journalistic practices tend to take the official view as a reference point. But when the status quo is upset, journalists must try to "normalize," reconcile, and assimilate anomalies into their perspectives.[63] They explain the anomalies as exceptions to the "rule." But if anomalies keep piling up, exceptions may not be exceptions and cannot be assimilated on an ad hoc basis. Journalists might have to adjust their fundamental assumptions to "fit the reality." Journalistic paradigms undergo major shifts when the power structure is sharply divided and when core social values are deeply disrupted.[64]

To provide a quantitative check, we undertook a content analysis of the following nine papers: *Ta Kung Pao* and *Wen Wei Pao* (ultraleftist); *Ming Pao, Sing Pao,* and the *Oriental Daily News* (centrist); *Sing Tao Jih Pao* and *Wah Kiu Yat Pao* (rightist); and *Kung Sheung Yat Pao* and *Hong Kong Times* (ultrarightist). We compared a random "constructed week" prior to the Sino-British Joint Declaration (between July 1, 1983, and April 30, 1984) with another "constructed week" after it (between July 1, 1985, and February 28, 1986).[65] The "constructed week" sampling is an application of stratified random sampling; increasing the sample size beyond 12 issues of each newspaper does not produce significantly more accurate results.[66] We focused on the public affairs news printed in the local news pages that were related to the Hong Kong government's activities and policies, China's policies on Hong Kong, and Xinhua's activities. Excluded from analysis were news stories exclusively about China but unrelated to Hong Kong; they were usually carried in the international news or separately in the China pages, rather than in the local news pages.

Several observations are in order:

Firstly, despite its decline in authority after the Sino-British accord, the Hong Kong government remained dominant in setting the news agenda. The press anchors its reportorial staff in the government agencies. The Hong Kong government maintains an efficient information arm to provide the press with a stream of news supply, which forms the staple of the local coverage by many papers. The mainstream (rightist and centrist) press remains cordial with the government, the ultrarightist press has to support it as a deterrent to the Communist inroads, while the ultraleftist press does not intend to weaken it to the extent of endangering a smooth transition of power.

Table 5–1 shows that the Hong Kong government accounted for the bulk of news sources (5–8 out of 10) before and after the accord. The Hong Kong government held solid ground in terms of the news hole size (as shown in Table 5–2) and the number of leading articles (see Table 5–3) and continued to be favorably covered (see Table 5–4).

Secondly, although Xinhua was still playing a second fiddle at the time of the analysis, it gained substantial grounds in terms of the num-

TABLE 5–1. Power Centers as Main News Source, by Press Ideology

Press types	Hong Kong Government[a]		Xinhua (China)[b]		Others[c]		Total (N)[d]	
	Pre-accord	Post-accord	Pre-accord	Post-accord	Pre-accord	Post-accord	Pre-accord	Post-accord
Ultrarightist	75%	79%	2%	3%	23%	18%	94	105
Rightist	74%	70%	5%	3%	21%	17%	269	328
Centrist	78%	62%	7%	24%	15%	14%	151	284
Ultraleftist	56%	53%	9%	23%	35%	24%	127	262

[a] Includes the government's affiliate institutions and their officials.
[b] Includes Xinhua News Agency, the transitional political institutions that it has set up, Chinese officials, and China-based institutions.
[c] Includes social leaders, social institutions, business groups, pressure groups, individuals, and the like.
[d] N = number of public affairs news articles

ber of sources attributed (Table 5–1), the news hole size (Table 5–2), the number of leading articles (Table 5–3), and the extent of favorable coverage (Table 5–4). But only negligible gains were made with the ultrarightist press. While Xinhua made gains with other papers in terms of news sources attributed and the number of leading articles, the colonial regime experienced corresponding declines and thus had to share the limelight with Xinhua. It is noteworthy that the ultrarightist and the rightist press had registered a 19% and 23% decline in unfavorable coverage, an act which could be viewed as subtly acquiescing to political reality.

TABLE 5–2. Power Centers in News Hole Allocation, by Press Ideology

Press types	Hong Kong Government		Xinhua (China)		Others		Total news hole[a]	
	Pre-accord	Post-accord	Pre-accord	Post-accord	Pre-accord	Post-accord	Pre-accord	Post-accord
Ultrarightist	38%	40%	1%	2%	61%	58%	20,458	23,214
Rightist	32%	39%	0%	11%	68%	50%	69,266	60,673
Centrist	25%	35%	1%	29%	74%	36%	39,107	46,296
Ultraleftist	22%	27%	4%	23%	74%	50%	36,923	59,892

[a] "Total news hole" covers all the newspapers' local pages in a week and is measured in square centimeters. For explanation of other categories, see Table 5–1.

TABLE 5–3. Power Centers in Leading News Articles, by Press Ideology

Press types	Hong Kong Government		Xinhua (China)		Others		Total (N)[a]	
	Pre-accord	Post-accord	Pre-accord	Post-accord	Pre-accord	Post-accord	Pre-accord	Post-accord
Ultrarightist	62%	92%	0%	0%	38%	8%	13	12
Rightist	75%	72%	2%	16%	33%	12%	55	50
Centrist	100%	71%	0%	21%	0%	8%	12	34
Ultraleftist	19%	40%	19%	40%	62%	20%	21	30

[a] N = number of leading public affairs news articles. For explanation of other categories, see Table 5–1.

A third observation that can be drawn is that the commercial, middle-of-the-road, mainstream press, being ideologically and organizationally more flexible, was expected to exhibit a greater readiness than the ultrarightist press to accommodate China/Xinhua. The ultrarightist press, holding extreme positions, had less latitude of movement.

Table 5–1 shows that the centrist press and the rightist press registered larger increases (17% and 8% respectively) for China/Xinhua than did the ultrarightist press (1%). Furthermore, as Table 5–2 discloses, the centrist press increased its news holes for China/Xinhua by as much as 28%, the rightist press had a corresponding 11% rise while the ultrarightist press almost stood unchanged. In the pre-accord period, according to Table 5–3, only the ultraleftist press (19%) and the rightist press (2%) ever treated China/Xinhua in the leading article positions. In the post-accord period, the centrist press had a notable 21% increase for China/Xinhua, while the colonial government experienced a corresponding decline (− 29%).[67] The rightist press had a rise of 14% for China/Xinhua. In contrast, the ultrarightist press has never featured China/Xinhua in the leading article positions either before or after the accord. Some of these statistics may not be taken literally because of the small number of observations, but the direction is consistent. Table 5–4 shows that increases in favorable coverage of China/Xinhua by the centrist press (5%) and the rightist press (6%) were modest, but these papers were about equally favorable towards both power centers. Although the ultrarightist press scored no favorable gain for China/Xinhua, there was a rise in neutral coverage (19%) alongside a similar drop in unfavorable coverage.

The fourth observation concerns the comparison between the ultraleftist press and the ultrarightist press. Our expectation that the ultra-

TABLE 5–4. Press Evaluation of Power Centers, by Press Ideology

Press types	Hong Kong government			Xinhua (China)		
	Pre-accord	Post-accord	Change	Pre-accord	Post-accord	Change
Ultrarightist press						
Favorable	51%	58%	+7%	0	0	0%
Neutral	45%	30%	−15%	0	19%	+19%
Unfavorable	4%	12%	+8%	100%	81%	−19%
(N)[a]	(74)	(90)		(14)	(16)	
Rightist press						
Favorable	50%	48%	−2%	43%	49%	+6%
Neutral	41%	41%	0%	14%	30%	+16%
Unfavorable	9%	10%	+1%	43%	20%	−23%
(N)	(209)	(242)		(14)	(69)	
Centrist press						
Favorable	46%	53%	+7%	45%	50%	+5%
Neutral	48%	34%	−14%	36%	38%	+2%
Unfavorable	6%	13%	+7%	19%	12%	−7%
(N)	(120)	(180)		(11)	(86)	
Ultraleftist press						
Favorable	21%	40%	+19%	89%	75%	−14%
Neutral	57%	48%	−9%	6%	23%	+17%
Unfavorable	22%	12%	−10%	6%	2%	−4%
(N)	(82)	(165)		(18)	(93)	

[a] N = number of news articles on a power center in a period of time.

rightist press has little choice but to look to the Hong Kong government as a deterrent to the Communists does not obtain strong support in the data. Although the ultrarightist press registered a 30% gain in the number of leading articles, the cases were too small to be taken literally. The ultrarightist press seemed to exhibit a certain ambivalence toward the Hong Kong government, as the 15% decline in neutral coverage was equally split into the "favorable" and "unfavorable" categories. The ultrarightist press was disappointed by the Hong Kong government backtracking from some of its more resolute positions (such as democratic reform).

On the other hand, we expect the ultraleftist press to toe China's Party line *and* to accommodate the colonial regime in the interest of power transition. Therefore, the ultraleftist press should moderate its anticolonial overtone and increase the amount of coverage and the amount of favorable evaluation for the Hong Kong government. That seemed indeed the case: the ultraleftist press increased its source attribution (14%), news hole size (19%), number of leading articles (21%), and favorable coverage (19%) to the Hong Kong government. This press remained overwhelmingly favorable (75%) to China/Xinhua, although there was a 14% decline in favorable coverage, presumably to "neutralize" its rigid press image (Table 5–4).

CONCLUSIONS

This chapter examines the paradigm shift of the press in relation to the changing configuration of political power. In the context of Hong Kong's political transition, the press has shifted its worldviews, whether in editorials or in news coverage, in regard to the dualistic power structure. Once political reality was redefined in terms of British withdrawal, mass media have constrained their discourse within the parameter of the "one country, two systems."

The shift of journalistic paradigms varies with the press's political ideology or affiliation. As expected, the centrist and rightist newspapers, because of organizational/ideological flexibility and market interest, have shown much greater accommodation to Xinhua than have the ultrarightist newspapers. Particularly notable is the former's shift from an initial preference for continued British rule to final acquiescence to, and even an endorsement of, China's takeover. The two ultrarightist newspapers, *Kung Sheung Yat Pao* and the *Hong Kong Times*, have adopted different paths of adaptation. *Kung Sheung Yat Pao* has chosen to opt out while the *Hong Kong Times* has chosen to stay (at least for now) and has softened its hard-line anti-Communist rhetoric. As 1997 draws nearer, there will be soaring pressure put on the *Hong Kong Times* toward conformity. The paper may respond by accommodating Xinhua as a legitimate power center, or remain faithful to its position until the date when it must quit. Finally, the ultraleftist newspapers, under the direction of Xinhua, have moderated their anticolonial overtones. The emergent cordiality between the Communist press and the colonial regime is to continue, in view of the promise by China in the Sino-British Joint Declaration to provide cooperation in the interest of stability and prosperity. Since Hong Kong's transition is gradually phased in, the media will shift their journalistic paradigms in a cumulative and incremental fashion. The new journalistic paradigms are born of the old, showing both continuities and discontinuities. The paradigm shift is as yet incomplete and will be elaborated until long after the change of power in 1997.

Will pluralistic media voices be lost? The political boundary, as previously analyzed, has narrowed. But given Hong Kong's vibrant market economy and China's promise of preserving Hong Kong's capitalism beyond 1997, we do not believe that Hong Kong will lose its pluralistic media in toto. The press has undoubtedly reshaped its journalistic paradigms, largely moving toward the center of gravity and accommodating the twin power structure. But journalistic paradigms, like political development, are dynamically changing and may take unexpected turns. Will the Beijing leadership remain stable? Will China keep its promises? How will Hong Kong's social formations be shaped? How will the media maintain their relative autonomy? All these questions will determine the content of journalistic paradigms in the future.

Chapter 6

"Two Systems" within "One Country": The Case of the Daya Bay Nuclear Plant

Since 1984 the main political discourse in Hong Kong has shifted from the contradiction between British rule versus Chinese rule to the contradiction between central control versus local autonomy. Yet political change, including the present one, does not follow a grand script with everything figured out in advance. The Sino-British Joint Declaration, at best, set a basic structure and laid out a set of highly abstract, theoretical principles—or perhaps even an irreversible trend—but it will take an arduous process of practical struggles and continual negotiations to work out the details that would give those principles any substantive and concrete meaning. The Basic Law Drafting Committee embodies the official process of transition, with its major task to define the boundaries of what Hong Kong can and cannot do as a "special administrative region." But the "struggles" and "negotiations" take place more broadly at the unofficial level, too.

Local interests will partially be a limiting condition for the extent to which the press accommodates the new political order and the extent to which the press shifts journalistic paradigms. No, the Hong Kong press has not unconditionally bent with the political wind or subjugated itself to be China's mouthpiece. Far from it. Hong Kong's market environment is antithetical to communism and may loathe a press that embraces the new power in a thoughtless and self-destructive way. The press, as a business, is deeply intertwined with local enterprises and other social institutions perpetually fearful of China impeding Hong Kong's interests. Therefore, while having come to terms with China, the press will stand up to defend Hong Kong's interests in the face of China's pressure.

When China collides with Hong Kong, the ultraleftist press in Hong Kong should be expected to toe China's Party line but also to air local grievances to the extent that they can be defused. The ultrarightist press, on the contrary, should seize upon the opportunity to politicize the issue, casting doubt on the feasibility of China's "one country, two systems" design. The rightist and the centrist press, while having acquiesced to China's blueprint to retake Hong Kong, should show a varying degree of altercation with China's stance. But all in all, these presumed "struggles" have to observe China's limits of tolerance.

To illustrate, this chapter will examine the controversy over the building of the Daya Bay Nuclear Power Plant, just 70 miles off Hong Kong. Regarding it as a potential safety hazard, the local population petitioned against its construction and thus pitted Hong Kong against China. Which side—the side of the future master or the local people— was the Hong Kong press on? Through this example we can gain a better sense of the limits of the "struggle."

THE CASE

On April 26, 1986, a major nuclear plant accident claimed many Soviet lives in Chernobyl and caused contamination of water, air, and food throughout Europe.[1] No one could have predicted that this accident would produce a rippling effect in Hong Kong thousands of miles away. Plans had been underway for some time to build a nuclear power plant at Daya Bay to testify to Hong Kong's continued economic prosperity and its closer cooperation with China. Suddenly Hong Kong caught the Chernobyl fever, turning the nuclear plant issue into a bitter friction.

The world oil crisis of the 1970s sent Hong Kong on its first journey searching for cheaper energy alternatives. After different efforts, a final solution seemed to be found in constructing a nuclear power plant at Daya Bay, located on the Chinese side but only 70 miles away from Hong Kong. The Hong Kong government promised not only to guarantee the loan but also to purchase 70% of the power to be generated. The China Light & Power Company (in Hong Kong) reached a joint venture agreement with the Guangdong provincial government in March 1986.[2]

China looked keenly to the Daya Bay nuclear plant as a vital source of electricity and transferred technology. China's power shortage is so severe that electricity has to be rationed even in major cities. The World Bank projected that China would require an annual 7% growth in power supply between 1980 and 2000 if the goal of rapid industrialization was to be attained.[3] China was already building a nuclear plant in Zhejiang, but the Daya Bay plant would generate six times more power and promise to hand over the much-needed Western technology and international capital to China on favorable terms.[4]

Everything was moving forward without much fanfare. Only feeble, scattered dissension was heard when both parties signed a letter of intent in March 1986.[5] Then the Chernobyl accident exploded on April 26. The previously ignored safety concerns suddenly became a rallying cry for antinuclear protesters. By May 31, a Joint Conference for the Shelving of Daya Bay Nuclear Plant was formed by 117 organizations. This body, though loosely organized, managed to compile one million signatures from the public by July to express opposition to the plant construction. Delegates of the protesters requested an audience with the Chinese officials in Beijing, but the demand was rejected.

The Hong Kong government refused to withdraw from its commitment to the project. In the Legislative and Executive Councils, most appointed members endorsed the government's stance but the elected members opposed it. A delegation was sent abroad by the Councils. Upon return to Hong Kong, the delegation issued a lengthy report listing the safety measures adopted by foreign plants. The report was also presented to the Beijing authorities, which promised to consider it fully in order to augment plant safety at Daya Bay.

The dispute divided the plant supporters and its opponents. The supporters included both the Chinese and Hong Kong governments as well as their business allies, who were pitted against the amorphous Hong Kong population at large as represented by the Joint Conference. The supporters won the battle when the Daya Bay contract was signed in Beijing on September 23, ending a five-month rancorous debate.

EDITORIAL PARADIGMS AND PRESS IDEOLOGY

The Ultraleftist Press

During the five-month period, *Wen Wei Pao* only carried three editorials and *Ta Kung Pao* only printed two on this issue. None of them appeared before the protesters had raised too loud a voice to be ignored. This calculated silence served to marginalize the issue as unworthy of serious attention.

In short, the Communist press relegated the plant safety issue to being a "technical" matter to be resolved by experts rather than by the public. "In the last analysis," *Ta Kung Pao* insisted, "building a nuclear plant is undoubtedly a question for science."[6] To augment this conclusion, both papers advanced the following arguments: (1) The nuclear plant will be built with advanced Western technology and international aid;[7] (2) China will ensure the plant safety and has taken every measure to do so;[8] and (3) China has a credible record in nuclear technology and will manage the plant properly.[9] As *Ta Kung Pao* said, "The probability of a serious meltdown for the Daya Bay Nuclear Plant . . . is very remote. Even if it happened, it would not affect Hong Kong."[10] Expounding the financial advantages of the nuclear plant, *Wen Wei Pao* argued, "The cost of nuclear energy is relatively low. Experts have pointed out that within twenty years, the plant would have saved HK$30 billion. . . . As the prices of oil and coal will rise sharply in the nineties, the use of nuclear energy is inevitable."[11]

The significance of the one million anti-plant signatures was discounted. *Wen Wei Pao* argued that the public signed their names out of ignorance about nuclear energy and did so only under the agitation of a handful of people after the Chernobyl accident.[12] *Ta Kung Pao* said that plant relocation or termination should follow scientific evidence rather than "backward [public] opinions."[13] *Ta Kung Pao* charged that the antinuclear movement leaders "turned a deaf ear to experts and scholars, undermined scientific evidence with polemics," and "exploited nuclear fear, collected some signatures, and inflated their own ego."[14]

The Communist press moved in quickly to patch up the differences with the public when a letter of intent was signed for the plant construction. *Wen Wei Pao* claimed that nuclear safety was a common interest, whereas *Ta Kung Pao* lauded the project as a symbol of "growing trust" and "synchronized development" between China and Hong Kong.[15] Countering the criticism that Beijing had been heavy-handed, the papers claimed that the plant construction was a "collective decision" reached after extensive consultation with experts and the educated.[16] *Ta Kung Pao* maintained that in fact China had accorded a top priority to the plant "safety and quality."[17]

Departing from its long-standing refusal to recognize the colonial Legislative and Executive Councils, the Communist press applauded the Councils' overseas inspection team report in order to legitimize China's actions.[18] Quoting Chief Secretary Sir Akers Jones, *Wen Wei Pao* praised that the report would "enhance the Hong Kong people's understanding of the issue and provide an invaluable help."[19]

On the eve of the contract signing in Beijing, *Ta Kung Pao* summarily put a full stop to the controversy:

> Given the guaranteed technological safety and the economic benefits, it becomes unreasonable for anyone to continue opposing the Daya Bay nuclear plant. . . . Any suggestion to stop or relocate the plant should evidently be questioned.[20]

The Centrist Press

The *Oriental Daily News*—the paper that does not carry any editorial and deliberately dodges political controversy—was mute about the Daya Bay issue. *Ming Pao*, however, strongly opposed the nuclear plant construction. *Ming Pao* was, from the beginning, apprehensive about possible management error that might create a nuclear havoc. "No matter how precise the design of mechanical equipment is," it said, "errors are inevitable as far as they are run by humans."[21] The paper addressed human error in a general way, unlike the *Hong Kong Times* which attributed the problem to incompetence of the Communist government. *Ming Pao* said that no guarantee could be provided for nuclear safety despite China's expressed concern, and unless safety can be absolutely certified, Hong Kong could not risk a nuclear accident at Daya Bay.[22] Such an accident would not only inflict human pain, cause environmental pollution, and contaminate Hong Kong's food supply, but would blow Hong Kong's position as a leading international financial center, thus jeopardizing China's "one country, two systems" experiment.[23]

While *Ming Pao* argued for the local interests, it characteristically took an empathetic perspective of the Beijing authorities. To calm Beijing, *Ming Pao* explicitly stated that the antinuclear movement should not be thought of as directed against the central authorities.[24] The paper said that it did not oppose nuclear power as long as the plant was built outside Hong Kong's vicinity.[25] *Ming Pao* argued that what the public cared about most was neither economic efficiency nor technical details, but safety.[26] According to the paper, public opinion was decidedly against the plant.[27] When the contract for building the plant was about to be signed, *Ming Pao* commented: "The Hong Kong people tend to be resigned when they fail to get things changed, but [public silence] does not mean that their hearts are at ease."[28]

Even though the Chinese authorities should bear the final responsibility for building the plant, *Ming Pao* was most critical of the Hong Kong government. In an appeal to Beijing, the paper rationally outlined the political and economic risks involved in building the plant adjacent to Hong Kong. But the paper raised its voice when it berated the Hong Kong government for abusing public trust in deciding to publicize the safety of the nuclear plant even after the British Nuclear Commission revealed that it was not that safe.[29] This represented quite a serious accusation for a paper noted for its close ties with the government. The Legislative and Executive Councils' foreign inspection team report was branded a "public relations gimmick" designed to convince the people of the safety of the Daya Bay plant and to enable the government to dodge the issue.[30] Both councils did nothing but "to accept the Chinese authorities' decision on behalf of the Hong Kong people."[31]

Sing Pao, on the other hand, did not see any real threat to the plant safety.[32] It said, for example, "Even in case of a serious accident, the safety dome of the nuclear plant should be able to contain the radioactive material. The chance for a Chernobyl-type accident to happen . . . is very remote."[33] Given the nuclear experts in China and Britain, it claimed, the safety of the Daya Bay nuclear plant would be assured.[34] When the contract for plant construction was about to be signed, the paper slighted the issue by stating that people should not demand "100% safety."[35]

Sometimes *Sing Pao* was self-contradictory. At one point, it said that safety concern was justified in view of the poor performance of China's service industries;[36] at another point, it praised China's world-class sophistication in rocketry for satellite launching.[37] The one million antinuclear signatures, *Sing Pao* said, were rendered suspect by some "overzealous" organizers who had collected signatures from "old women" and "primary school pupils" ill-informed about the issue.[38] The paper quoted poll results from unnamed sources to argue that more and more people were supporting the nuclear plant.[39] The uproar over the plant was thought to be more a result of public ignorance than a real threat. *Sing Pao* echoed the Communist press to call for more public education on nuclear power to help alleviate fear.[40]

Sing Pao tried to bury the issue as soon as the agreement for plant construction was signed. Calling to end the antinuclear movement, the paper advised that Hong Kong should concentrate its effort on training local nuclear experts to ensure nuclear safety.[41] In fact, *Sing Pao* proceeded one step further to claim that whether to establish the plant or not was "a question of China's sovereignty," whereas Hong Kong could only decide whether to buy electricity from China or not.[42] The paper stated, "While the struggle to stop the plant is destined to fail, we should aim lower for a safer nuclear plant and take part in monitoring its safety."[43] On several occasions *Sing Pao* portrayed China as a power that heeded Hong Kong's public opinion by emphasizing nuclear safety.[44] It was a "move toward democracy" to allow the antinuclear movement leaders petition their concerns in Beijing.[45] Even though the Hong Kong government's handling of the issue was not a frequent topic for *Sing Pao,* the paper generally endorsed its position. For example, the paper sided with the governor in rejecting a request by Martin Lee, a vocal Legislative Councillor, that a special session be called to debate on the nuclear power issue.[46]

The Rightist Press

Both *Sing Tao Jih Pao* and *Wah Kiu Yat Pao* opposed the plant even if chances for a nuclear catastrophe were perceived to be remote. Like *Ming Pao*, they tended to attribute the potential nuclear misfortune to human error or management failure rather than to technological obstacles.[47] Both papers warned that Hong Kong could not afford the risk of having a nuclear accident on its doorstep—as *Wah Kiu Yat Pao* put it, "a slightest neglect may result in an accident that will destroy Hong Kong in its entirety."[48] They also disputed the alleged need for nuclear power and its supposed economic benefits. They maintained instead that the coal- or oil-generated electrical supply could meet Hong Kong's future needs and that the economic gain was not worth the risk.[49]

Both papers sympathized with public opinion that surged against plant construction. *Sing Tao Jih Pao* asserted that participants in the antinuclear movement were neither "blind" or "neurotic," but were inspired by a "concern for survival."[50] The appeal to have the plant relocated was regarded as rational and justified.[51] *Wah Kiu Yat Pao* was less consistent. It scolded the Hong Kong people for being "emotional," but then defended their concern as legitimate in view of the Chernobyl accident.[52]

Among the mainstream newspapers, *Sing Tao Jih Pao* stood out as most scathingly critical of the remarks made by the Chinese officials. Denunciation by the Chinese officials of the antinuclear movement as "politically motivated by ulterior goals," *Sing Tao Jih Pao* retorted, typically reflected China's domination over Hong Kong.[53] It said:

> The negative impact of the nuclear power question on the CCP's "one country, two systems" . . . will long last. The Chinese Communists' blunt decision [to build the plant] not only denies the will of one million and forty thousand people who have petitioned against the nuclear plant but disregards Hong Kong people's sense of democracy.[54]

Wah Kiu Yat Pao was less derogatory. But as the antinuclear movement was winding down, the paper maintained that the Hong Kong people were not just upset by potential technological hazards but by China's indifference to public opinion. The paper predicted that China's neglect of public opinion would lead to further erosion of the already very low public confidence in Hong Kong's future.[55]

Sing Tao Jih Pao, famous for its warm ties with the Hong Kong government in the past, reprimanded some Executive and Legislative

Councillors for trying to appease China at a rapid pace. It said," [They] have gone too far when they defied their past record and the will of the public to please the [new] boss."[56] The paper even chided the Hong Kong government as a "lame duck" that always "says yes" to China.[57] *Wah Kiu Yat Pao*, again, was less critical, only complaining that the Hong Kong government failed to keep the public sufficiently informed about the nuclear plant.

Both papers were sympathetic to the antinuclear effort and wanted the nuclear plant to be delayed or relocated elsewhere. *Sing Tao Jih Pao* was, however, more consistent and persistent than *Wah Kiu Yat Pao* in arguing against the plant and in criticizing the way China and the Hong Kong government handled the matter. Upon approval of the contract for building the plant, both papers rushed to commend the inspection report amassed by the Legislative and Executive Councils that made a series of suggestions to improve the nuclear power plant safety.[58] *Wah Kiu Yat Pao* commented, "The Nuclear Power Energy Inspection Tour . . . offered a compromise for the deadlock. It helped the Chinese government to shed its dictatorial image and provided a chance to cool down the intense public opinion."[59]

The Ultrarightist Press

While raising safety as a core issue, the *Hong Kong Times* explicitly attributed the peril to "the corrupt and inadequate Chinese Communist bureaucracy" and to "the low standard of its technical personnel."[60] Speaking in the name of the Hong Kong people, the paper maintained that it was more advisable to pay a higher electricity bill than to endure a "timed nuclear bomb only 70 miles away that may explode any time."[61] A nuclear accident at Daya Bay would spell the "death of the Hong Kong harbor."[62]

The *Hong Kong Times* had been fiercely suspicious of social movements, fearing that putting too much pressure on the colonial government might tip the power balance in favor of mainland China. Since the onset of the political transition, however, the *Hong Kong Times* has been sympathetic to similar movements that tend to make demands on the Communist authorities. This time, the paper dismissed the charge that the public was ignorant about nuclear power, asserting that the real issue lay in the Chinese Communists' lack of modern skills in nuclear management.[63] The *Hong Kong Times* again accused the CCP of its "bureaucratism," of "placing leadership in the hands of the ignorant rather than the knowledgeable," and of their "excessive concern about keeping the power."[64] While the *Hong Kong Times* politicized the issue against the Communists, it characterized the antinuclear movement as "not based on political reasons or bias" but motivated by the "concern for safety and the property" of the Hong Kong people.[65] In addition, the paper scolded the Hong Kong government for "slighting public opinion" and collaborating with China.[66]

On several occasions, the *Hong Kong Times* regarded the nuclear dispute as a "litmus test" of the "one country, two systems" policy. The paper argued that "two systems" would not stand a chance and will be collapsed into "one system."[67] The aloofness displayed by the refusal of ranking officials to receive the antinuclear leaders in Beijing, the *Hong Kong Times* said, should awaken those who still held wishful thoughts about the Communists.[68] The nuclear issue, in short, gave the *Hong Kong Times* another anti-Communist opportunity.

DISCUSSION AND IMPLICATIONS

The Daya Bay issue reveals the way that the Hong Kong press might behave when there is a potential conflict of interest between China and Hong Kong or, more broadly, between "one country" and "two systems." It came as no surprise that the Communist-controlled *Wen Wei Pao* and *Ta Kung Pao* would echo China's established policy, while the *Hong Kong Times* seized another chance to rehash its anti-Communist rhetoric. *Sing Pao* and *Wah Kiu Yat Pao* (to a lesser extent) appeared to conform to the Chinese position but made a plea to relocate the plant. *Ming Pao* and *Sing Tao Jih Pao* were quite persistent in their demand for plant relocation. Overall, the commercial press is particularly sensitive to public opinion when the issue has important bearing on Hong Kong's interests and autonomy.

Although many papers continued to be distressed by China's "one country, two systems" policy, none has refuted its premises. On the contrary, most of the struggles seem to be fought in terms of this framework, demanding China to uphold the integrity of the Joint Declaration, in letter and spirit. In fact, most papers simply wanted China to move the plant away from Hong Kong—to Shanghai, Guangzhou, anywhere—rather than to stop its construction.[69] As China attempted to attribute the nuclear opposition to "exterior motives," most papers carefully denied that allegation and said that China should not view differences of opinion as antagonistic to Beijing.

The press will reduce its loyalty to the Hong Kong government with each day that goes by. This was clearly manifested in the Daya Bay conflict when its traditional allies, particularly *Ming Pao* and *Sing*

Tao Jih Pao, vehemently challenged the colonial regime's decision to concur with the Chinese position. It was ironic that the Hong Kong government drew its comforting support from the Communist press.

The Daya Bay controversy is a test case of the way that conflicts between China and Hong Kong can be resolved. Although theoretically China has the power to make a decision irrespective of Hong Kong's public opinion, this would have resulted in the further erosion of the already low public trust. To consolidate its legitimacy, China adopted what Herbert Simon calls a "coactive" approach rather than a "combative" approach, with its emphasis on rationality and search for common grounds among conflicting parties.[70] While persistently placing emphasis on "rational" discussion, China tried to "localize" the whole issue to safety enhancement. China also made minor concessions by dispatching a low-ranking official to greet the movement representatives and by agreeing to set up an advisory board to monitor the plant safety.

Given China's lopsided power, the logical outcome of the conflict is, in the word of Louis Kriesberg, "implicit" in nature: both parties agree that the conflict is formally terminated, yet compliance is forced upon the weaker side.[71] The conflict over plant construction has ended with the signing of the contract, although the movement leaders vowed to continue the struggle. After 1997 the conflicts between China and Hong Kong will have to be resolved in an institutionalized framework of the Basic Law, but open confrontations cannot be ruled out.

Chapter 7

Closing the Ranks: Thunder of Tiananmen

The thunder of democracy and freedom exploded in Tiananmen Square and was heard throughout the world, thanks in part to the power of modern media. For two spring months in 1989, the world was holding its breath for, exalting at, and then shocked in disbelief by the events unfolding in Beijing, China's capital. The yearning for democratic reform was unprecedented in scale since Mao came to power in the world's most populated land in 1949. What started out as a peaceful demonstration ended with one of the most brutal and tragic massacres in modern history. Voices once raised in joyous acclamation of democracy and freedom have at least temporarily been silenced by bursts of gunfire; the crush of tanks; the rounding up of dissident students, intellectuals, and workers; and by strict control of information. While pro-democracy students in Beijing cried out to "tell the world," China's aging leaders wasted no time in rewriting their version of history in Tiananmen Square.

This chapter examines how the Hong Kong press shifted its journalistic paradigms while China experienced a power vacuum during the 1989 Tiananmen incident. What began as an expression of student discontent escalated, by no one's design, into a theater where the drama of a top-level power struggle within the Chinese Communist Party was played out. The power uncertainty in Beijing left Xinhua News Agency, China's command post in Hong Kong, temporarily confused and impotent to enforce ideological conformity. Hong Kong's Communist press broke party ranks to endorse the student movement in China, whereas the non-Communist press regressed into an anti-Communist framework. To wit, the centrist press and the rightist press were initially tentative but finally joined the chorus condemning Beijing. The ultrarightist press was critical of the Beijing regime from the beginning to the end. The Hong Kong press was inadvertently, if also temporarily, united in condemnation of the Beijing massacre.

The announcement of the Sino-British Joint Declaration in September 1984, as previously analyzed, has set off significant paradigm shifts among the Hong Kong press. The press, having sided with the British, has come a long way to acquiesce to China's legitimacy in Hong Kong.

Political discourse is redefined within China's policy of "one country, two systems." The Tiananmen protests, however, mark a decisive though temporary departure from the newly constituted press paradigms. This illustrates that paradigm shifts—or more accurately, reshifts—may result from a power vacuum, a collapse of elite consensus, as well as major social crises, any of which renders the press greater leeway to steer its editorial course.[1] This editorial course is often rooted in and intertwined with press ideology, which imparts the reality with a distinctly different significance. But even these reshifts, however radical or shocking, have severe limits.

THE CASE

First Stage

Student protests broke out on April 15, 1989, to mourn the death of Hu Yaobang, who lost his post as Party general secretary in 1987 for advocating tolerance toward similar protests. The students petitioned to have Hu's name restored, and to have the campaigns against spiritual pollution (1983) and bourgeois liberalization (1986–1987) repudiated. They also called for greater freedom of the press, more funds for education, better treatment for intellectuals, and disclosure of bank accounts of high-ranking officials and their children. Getting no response from the government, students boycotted classes and sat in at Tiananmen Square, near the heart of China's government. The officially controlled media, meanwhile, gave no inkling of these protests.[2] The dismissal of Qin Benli as editor of Shanghai's reformist *World Economic Herald* heightened the demand for press freedom.[3] Following Deng Xiaoping's directive, the *People's Daily* denounced the student movement in its April 26 editorial as "a planned *conspiracy*, a *disturbance* . . . instigated by a handful of people." (These same terms were later used to justify the crackdown and purges following June 4.)

Second Stage

The *People's Daily* editorial touched off a flurry of demonstrations. Seeking to exonerate their cause as peaceful and patriotic, the students demanded a televised dialogue with high-level officials and an official promise that there would be no retribution against them. Yuan Mu, spokesman of the State Council, told the students to air their grievances "via regular channels." On May 4, the moderate Party General Secretary Zhao Ziyang said that he did not see the student movement as a "disturbance," since the students sought reforms within the system rather than the overthrow of the Party. On May 8, more than 1,000 journalists petitioned the Politburo to demand greater freedom of the press.

Amid escalating student protests and Soviet President Gorbachev's summit visit, there were clear signs of a power struggle between Zhao and Premier Li Peng. Furious at the government's decision to turn a deaf ear to their demands, 3,000 students went on a hunger strike on May 12. Some 1,000 foreign reporters who arrived in Beijing to cover the summit between leaders of the two greatest Communist powers were incidentally on hand to focus world attention on, and to dramatize, the Tiananmen protests. Zhao asked the students for self-restraint to save national dignity, but acknowledged that their grievances were legitimate and should be addressed. In what was later to constitute the heinous crime of "leaking a state secret," Zhao disclosed to Gorbachev that Deng Xiaoping held ultimate veto authority in the Politburo. The demonstrations mushroomed to 20 major cities across China. On May 17, Zhao urged students to maintain "coolness, reason, restraint, and order," and assured them that the government would not retaliate against them. Meanwhile, two-thirds of the fasting students had lost consciousness, striking a cord in the hearts of the common people, one million of whom poured into the streets of Beijing shouting slogans and calling for Deng and Li to resign.

Under pressure, Li held a televised meeting with student leaders on May 18, in which he sternly warned them to stop fasting but refused to discuss substantive issues. The following day, one million residents of Beijing marched again, this time echoed by another million marching in Shanghai. In what turned out to be his last public appearance, a tearful Zhao visited students in Tiananmen Square and apologized for failing to heed their voices in time.

Third Stage

Premier Li imposed martial law in Beijing on May 20. The next day in Hong Kong, one million people took to the streets, to be followed a week later by another demonstration of one and a half million people, including many pro-China union members and journalists from the Communist press. (Throughout the movement, Hong Kong provided enormous material and moral support in various forms.) For almost two weeks, the crowd in Beijing defiantly barred the army's entry into Tiananmen Square with walls made up of trucks, buses, and their own bodies. Satellite transmission was disconnected, then briefly resumed, and halted again. Zhao was dismissed. The troops and tanks forced their way into Tiananmen Square during the late hours of June 3 and the early hours of June 4, killing a huge but undisclosed number of people. The state media claimed no student casualties.

That Deng had not been seen in public since mid-May gave rise to hope that he might not have been responsible for the massacre. But any doubt about his role was scrapped once and for all on June 9 when he reemerged on television to congratulate the Liberation Army for a job well done. Meanwhile, somewhat astonished at the strongly negative reaction from the rest of the world, China lashed out at the United States (especially the Voice of America), Hong Kong, and Taiwan for instigating the unrest.

EDITORIAL PARADIGMS AND PRESS IDEOLOGY

The Ultraleftist Press

In the past, when the Xinhua-controlled ultraleftist newspapers in Hong Kong wished to express their rare disapproval of China's official line, news was subtly placed in a less prominent position or attributed to Xinhua.[4] In line with China's "one country, two systems" policy, these newspapers have tried since 1984 to enhance their competitive capability in Hong Kong's market, and hence have chipped away at some of their ideological inhibitions. This time when the protests broke out, their first reaction was to urge that the Chinese authorities and students communicate with each other. But as the movement gathered support and the top leadership appeared to be locked in a ferocious power struggle, these newspapers threw their weight behind Zhao and ended up condemning Premier Li. During the movement, both papers were circulated in Tiananmen Square and cheered up the protesters by informing them of the worldwide support for them.

At the outset, *Wen Wei Pao* was fearful that the rally might lead to chaos and counseled both sides to resolve the predicament through "dialogue and mutual compromise."[5] While urging the students to "cool down in view of the paramount importance of unity and stability," *Wen Wei Pao* asked the government to be more generous and tolerant toward the students and to search for harmonious solutions to the demonstrations.[6] Similar views were uttered by *Ta Kung Pao*.[7] Neither of these papers echoed Beijing's *People's Daily* in characterizing the movement as a "disturbance"; both endorsed Zhao's May 4 speech, in which he urged government corruption be resolved "in a cool, rational, restrained, and orderly fashion by democratic and legal means."[8]

In early May, both newspapers began to stray from the Party line, heartened by the student's hunger strike and by the reports of 1,000 journalists in Beijing marching for press freedom. On May 16, *Wen Wei Pao* attributed the cause of the movement to rampant government corruption and praised the protesters for "hurling China onto a new stage" of development which would help implement reforms and root out corruption.[9] *Ta Kung Pao* was similarly moved by the sight of one million citizens marching through Beijing on May 17, and blamed the authorities for ignoring those students whose lives were menaced by the hunger strike.[10]

For its May 21 editorial, *Wen Wei Pao* departed from its usual densely printed layout to comment on the imposition of martial law by marooning four characters in a sea of white space: *tongxin jishou* (heartstricken).[11] This tactic of *kai tian chuang* (windowing), leaving a blank space in a publication to show something has been censored, was used by pro-Communist papers against the KMT before 1949. Never before had a Communist newspaper been known to have resorted to this technique against the Communist authorities.

Witnessing the courageous blocking of the army by Beijing citizens, *Wen Wei Pao* expressed its hope that the Zhao-led "healthy voice" would take advantage of public opinion to further the goals of reform. In a milder statement, *Ta Kung Pao* took the Chinese authorities to task for failing to avert escalation of the conflict.[12] Predicting that the tide of democracy, and Zhao, would win the power battle, *Ta Kung Pao* wrote that the few that stood opposed to the people would be reprimanded.[13]

The situation, however, took an abrupt turn. To mourn those killed in Tiananmen Square on June 4, *Wen Wei Pao*'s usual red masthead was printed in black. The paper said that the "Li-Yang Clique" (Premier Li and President Yang)—"thieves of the nation" and "shameless liars" who grabbed national leadership—should not only be discharged but be put on trial. The editorial said:

> Since the student movement began, this newspaper has consistently tried to persuade the [Chinese] authorities to have genuine dialogue with the students so as to prevent aggravation of the situation. Even after [Premier] Li Peng's blood-thirsty speech on May 19, we risked ourselves in urging the authorities to exercise restraint . . . unfortunately, [we] failed to stop a handful of people from committing violence. Inevitably, people must ask: *What is wrong with our system? What can be done when national leadership is grabbed by a handful of butchers?*[14] (emphasis added)

Urging the people to "rise up to punish the thieves who usurp the country," *Wen Wei Pao* accused the "frenzied Li-Yang clique" of manufacturing despicable lies, including repeated showing of television pictures that "called murderers victims."[15]

> The Li-Yang clique has pushed the clock back by bathing Beijing in blood, and has been grievously and angrily opposed by people throughout China and by overseas Chinese, and justly condemned by countries around the world. . . . With the usurped power and "the emperor's [Deng's] consent," the clique continues to slaughter unarmed, innocent citizens. With tanks rolling in to show [the clique's] might and gunshots fired unendingly, Beijing is in a state of terror. . . . [T]he frenzied Li-Yang clique confounds right and wrong as well as manufactures despicable lies.[16]

Publisher Lee Tse-chung, a 40-year follower of the Communist Party, was no less condemnatory in signed articles.

Ta Kung Pao's repugnance, milder than *Wen Wei Pao*'s, was expressed in signed columns and special commentaries, rather than in editorials. Comparing the Beijing slaughter to fascist crimes during World War II, the paper said that the people, once awakened, will finally prevail.[17] *Ta Kung Pao* argued that the crackdown was disastrous to China's economy, internal order, and its international image.[18]

Causes of Deviation

What caused the ultraleftist press to deviate editorially from the Communist Party line? First, the student movement's avowed goals to end official corruption by peaceful means and to strive for basic constitutional rights earned sweeping admiration. Kam Yiu-yu, former editor-in-chief and now a board director of *Wen Wei Pao*, said, "We were deeply moved by the students' disciplined behavior and selflessness."[19] In view of public enthusiasm for the April 27 march (the day after the *People's Daily* editorial denounced the movement), *Ta Kung Pao* told its Beijing correspondents not to censor themselves, but rather to let the editors in Hong Kong decide what was fit to print.[20] Long-time followers of the Communist Party were heart-stricken by the state-sanctioned violence against the demonstrators.[21]

Beijing's struggle for press freedom was another source of inspiration. The dismissal of Qin Benli, editor of Shanghai's *World Economic Herald,* was strongly repudiated by the *Wen Wei Pao* leadership (including Lee Tse-chung) in an open letter. For several days in mid-May, the *People's Daily* covered the student movement more fairly than earlier or later, which partly reflected a paralysis of the control mechanism caused by strife among the top leadership. It would have been a self-caricature if the Hong Kong press had adhered to the Party's rigid stance while journalists in Beijing put themselves on the line for press freedom.

Public enthusiasm, which reached an awesome level both in Beijing and in Hong Kong, further justified the Communist press' pull away from the official line. Journalists were hard-pressed not to be touched by the bravery of ordinary citizens, who joined the students to confront the army and police in Beijing. The Hong Kong people were traditionally apathetic to politics, but this time aghast at the implications for 1997, one of every six citizens marched to show their solidarity with the students in Beijing. How could the press contradict the seemingly invincible "people's power" impressed on the Hong Kong citizens by television night after night?[22]

The thriving student movement sharpened the power division within the Communist Party. Facing the hard-liners' efforts to discredit the student movement as a "disturbance," the conciliatory Zhao lauded the students' initiative for sparking the long-overdue reforms. (The winners of the power struggle late accused Zhao of creating "two headquarters" that spoke in "two voices.") The power struggle left regular control mechanisms, both in Beijing and in Hong Kong, temporarily paralyzed while rumors were circulating unchecked as to who was gaining an upper hand. The intermittent cancellation and resumption of satellite transmission in Beijing testified to a lack of unified central control.

Cautiously waiting on the sideline, Xu Jiatun, Xinhua's head in Hong Kong, was conspicuously absent from the public scene for an extended period of time. Given the power uncertainty, it would have been embarrassing if Xu took one side only to switch sides later.[23] Xinhua could not enforce strict editorial guidelines while waiting for the dust in Beijing to settle; the ultraleftist newspapers were allowed to formulate their own editorial lines. Therefore, in the absence of unified power from above, the press was more susceptible to influences from within and from other social groups.

Cross pressure arose from within. The political transition to 1997 had already caused the Communist press to pursue a localization policy. *Wen Wei Pao* has recruited a contingent of local staff to improve its professionalism, and this group stood firmly behind publisher Lee to oppose Beijing's hard-liners. Similar pressures were felt inside the *Ta Kung Pao* hierarchy. Insofar as the "safe" editorial line was unclear, the local staff had a more direct role to play.[24]

Tightening the Rein

Furious at *Wen Wei Pao*, President Yang indicted it as "more counter-revolutionary than counter-revolutionary [KMT-owned] papers," to which Premier Li added: "We have taken good care of *Wen Wei Pao* for 40 years. How can it turn against us?"[25] Xu Jiatun, Xinhua's director, was summoned to Beijing in late May to explain the revolt of *Wen Wei Pao* and other state-owned agencies. Upon his return to Hong Kong, Xu tried to make peace with publisher Lee, to no avail.[26] Following the paper's political turnaround during the protests, *Wen Wei Pao* tripled its circulation to a peak of 220,000 copies before slipping again after the crackdown. Xu understood that reverting to the old stance without alienating readers would be difficult for this paper; therefore he suggested that *Wen Wei Pao* "come around slowly," to make the return less obvious and less painful.[27]

Wen Wei Pao could not and would not break off with China permanently. The paper receives an annual subsidy of US$1.3 million from China, not to mention the substantial advertising revenues garnered from China-owned concerns in Hong Kong.[28] The likelihood that *Wen Wei Pao* would sever such ties and strive to stand on its own feet in the market seemed slim. For one thing, 92% of newspaper circulation is accounted for by the centrist and the rightist press; unless *Wen Wei Pao* offered an extraordinarily attractive alternative, it would be difficult to gain a foothold. For another, some journalists regarded working for the two Communist newspapers, which are allowed to circulate in China and are allegedly read by 100 national leaders, including Deng himself, as a noble calling.[29] Ideologically, both papers hoped that the "healthy force" within the Party would eventually regain power.

After a pause, Xinhua tightened its reins. *Ta Kung Pao* reverted to the Party line by publishing articles on July 6 and after, harshly critical of Zhao's role in inciting the movement. Publisher Yang Qi, a former secretary-general of Xinhua (Hong Kong branch), who had supported *Ta Kung Pao*'s pro-student policy in the hope that Zhao Ziyang would win the power struggle, now argued that a change of position was justified. The older staffers were threatened with having their pension funds withheld if they remained defiant.[30] At *Wen Wei Pao*, meanwhile, the storm was not over. A flurry of chain reactions was triggered by the paper's Deputy Director Chen Bojian, a former deputy director of Xinhua, when he demanded that the staff toe the Party line. Publisher Lee attempted in vain to fire Chen, only to find that Lee himself had been dismissed by Xinhua. More than 30 reporters and editors, including a deputy editor-in-chief and editorial writer, resigned in support of Lee. *Wen Wei Pao* returned to Communist control.[31] As part of the attempt to unify "correct" thought, Xinhua distributed documents to every pro-China unit in Hong Kong, required high-level staff to participate in "study classes" held in Hong Kong and China, and rebuked those who drifted from the Party line during the pro-democracy movement.[32]

The Centrist Press

The centrist newspapers printed a sizable number of wire copy when students gathered to mourn Hu Yaobang's death, and then sent their own reporters to Beijing as the mourning spiraled. But editorially they took different paths to the final condemnation of the Chinese authorities.

Ming Pao

Ming Pao, indisputably the premier intellectual newspaper in Hong Kong, owes much of its success to attacks on Communist China during the Cultural Revolution. *Ming Pao* was initially skeptical about China's plan to claim Hong Kong. Once the Joint Declaration was concluded, however, the paper shifted its position, even to the point of hailing China's "one country, two systems" policy as being "far-sighted and grand in scope" and deserving to serve as a model of conflict resolution for the whole world.[33] Moreover, the paper has lauded Deng Xiaoping's policies since 1979, and publisher Louis Cha has forbidden any personal attacks on Deng by name. Sensitive to the charge of bending with the political wind, Cha defends himself by saying that his change of position was not a result of self-censorship, but based on a rational judgment that Deng's "open and reform" policy deserved encouragement.[34]

Cha plays a pivotal role in the Basic Law drafting and Consultative committees. He drafted a controversial "mainstream resolution" for the committees, which proposed letting a referendum decide whether the chief executive of Hong Kong be directly elected during the period from 2009 to 2012, more than 10 years after the colony's reversion to China. The proposal drew heavy criticism from those who argue that Hong Kong must hasten the pace of democratization in order to ward off Communist intervention. Answering his critics, Cha argued that to avoid China's interference, Hong Kong must not change rapidly, since with the organizational resources at its disposal, China would be a sure winner in a direct election.[35] Refusing a request by the Hong Kong Journalists Association to resign from the Drafting Committee, Cha denied any political ambition and said he preferred to be vindicated by history. Cha justified his position by alluding to his own experiences working for a Communist paper.[36]

Given Cha's conservative and pragmatic outlook, he would have been expected to voice caution about the student movement, at least initially. And that indeed was the case. While endorsing students' intentions, *Ming Pao* feared that a disturbance might be created.[37] Considerate of Chinese officials, Cha wanted the protesters to understand the "simple truth" that it took time for the authorities to respond to their demands. Cha claimed that the soul of Hu Yaobang would loathe seeing activities mourning him turned into a disturbance.[38] After the *People's Daily* published the severe editorial on April 26, *Ming Pao* even mentioned that "China's keen intent of preventing loss of control is understandable."[39] The paper predicted the liberals would prevail when the situation was under control, while noting that the hard-liners would antagonize the people and hinder China's development.

Describing the April 27 march as "patriotic," *Ming Pao* praised the current Chinese leadership for not resorting to violent suppression and for differing from their predecessors who did not care about public opinion or students.[40] In the wake of a televised dialogue between the authorities and the students, *Ming Pao* said, "After this, people in Hong Kong have vastly improved their impression of the Beijing government; they also have greater confidence in the future of China and Hong Kong."[41] In early May, *Ming Pao* reiterated Zhao's restrained approach to the student movement at great length, while disapproving of hard-line bureaucrats who "made a very bad impression on the masses."[42]

When the students went on a hunger strike in mid-May, *Ming Pao* continued to describe the movement as "patriotic," though objecting to some of its tactics.[43] But later moved by the dedication and bravery of the students and Beijing residents, the paper said, "It is difficult for any country to arouse its people to dedicate themselves so selflessly. . . . The Chinese people have shown what other nations have failed!"[44] *Ming Pao* appealed to Deng to harness this social vigor to the cause of reform.

But the paper's last hope was smashed by the May 20 imposition of martial law, prompting Cha to resign from the Hong Kong Basic Law Drafting and Consultative Committees on the same day. "Heartstricken and painfully grieved," Cha accused Deng in the next morning's editorial of not siding with the people to lay the foundation of national stabilization.[45] Illustrative of his disappointment, Cha said that the successive dismissal of Hu and Zhao, two reformist leaders, must have received the nod from Deng, who Cha had once so respected and supported.[46] *Ming Pao* started to call Li Peng a "liar" who failed to measure up to the morality and ability required of a premier.[47] Vowing not to be content with Li's overthrow, Cha said he would like to see the abolition of the feudalistic system that had made the rise of such a mediocre person as Li Peng possible.[48]

Ming Pao's disappointment turned into anger with the crackdown on June 4. It sarcastically compared the brutality of the "People's Government" and the "People's Liberation Army" to the Japanese massacre of Chinese in Nanjing in 1937, and to Soviet suppression of uprisings in Hungary and Czechoslovakia in 1956 and 1968.[49] The crackdown was a premeditated and bloody slaughter, the paper argued, completely irrational and inhuman and serving only the privileged members of a small clique. In *Ming Pao's* assessment, the troops had slain not only the students and the masses but also public support for this government. Looking into the future, *Ming Pao* envisioned that a relatively enlightened and popular force would arise within the Party to replace Deng's dictatorship.[50]

Cha had wishfully rationalized Deng's absence from the public scene as an indication that he might not have been personally involved in the brutality. But when Deng broke his silence on June 9 to laud the Liberation Army for the massacre, Cha could no longer conceal his profound anger and despair:

Is Deng, the man who has commanded our respect for the last ten years, responsible for this? When will the country and the people who we deeply love have a bright future? Were the inspirations and convictions of the last decade nothing but a dream and an illusion? Hu Yaobang, who we respected and admired, was brought down and died a melancholy death because he spoke up for intellectuals. Zhao Ziyang, who did much for economic reform, disappeared mysteriously because he opposed military suppression of the students. Wan Li, who has always come across as liberal and capable, was all smiles when he appeared at a function in honor of the officers commanding the troops. He once told me himself that the future for reform was bright. . . . I always trusted these leaders and was convinced that, with full support from Deng, they would do many good things for the people and put China on the road to prosperity and high repute. But they have all either died, been deposed, or changed their stand, and the political situation in China has changed all of a sudden. Ideals have been shattered in the space of less than a month.[51]

A tearful Cha declared on television that while he used to keep "a respectful distance" from the Communist Party, he would now "dodge" it completely.[52] Describing the Beijing leadership as "having gone mad," Cha urged the outside media to spread the news about the massacre across the interior of China.[53] Denounced as an "old-time anti-Communist" by Beijing, Cha said that his family was fearful but he had no concern for the consequences of being truthful.

In short, *Ming Pao* ran 51 editorials—more than any other newspaper—on China's student movement. *Ming Pao* did not wane in its sympathy for the Chinese government until after the imposition of martial law on May 20. In a signed June 11 editorial, Cha admitted that the paper had restrained itself in part because he wanted to maintain the paper's circulation, however limited, in China. Cha said,

> In the last few years, limited copies of *Ming Pao* could be taken into China on the quiet. High and middle-ranking cadres, university professors, lecturers, research scholars and newspaper editors were able to read it every day. We wanted to bring news of the outside world into China to help those who wielded influence over the country's future to gain a better understanding of world issues and help put China on the right track. Although we could do very little, we were convinced that we were doing our bit for the country and people. . . . After the announcement of martial law, the mobilization of troops, and the Tiananmen massacre, *Ming Pao* can no longer exercise self-censorship for the sake of being allowed limited circulation in China.[54]

Cha also admitted that he had tried to stay within China's limits of tolerance in drafting the "mainstream resolution" for the Basic Law Drafting Committee, only to discover that limit to be much lower than he expected.[55]

Oriental Daily News

The *Oriental Daily News,* an apolitical mass-circulated daily newspaper that carries only one short editorial per day, shied away from political controversy as usual. The paper kept completely silent about the Tiananmen events for five weeks until May 21, the day one million people turned out in Hong Kong in a march to protest the imposition of martial law in Beijing.[56] The paper then commended the Hong Kong people for their bravery, patriotism, love of freedom, and righteousness, saying that Hong Kong should join the people's struggle in China, or else all people would suffer. Viewing China and Hong Kong to be "as closely related as flesh and blood," the paper asserted that it was the Hong Kong people's responsibility to take part in China's affairs and to wield political clout.[57]

Brief signs of relaxation toward the students led the paper to praise the Chinese authorities for bringing new hope to the Hong Kong people.[58] Such premature optimism gave way to anger and dismay when the Beijing massacre occurred. The paper proclaimed that the bloodshed in Beijing had awakened the Hong Kong people, who should "support our compatriots forever."[59]

Sing Pao

Unlike Communist papers or other centrist papers, *Sing Pao* was suspicious of the Chinese authorities from the beginning and strengthened its critical stance toward China's hard-line course. As early as April 17 *Sing Pao* warned that there were plainclothes police among the ranks of students mourning Hu's death.[60] While *Ming Pao* said Hu would loathe unrest, *Sing Pao* argued that, "if Hu's death could push democracy forward, he would be as weighty as the Mt. Tai."[61] *Sing Pao* also came out on April 21, long before its peers, to extol the students' patriotism and their "concern for the country and for the people," adding that "the office-holders should be proud to find so many Chinese youth who are not afraid of sacrifice and dare to state their political demands."[62]

The paper was quick to criticize the *People's Daily*'s antagonistic label of the student movement as a "disturbance."[63] A disturbance would actually break out, argued *Sing Pao,* if the Party stood opposed to the students. The paper backed the student demands for televised dialogues with the government and for an official promise not to take vengeance against them.[64] Commenting on Zhao's disclosure to Gorbachev that Deng held supreme power in the Party, *Sing Pao* accused Deng of posing an obstacle to reversing the *People's Daily*'s "disturbance" verdict.[65] The imposition of martial law prompted *Sing Pao* to doubt that the Communist Party could lead China on the road to modernization, democracy, freedom, and prosperity.[66] Instead, the paper chided the corrupt Communist regime as being worse than the pre-1949 KMT.[67]

Outraged by the Beijing massacre, the paper said that the first bullet fired on June 4 shattered public confidence in the Communist Party and wrecked its legitimacy.[68] To continue urging the "Beijing gunners" to be rational would be "utterly fruitless."[69] Prodding people in China and Hong Kong to stand up against the massacre, *Sing Pao* said, "In Hong Kong, we should unite and break our silence. Besides communicating our anger and condemnation through sit-ins, marches and the like, we should donate whatever we have—money and blood." When Deng appeared on television on June 9 to end a suspenseful silence and to signify a consolidation of power, *Sing Pao* concluded that "[although] the democracy forces had been crushed, those few who opposed the tide of the times were sitting on the top of a volcano."[70]

The Rightist Press

Both of the rightist papers studied here, *Wah Kiu Yat Pao* and *Sing Tao Jih Pao*, have been loyal to the British colonial regime. They supported a continued British rule throughout the Sino-British negotiations but were eventually forced by the Joint Declaration to acquiesce to China's resumption of power in Hong Kong after 1997. However, *Wah Kiu Yat Pao* has switched its editorial position more swiftly and more favorably toward China than *Sing Tao Jih Pao*. This is partly because the family-owned *Wah Kiu Yat Pao* has less room for maneuver in coping with the political change than does *Sing Tao Jih Pao*, a public corporation that has moved its headquarters to Australia and divested its interests into other enterprises.

Wah Kiu Yat Pao

Like the *Oriental Daily News, Wah Kiu Yat Pao* was mute about the student movement during the early stages; the few comments that were printed tended to side with the Beijing authorities. At the peak of student mourning of Hu Yaobang, *Wah Kiu Yat Pao* was confident that the situation would remain under control. Citing the Tibetan riots of 1987–88, it argued:

> Once the Beijing authorities ordered the Liberation Army to suppress the demonstrators and to impose martial law, the "Tibet Incident" was solved and order was restored—not to speak of the fact that the current event occurs in Beijing, the administrative center.[71]

In a commemorative editorial, the paper equated the spirit of the May Fourth Movement of 1918 with "unity, progress, and cooperation" and warned the students against causing divisiveness with the government.[72] Lukewarm toward demonstrators' pleas for support, the paper remarked, "Beijing students might have high expectations of the Hong Kong people, but we view national events differently."[73]

But *Wah Kiu Yat Pao* was obliged to reassess the situation in view of the hunger strike, the mass marches, and the overwhelming support for the movement from within China and Hong Kong. Commending the Hong Kong people's generous support for Beijing's students, the paper said that the peaceful struggle by the latter "should be seen as a mission to rescue the nation and an effort to right the wrong."[74] Rebutting China's official line that the students initiated a national disturbance, *Wah Kiu Yat Pao* said that "this is like giving a dog a bad name and hanging it" and that this tactic would fool no one.[75] *Wah Kiu Yat Pao* then characterized the suppression in Beijing as a "bloody crackdown" which proved that "the Communist Party is bankrupt and the people yearn for a change."[76] *Wah Kiu Yat Pao* predicted a new force would inevitably replace the old, saying that the dead have planted seeds of change.

Sing Tao Jih Pao

At the outset, the rightist *Sing Tao Jih Pao* shared the concern of Communist China about the methods used to mourn Hu, even comparing some slogan-shouting "radical" students to "separatists" in the Tibetan riot.[77] However, *Sing Tao Jih Pao*'s reservations soon melted as the mourning turned into a "political movement for democracy and freedom." Arguing that political reforms were essential for national stability, *Sing Tao Jih Pao* hoped that the demonstrations would push the reforms forward.[78]

Construing the April 26 editorial of the *People's Daily* as a pretext for an extensive crackdown, *Sing Tao Jih Pao* appealed to the Communist Party "to value and protect the students."[79] The mood turned hopeful on April 27 when an estimated 100,000 students defied government orders, marched peacefully in Beijing, and were greeted by another one million people lining the streets. While advising the students not to step beyond the tolerance limits of the Communist Party, the paper commended Party authorities for exercising self-restraint.[80]

Sing Tao Jih Pao's hopes for a peaceful resolution were overturned by the imposition of martial law on May 20. The paper attributed the escalated conflict to the authorities' lack of sincerity and failure to respond in a timely fashion.[81] Feeling betrayed, *Sing Tao Jih Pao* confessed that its earlier hope for China to achieve economic reform was misplaced. The root cause of China's corruption and bureaucratic privilege, one editorial suggested, was a dictatorship that forbade political reforms. The paper declared that Li Peng's imposition of martial law was unconstitutional without the approval of the People's Congress standing committee.[82]

Referring to the June 4 bloodbath, *Sing Tao Jih Pao* declared that the Chinese government "had gone [so] mad" that there was no use reasoning with it.[83] The extent of China's "ultraleftist" measures not only antagonized Chinese globally but would have "astonished [the ultraleftist] Mao Zedong [himself]."[84] Predicting the downfall of the hardline regime, *Sing Tao Jih Pao* wrote that the Communist dictators had gone against the people's hearts and were "destined to meet their historical fate."[85]

The Ultrarightist Press

Since the Joint Declaration, the ultrarightist *Hong Kong Times* has taken a defensive posture and tactically replaced its hard-line anti-Communism with milder rhetoric. The Tiananmen protests proved opportune for the paper to vent some of its frustrations.

Among the first to hail the students' mourning march as a "historic" democracy movement, the *Hong Kong Times*' anti-Communist rhetoric gained momentum with each twist and turn of the movement. Declaring Beijing's reform and open policy "fraudulent," the paper said that none of the Communist promises, including that of "one country, two systems," should be trusted. Early on, the paper concluded that the Communist Party would not accept the students' demands and that the students would "pay the price of blood." [86] The harsh editorial in the *People's Daily* on April 26 was characterized as the Communist authorities' stubborn and savage effort to uphold a fascist dictatorship by violence. [87]

Ironically for a newspaper that often shares the KMT's aversion to student movements, the *Hong Kong Times* pleaded with the Hong Kong people to lend concrete support to Beijing students. [88] Commenting on Beijing's seemingly more relaxed attitude toward the students in early May, the *Hong Kong Times* suspected that the Communist Party was making a "tactical compromise to await a chance for crackdown." The *Hong Kong Times* said that Communist bureaucratism and arrogance had escalated the movement. [89]

The *Hong Kong Times* readily concurred with the protesters in their attacks on Deng Xiaoping's dictatorial rule. The paper said that Deng should quit being "an emperor behind the curtain" and should be held responsible for such a tense situation as well as for the April 26 editorial in the *People's Daily*. [90] The massacre "committed by a handful of mad fascists," according to the *Hong Kong Times*, was similar to the 1956 Soviet slaughter in Budapest and exposed the "deceiving, brutal and blood-thirsty" nature of the Communists. [91]

DISCUSSION AND IMPLICATIONS

The press mirrors and intervenes in relations of social power. A journalistic paradigm has inertia and is resistant to change. As such, the press is prone to see the world through conventional suppositions. But, to use Lippmann's metaphors, the press will change "the pictures in our head[s]" when there is a fundamental break with "the world out there." [92] Examples include the Tonkin Gulf combat, which shook the basis of American elite consensus about the Vietnam War; the Iranian revolution; and other major, unexpected occurrences. [93] Under such circumstances, conventional suppositions prove futile. Reality must be redefined anew. In the case of Hong Kong, the Sino-British Joint Declaration signified a fundamental break with the century-old colonial rule, and the Tiananmen bloodbath served to shatter the pro-China premises that had been fostered since 1984 in the spirit of the Joint Declaration.

The student protests handed convenient ammunition to the ultra-rightist press, which applied its old anti-Communist rhetoric to snipe at Communist dictatorship. The rest of the press reacted cautiously: while positive about the students' goals, it remained reserved about their seeming radicalism. The Hong Kong press tried to repair some of its perspectives while clinging to, or saving, its paradigmatic structure. But with mass turnout, the protests gradually came to be perceived as spontaneous and peaceful, and thus deserving of press sympathy. As the situation went from bad to worse, the press finally regressed to the anti-Communist canon typical of the dominant journalistic paradigm before the Joint Declaration was concluded. Because of their ideological and organizational flexibility, the mainstream newspapers are more prone than the partisan press to undergo paradigm shifts as the situation dictates. They thrive on market vibrancy and owe their primary loyalty to Hong Kong's stability and prosperity. Their reaction to the Tiananmen events was partly market-based. Simply put, Tiananmen became a principal obsession of the Hong Kong people: television instantaneously brought scenes of joyous marches, hunger strikes, and tanks into their living room, as a powerful reminder that whatever China did in Beijing was inescapably pertinent to Hong Kong's well-being. The press had an obligation to satisfy the reader's voracious demand for more, even sensational, reportage.[94] The press was so emotionally involved in the ups and downs of the movement that it added oil to the fire of public outrage against the Chinese government's indifferent-turned-violent response to peaceful protests. In view of the 1997 reversion, Communist China's hard-line policy was Hong Kong's worst dream come true.

Further, the press was deeply touched by the patriotic appeals and peaceful tactics of the protesters. Hong Kong reporters in Beijing were not neutral observers; they were ardent participants and supporters of the movement, thus injecting passion into their stories. Consequently, advocacy rather than accuracy became their foremost concern. They wishfully portrayed an invincible student movement while failing to analyze the complex causes (including the movement's internal division) that led to its own demise. Worse yet, in the aftermath of the massacre, the Hong Kong press printed many unconfirmed stories wildly speculating about Li Peng's being shot or stepping down, Deng's death, and an imminent civil war. None of these stories proved accurate or founded in facts, thus making press credibility a main target of Beijing's vehement attack. No doubt such blunders originated from the tight news control after June 4 that made reporters doubly liable to manipulation, but these misjudgments also graphically reflect their subconscious and wishful thinking as to how events might, or should, unfold.[95]

Besides the powerful impact of patriotic appeals and the peaceful tactics of student demonstrators, the paradigm shift of the Communist press is due further to the leadership's power struggle in Beijing. The power vacuum made it easier for the newspapers to lean toward Zhao when Li imposed martial law. After the June 4 slaughter, *Wen Wei Pao* stepped up its criticisms of Beijing's hard-line leaders to the point of calling them fascists. But no sooner had the hard-liners consolidated power and tightened the rein than the Communist press toed the line. It had nowhere to go.

This case study demonstrates how far—or how little—the Hong Kong press, in China's orbit, can stretch. While issues of significance to the China–Taiwan rift inevitably sparked off partisan coverage by the Hong Kong press, the Beijing democracy movement transcended that rift. For the first time in Hong Kong's history a political issue of such significant magnitude was met with a unified response from the entire ideological spectrum of the press. Never before did such a solid anti-Beijing front exist. Not during the Anti-Rightist Movement (1957), not during the Cultural Revolution (1966–76), not during the 1967 riot in Hong Kong, not even during China's similar student protests in 1986–87 that resulted in Hu Yaobang's demise. But the alliance was short-lived. It dissolved as soon as the hard-liners tightened their grip.

The paradigm shifts in 1984 (the Joint Declaration) and in 1989 (the Beijing massacre) exhibit continuity and discontinuity. The Joint Declaration set the foundation for China's "one country, two systems" policy, which is irreversible even though confidence in China sunk to an all-time low in Hong Kong after the massacre.[96] No matter how much paradigms have shifted, the political discourse is structurally bound within the parameter of the Joint Declaration and the Basic Law. In fact, the whole press spectrum urged China to behave responsibly in the spirit of the Joint Declaration, which is about the best protection Hong Kong can hope for. Nor did Beijing waste time in reiterating its commitment to the "one country, two systems" policy, amid harsh warnings that Hong Kong should not be used as an anti-China base and should not attempt to transplant capitalism to the mainland.[97]

Since June 4, 1989, China has set forth guidelines toward Hong Kong outlawing the use of Hong Kong as "a subversive base against China," suppressing the pro-democracy forces in the colony; continuing to coopt industrial and business leaders; and fortifying the control of leftist units. *Wen Wei Pao* and *Ta Kung Pao* returned home to tighter norms. The *People's Daily* attacked Martin Lee and Szeto Wah, two outspoken critics of China's policy, who were subsequently barred from participating in the Basic Law Drafting Committee. Hong Kong's leftist bookstores were forbidden to sell "counterrevolutionary" books or those by pro-democracy writers.[98]

Subduing the pro-China units, Xinhua has resumed its cooptative work in the worst possible circumstances. China had previously appealed to the Hong Kong press not to look retrospectively at its atrocious past but to look ahead to a bright future. Many journalists were willing to give China the benefit of the doubt. But the tanks and guns of the People's Liberation Army have undermined China's credibility in Hong Kong. Since June 4, Beijing has repeatedly blasted the Hong Kong press as a rumor mill. Xinhua, however, cannot afford to burn the bridge with the Hong Kong press. The more hawkish Beijing is, the less stable Hong Kong will be. Where possible, therefore, Xinhua has tried to renew friendship with Hong Kong's press circle but has found the response to be at best lukewarm.[99] Meanwhile, Xu Jiatun, Xinhua's director in Hong Kong, has been replaced by Zhou Nan, who is believed to be more hawkish. Some frightened papers rationalize that it is best for Hong Kong to mind its own business and not to meddle with China's internal affairs. How soon and to what extent Xinhua can repair the carefully woven network of relations with the press and the public remains much in doubt. Only deeds, not words, will redeem China from the despairs and doubts of the people of Hong Kong; and only time will heal the deep wounds left by the Tiananmen massacre.

Chapter 8

Journalistic Paradigms in Flux: Retrospect and Prospects

This book has focused on how the Hong Kong press, in China's orbit, acts and reacts to political transition. This final chapter will address four different questions: First, what are the conditions of the political transition and what are the options open to Hong Kong? Second, as Hong Kong reverts to China in 1997, what are the conditions of journalistic paradigm shifts and what are the limits of such shifts? Third, what political effects does the Hong Kong press have on China? Fourth, what are the implications of this project for future cross-cultural comparisons?

HONG KONG'S OPTIONS

In the political transitions of most of the crown colonies, the people strongly rejected British rule; only in Hong Kong do the people plead the colonial masters not to "abandon" them to "sovereign" Chinese rule. None of the many proposals made with regard to the future of Hong Kong proved realistic. The Hong Kong people did not get what they wanted; they will become, against their wishes, the subjects of the People's Republic in 1997. What other options have been proposed?

1. *Independence.* Out of the question. Legally, Hong Kong is part of China. Practically, Hong Kong depends on China for a steady supply of daily necessities, including drinking water. Economically, Hong Kong could not be viable should its symbiotic connections with China be cut off. Militarily, China could crush Hong Kong as easily as "a stone smashes an egg." The proposal received scant press attention and was never taken seriously.

2. *International trusteeship.* The odds of putting Hong Kong un-

der the United Nations trusteeship were close to none because China holds a veto power in the security council of that body. In fact, the United Nations, at China's behest, removed Hong Kong and Macao off the list of colonies in 1972. There was scattered press support for this proposal before Sino-British negotiations began but it died down soon afterwards.

3. *Extension of lease.* Britain, apparently with the support of people in Hong Kong, called for China to renegotiate a lease extension beyond 1997, only to be scornfully rejected by China. The press, save the Communist papers, enthusiastically promoted this proposal to begin with but was forced to give it up (see Chapter 5).

4. *British administration.* Failing to secure a lease extension, Britain longed to preserve the right to administer Hong Kong under Chinese sovereignty after 1997, again to no avail. The press also championed this "second-best" but equally improbable proposal (see Chapter 5).

There was nothing that Britain could have done other than sign a Joint Declaration in 1984 to give Hong Kong back to China, which promises Hong Kong a high degree of self-autonomy and maintenance of a capitalist way of life for 50 years after 1997. What remained for the British would be an honorable exit from the colony, and in the process Britain must contend with the following problems:

1. *Legitimacy crisis.* The British colonial regime, now a crippled lame duck, is eager to project itself as effective, open, and prepared to serve Hong Kong's interests. The government has mobilized its information bureaucracy and enlisted the support of the press to construct a positive image of Hong Kong as a measure to shore up the investor's confidence (see Chapter 3). But there are severe limits as to what it can do. Since 1986 the Hong Kong government has attempted to speed up democratization but has balked each time on account of China's strong opposition (see below). Under these circumstances, Britain can maintain its legitimacy in Hong Kong only by forging a nonconfrontational tie with China. The press has been let down by the British many times but finds itself having to continue bolstering British initiatives for democratic reform and internationalization (see below).

2. *Cooperation.* The British have pledged to cooperate with China in bringing about a smooth transition, which will not only give Britain some "face" but protect its future interests in the region. As former Foreign Secretary Geoffrey Howe said,

It's always been recognized that the colony itself is so small when faced
with the huge mass of China, its people and its army on the doorstep, that
we have had to build the future of Hong Kong on cooperation and consent
between them and the local people.[1]

In return, China has tried not to overshadow the colonial regime in day-
to-day business but has never hesitated to oppose British policy on key
issues. The common interest that binds both regimes together also permits the press to play duplicity—or develop double loyalties—with them.

3. *Democratic reform.* Hong Kong under British rule has not been
a democracy. Civil servants govern it administratively, in consultation
with an appointed legislative council. But having lost battles to China,
Britain announced a white paper in 1984 aimed to install somewhat
ambitious measures of a more representative democracy in Hong Kong,
partly to save face and partly to forestall Chinese arbitrary interference
in the future. The press, except Communist papers, has supported Britain on this initiative.

Britain's motives do not escape China's attention. China protested
vehemently that such a move represented a departure from both the
colonial history and the Joint Declaration. To wit, China would like to
inherit the tradition set by the colonial regime that single-mindedly pur-
sues economic growth but discourages political activism. Mobilizing the
Communist press to launch an attack on the British, China abhors the
prospect of organized dissent and other uncertain, even uncontrollable,
factors. Once more, the colonial regime could do nothing but retreat
from its commitment, making the press even angrier.

A renewed attempt was made to press for Hong Kong's democratic
reform in the wake of Beijing's suppression of the democracy movement
in June 1989. Public opinion and the press favored more sweeping and
direct elections. The unofficial members (appointed by the governor but
holding no government positions) of the Legislative Council and Executive Council proposed that one-third of the Legislative Council be elected
in 1991, and entirely so by 2003. The colonial government, as in the
past, mobilized public opinion in support of it. But Beijing brushed the
model aside, saying that it had been instigated by Britain and did not
reflect the aspirations of the Hong Kong people. Other proposals were
made.

Instead, the Basic Law Drafting Committee adopted in February
1990 a conservative motion that allows only 10 of the 56 Legislative
Council members to be elected for the first time in 1991, and 50% of
its membership will be chosen in direct elections in 1997. Under the

Basic Law, half of the Legislative Council members will consist of representatives of functional constituencies (namely, various professions or sectors). To ensure "convergence" of pre-1997 and post-1997 political systems, Beijing and London agreed to create a "grand electoral college" in 1995 to choose 10 additional Legislative Council members. As a whole, the political system that emerges is characterized by the concentration of power in the hands of the chief executive, appointed by Beijing, with few checks and balances.

While conceding that the pace of political reform falls short of the aspirations of the Hong Kong people and Britain, British Foreign Secretary Douglas Hurd argued that the agreement is "in the interest of continuity" and "makes good sense for Hong Kong." Both Hurd and the colonial government maintain that they will continue to press China for speedier democratization, but Beijing insists that the Basic Law will not be amended before 1997.[2] Meanwhile, senior Executive Council member Dame Lydia Dunn urged the public to stop bickering and to work together to make the 1991 direct elections a success. Vowing to continue the fight for democratic reform, the largest political group has a membership of no more than 600 people.

4. *Internationalization.* Internationalization once referred to the growing integration of Hong Kong, as a free port and financial center, into the global economy. The concept has taken on new meanings in view of China's resumption of sovereignty: as illustrated in Chapter 4, many of Hong Kong's newspapers and other enterprises have sought to merge or establish reciprocal links with foreign corporations, as well as invest or relocate business in other nations, presumably as strategies to reduce uncertainty and risk.

Internationalization is also framed in the context of Hong Kong's emigration. Following a visit to Beijing by Governor MacLehose in 1979, Britain announced a white paper on the Nationality Bill the next year preemptively blocking the right of abode in Britain to the 3.5 million British passport holders of Chinese descent born in Hong Kong. This means that Hong Kong Chinese are treated differently from all other British subjects fearing involuntary absorption, as in the Falkland Islands and British Gibraltar.[3] This criticism was popular in the Hong Kong press.

Under domestic and international pressure mounted after the Tiananmen massacre, the Thatcher government finally decided to grant full British citizenship to 50,000 carefully selected Hong Kong families, who may choose to live in Hong Kong or Britain.[4] Most offers, under a points system, will go primarily to business managers, senior government workers, wealthy entrepreneurs, and secondarily to professionals.[5]

Thatcher also openly tried to rally support for Hong Kong at the Kuala Lumpur Commonwealth Conference in 1989. Thatcher claims that Hong Kong should continue to "internationalize" itself as a world city receptive to new ideas and able to stand up to global competition. In view of the severe brain drain, Britain argues that its measures serve to stabilize Hong Kong because people are more willing to remain as long as they have foreign passports. (The Labor Party has vowed to repeal this law if and when it comes to power. This—plus threats from China— has made those qualified to leave the colony do so at the earliest dates possible.)

China denounced such moves to "internationalize the Hong Kong issue" as an interference with China's internal affairs and a conspiracy to perpetuate British rule in Hong Kong beyond 1997.[6] Beijing warned that Hong Kong holders of British passports will neither be treated as British citizens nor enjoy consular protection. The Basic Law, announced in 1990, stipulates that people with right of abode in other countries should not be principal officials of the future Hong Kong, while limiting the Legislative Council members with foreign passports to 15%.

It is evident that Hong Kong's political reform can only abide by the blueprint of the Basic Law, which also defines the outer limits of the press. The press (except the Communist papers) has sided with the Britain's losing causes on just about every issue outlined above—be it lease extension, administrative rights, democratic reform, immigration—each time to be rebuffed by China. In the case of the British Nationality Bill, the Hong Kong press as a whole was quite critical of London for failing to do more. On the other hand, the press has been careful not to agitate Beijing because, after all, it will have to stay in Hong Kong after 1997.

PARADIGM SHIFTS: CONDITIONS AND LIMITS

Legitimacy Crisis and Cooptation

As mentioned earlier, Britain and China alike are beset by legitimacy crises in Hong Kong. Britain has no moral base to impose its rule on a population that is ethnically Chinese. The legitimacy of British rule has always been tacit and shaky: tacit because people in Hong Kong do not have the inclination to oust the British, shaky because this rule depends on China's deliberate tolerance in spite of vigilant challenges. Hong Kong has accrued profits from international politics including the Western blockade of Communist China during the cold war, the wars in Korea and Vietnam, and the international division of the labor market. Political stability and economic prosperity make Hong Kong compare admirably well to China and make the colonial rule tolerable or even desirable.

By contrast, although China is legally entitled to own Hong Kong after 1997, its own record of instability and tumult has been a source of legitimacy crisis in Hong Kong. It is not the *objective* (legal) but the *subjective* (consent) sense of legitimacy that is called into question. The Hong Kong people are ethnically Chinese but nonetheless refuse to be politically nor economically associated with Communist China. In fact, half of the population in the colony are mainland refugees who escaped the Communist revolution, and the majority share an antipathy to Communist rule. Therefore, China has tried to lure Hong Kong with what purport to be very generous terms (by China's standard) provided by the Joint Declaration and the Basic Law. The Hong Kong people did not have any voice in the negotiation over their life; the Joint Declaration was thrust upon them against their will. China has aimed to emulate the colonial status quo by absorbing largely the same previously pro-British elite circle into the Basic Law Drafting and Consultative Committees, thus to oppose democratic formations and to ensure minimum change.

To shore up legitimacy, both power centers—the colonial government and Xinhua—have vigorously coopted the press in the light of the new political order. Eager to inherit and embellish the colonial legacy, China has coopted Hong Kong's elite, including many of the key publishers and journalists, into its United Front scheme (see Chapter 3). Consistent with its domestic policy of the 1980s, characterized by the contradiction between economic liberalization and (though lessened) political control, China seems intent on being bequeathed with Hong Kong's political power but would leave economic and social domains relatively undisturbed.[7]

Accommodation and Paradigm Shifts

The preceding case studies (in Chapters 5, 6, and 7) show that the press has accommodated the new irreversible "reality," thus engendering vast shifts in journalistic paradigms. The political boundary is reset from British rule versus Chinese rule to China's "one country, two systems" policy, which promises Hong Kong high autonomy and maintenance of its present capitalist system. The press had insisted that China's "one

country, two systems" policy would be untenable and that Hong Kong's
stability and prosperity could only be sustained under extended British
rule. Now it has acquiesced to China's assumption of power in Hong
Kong, maintaining that if Britain must fade out, then it is best that
China phases in slowly and minimally. For Hong Kong's stability and
prosperity to continue, the press appeals to Beijing that China must
implement the "one country, two systems" policy unfailingly. The press
not only has gravitated toward the established framework of political
transition but also appeased the power centers.

Limits to Paradigm Shifts

Will the mainstream press accommodate Xinhua's power to the extent
of total submission to its dictates? No, far from it. The pace and extent
of the political shift by the mainstream press is subject to at least five
limiting structural factors:

1. Although the colonial regime has eroded in authority, it will
remain in power until 1997 and the press is not expected to sever cordial ties with it. Hong Kong remains a pluralistic society. Groups do
have varying interests; some can still afford a certain level of disagree-
ment with China.

2. China is legally bound by the Sino-British accord that promises
to maintain Hong Kong as a viable capitalist system, of which press
freedom is an integral part. This commitment is essential if the People's
Republic is to court Taiwan for ultimate unification.[8]

3. Many of the Hong Kong reporters were educated in Taiwan
and remain sympathetic to Taiwan. China cannot pressure the press
into severing ties completely with Taiwan without having its sincerity
to carry out the "open" policy cast into doubt. China has, in fact, urged
the KMT institutions and its press to stay in Hong Kong.

4. Hong Kong's vibrant market insulates the press from excessive
political intrusion or bars it from silencing dissent. Many publishers feel
that as long as the Communist operations (including the media) have to
compete in the market, the situation is tolerable and, in the words of
Ha Chu-jen, editor of *Pai Hsing Semimonthly*, "They cannot exert 100%
control."[9] Critical voices will continue to be heard, although they will
be directed more at policy implementation than at its goals; outright
attacks on China will probably be replaced with constructive criticisms.
Given Hong Kong's antipathy to Communism, the press does its credibility a disservice to embrace China too impetuously.

5. Market forces might deter the press from appeasing China at
the apparent sacrifice of Hong Kong's local interests. With Hong Kong's

political parameter reset, China has emphasized the aspect of "one country" whereas Hong Kong has advocated "two systems"; we expect the Hong Kong press to devote itself to the protection of Hong Kong's local autonomy from Beijing's encroachment.

Paradigm shifts are neither linear nor static. The Hong Kong press has oscillated, and will continue to sway, between shifting positions in line with the unfolding political scenarios. The press may undergo paradigm *regression,* in whole—to a former state—or in part, by readopting some of the original traits. This regression may likely be partial and temporary, as it was during the 1989 Chinese democracy movement. It is important to bear in mind how far the Hong Kong press has traveled to where it is now in the last decade, ideologically speaking. China does not intend to undermine Hong Kong's capitalism, so the Hong Kong press will not attack the core assumptions of the "one country, two systems" policy.

If the Communist press represented an editorial *defection* from the party hard-line during the short-lived democracy movement (see Chapter 7), it was also temporary. The deviation, to generalize, could result from the following conditions: (1) ambiguous power relations, (2) loosened organizational controls, (3) eruption of a critical event that defies the ideology subscribed by the press, (4) public revolt against the power center, and (5) availability of alternative channels of information (such as foreign broadcasts). But as power consolidated and the organizational rein tightened, the press was promptly brought back to line.

XINHUA: MANAGING THE FALLOUT

Since 1984, China has persisted in coopting, placating, and alluring public opinion in Hong Kong, even urging the pro-Taiwan forces to remain after 1997. A more cordial and stable tie was forged (see Chapter 3). But Beijing's democracy movement upset China's power equilibrium and its suppression of the movement completely shattered Xinhua's credibility in Hong Kong (see Chapter 7).

After the Tiananmen crackdown, the hard-line leaders that won the power battle reaffirmed the "one country, two systems" policy, but forbade Hong Kong in the Basic Law from turning into a "subversive base" against the socialist motherland. The authority of Xinhua's Hong Kong branch seems to have reduced, as the State Council's Hong Kong and Macao Office, loyal to Premier Li Peng, is more influential.[10] Xinhua, particularly Xu Jiatun, has been censured for failure to contain the anti-China sentiment in Hong Kong during the movement.[11] Xu was replaced by Zhou Nan, believed to be more hawkish, as Xinhua's boss in Hong Kong. (Most dramatic is Xu's unexpected and unapproved departure for the United States for fear of the hard-liners' reprisal—a subject to which we shall return.)

China is wearing two faces. One is to tighten control among the leftist groups, including the Communist press. Most notably, China has mounted strong attacks on the Hong Kong Alliance in Support of Patriotic Democratic Movement in China, an organization that has donated money to Beijing's demonstrators and rescued their leaders. Martin Lee and Szeto Wah, leaders of that organization, have been criticized by the *People's Daily*, barred from taking part in the Basic Law Drafting Committee of which they are members, and declared persona non grata by Xinhua. Accused of fanning the democracy movement, Hong Kong reporters' activities in China have been severely restricted.[12]

The other face that China is wearing is to step up its United Front activities in order to cancel the adverse effects of the crackdown. Xinhua gradually reactivated its cooptative web through established channels. The two Basic Law committees resumed operation; prominent social leaders were invited to meet with the Beijing authorities and journalists quickly became Xinhua's guests of honor. Journalists, in groups or as individuals, were invited to have meals over which the Xinhua officials reaffirmed the "one country, two systems" policy, explained that the Hong Kong people's protests were caused by ignorance about China's situation, and expressed their desire to restart the friendship.[13] But the frequency and enthusiasm of such encounters have sharply reduced after the crackdown.[14] It seems that Xinhua has to work again from scratch in some areas.[15]

The End of an Era: Xu Jiatun's Downfall

As previously mentioned, China during the Cultural Revolution was stridently antibourgeois, anti-imperialist, and anticolonial; and Xinhua viewed Hong Kong's elite and press as "running dogs" of the British colonial regime. It was during Xu Jiatun's 6½ years of reign that Xinhua drastically resorted to coopting them—and with considerable success. Xu, at root, faithfully implemented China's "open and reform" policy as well as its newly carved "one country, two systems" strategy, both of which require close cooperation of the elite and press in Hong Kong. Xu was said to enjoy special political ties with Hu Yaobang and Zhao Ziyang—two reform-minded Party general secretaries who fell victim to China's succession crisis—and hence could report to Deng Xiaoping without the mediation of the State Council's Office for Hong

Kong and Macao. After retiring from the central committee of the Communist Party in 1985, he was appointed to the influential Central Advisory Commission—a body set up by Deng to accommodate powerful Party elders—and was further made a member of the Standing Committee of the National People's Congress in 1988.

Xu's open rejection of Lenin's rigid interpretation of capitalism, urging China to abandon outmoded stereotypes and to learn selectively from capitalism, has won applause in Hong Kong but has solicited the suspicion of the conservative faction within the Chinese leadership.[16] More tolerant of criticisms toward China than perhaps any other Communist leaders, Xu did not seek to put down mass marches that erupted in Hong Kong—which were attended in huge numbers by pro-China enterprises, media, and units under Xinhua's jurisdiction—in support of the Beijing demonstrators in 1989, but he paid visits to the student hunger strikers. As soon as hard-liners in Beijing consolidated their power, it was Xu's turn to pay his political price. Beijing forced him to retire two months before his term expired, refusing his request to stay until after the passage of the Hong Kong Basic Law, a legislation for which he should be credited.

Most dramatic of all, Xu abruptly took off for the United States in early May 1990, without Beijing's authorization, for fear of recrimination by China's hard-liners.[17] There are different conjectures about his departure, but these theories do not matter much, because the "defection" of Xinhua's top man speaks louder than words. This, according to one commentator, amounts to a vote of no confidence in Xu's own work and the "one country, two systems" policy that Xu had enthusiastically tried to sell to the Hong Kong people. Xu's unauthorized departure also set off yet another wave of jitters in Hong Kong, already reeling from fears about its uncertain future after 1997. While Xu encouraged Hong Kong holders of foreign passports to return to Hong Kong, now Beijing vowed not to accord them with consular protection. A Hong Kong official was quoted as saying, "Xu is a very senior Chinese official who understands Hong Kong well and is probably the most sympathetic to our plight. If even he has to flee, what hope is there for the rest of us?"[18]

Xu's departure posed a vivid mockery of Xinhua's United Front work. His close aides became victims of organizational reshuffling, adding to further deterioration of the already battered morale within Xinhua. Moreover, Beijing's hard-liners confirmed their suspicion held against what they regarded as a corrosive capitalist influence from Hong Kong, while tightening security control of Chinese personnel working outside China.[19] China will be more adamant about imposing its will on Hong

Kong, seeing to it that Britain, the United States, Japan, Taiwan, and the "democratic forces" in Hong Kong do not take advantage of the situation in the colony.[20]

Despite the confidence gap, Xinhua has reactivated its cooptative machine. Zhou Nan, Xu's successor, continues to court the elite and the press with enthusiasm; he visited the *Oriental Daily News* and *Sing Pao,* wined and dined newspaper proprietors and senior news executives, and even organized a swimming party with reporters at a Xinhua villa at Stanley beach.[21] But Zhou has also paid more attention to grassroots organizations. A source close to Xinhua discloses that Xinhua has little trouble in wooing the rich and powerful with interests, but it is difficult to make the middle or lower classes "turn over their hearts" because "their minds are already made up."[22] It will undoubtedly take a long time before Xinhua's cooptative machine recovers its effectiveness—when China's reform surges again and people's memory begins to fade away.

PRESS FREEDOM REVISITED

If the Hong Kong people cannot trust Britain to deliver its own promises, they have an even deeper, possibly fatal, confidence gap in China. Memories of China's tumults, bloodshed, and purges of the previous decades, especially during the Cultural Revolution, linger vividly in the minds of the Hong Kong people. China's reform decade of the 1980s was also interspersed with campaigns against "spiritual pollution" and "bourgeois liberalization," each time making Hong Kong an easy target of attack. The Hong Kong people could not take China's reform into full confidence before the Tiananmen massacre, much less after it.

What options do the Hong Kong people have? A small proportion—professionals, business people, the skillful, and the rich—can leave or have left. Since the early 1980s, emigration from Hong Kong to Canada, Australia, and the United States has averaged 20,000 people per year, and the number has doubled in recent years.[23] Some of them have returned to take up jobs in Hong Kong after securing a foreign passport, but most have left with their own bank accounts and family roots.

The Hong Kong people supported China's democracy movement, but their dreams were shattered by tanks that lumbered through Tiananmen Square. The post-Tiananmen reaction is most instructive from the perspective of Hong Kong's press freedom in that the press, to survive in the market, must stay in tune—at least not too far out of step—with public opinion. Even though the Hong Kong people were so disil-

TABLE 8–1. Journalists' Evaluations of the Statement "Most Journalists Are Apprehensive about Criticizing the Chinese [or Hong Kong] Government Now." (1990)

	Chinese government (N = 522)	Hong Kong government N = 522)
Strongly agree	12%	3%
Agree	39%	17%
Uncertain	19%	14%
Disagree	23%	52%
Strongly disagree	2%	10%
No opinion	5%	4%

Source: See note 25.

lusioned after the Tiananmen incident that they would like to keep a respectful distance from China, most of them dare not "rock the boat" by provoking China because they do not have the ways and means to settle elsewhere. As the passion of the Tiananmen crackdown cools off, Hong Kong's political activists have increasingly come under public pressure for self-restraint. These activists have been, for obvious reasons, scathingly attacked by China and pressured by the business community in Hong Kong to "act responsibly." This time, sadly, they (such as Martin Lee, a vocal legislative councillor and critic of China) are told by the scared masses not to provoke China, thus weakening their claims on public interest as well as their moral ground to fight on.[24] This despair has acutely affected the press: no matter how intensely disenchanted, the Hong Kong press has refrained from agitating China. Future criticisms of Beijing will be scattered, tempered, and temporary.

A survey with a systematic sample of journalists from 25 news organizations conducted in the summer of 1990 reveals that self-censorship has haunted Hong Kong journalists, who are very concerned about the condition of press freedom in the future.[25] As Table 8–1 shows, 51% of our interviewees agree or strongly agree that "most journalists are apprehensive about criticizing the Chinese government now"; only 20% think their colleagues are apprehensive about criticizing the Hong Kong government. These proportions decrease to 23% and 10% respectively when the question is whether the interviewees themselves are apprehensive about criticizing either government. This self-censorship appears to be inspired by anticipatory fear of Xinhua and, to a lesser degree, the colonial regime to take offense at their criticisms and punish them now or later. Neither of the power centers has to exert overt pressure to bring about self-censorship of the journalists. In fact, in the same survey only 13% admit having experienced political pressure from the Chinese government to change news treatment, whereas 7% report pressure from the Hong Kong government.

Moreover, most journalists hold an uncertain view about Hong Kong's political future. The survey shows that while 22% of the journalists believe China's "one country, two systems" policy to be feasible, 27% rule it out as infeasible, and 40% express uncertainty. But all in all, 69% of them think that Hong Kong's press freedom will be "more restricted" after 1997, and 86% agree or strongly agree that the media should strive to maximize autonomy.

On the other hand, a totally bleak picture is not warranted either. We do not believe that China will hold out against change when it is already so deeply integrated into the global political economy, to the point where economic sanctions imposed after the Tiananmen crackdown represent a threat. We do not believe that China can hold out in light of the remarkable examples of democratic change arising from Taiwan, the Soviet Union, and Eastern Europe. It seems that economic reform of the 1980s has gone too far to be overturned. Even in China, as a result of this reform, the media display a broader diversity in terms of genres and content areas.[26] This does not rule out the prospect of policy reversals by China, which would hurt Hong Kong's press freedom.

If a post-Deng, more liberal regime emerges in China, it might be more tolerant of the Hong Kong press for "constructive criticisms." It is certain that the press cannot revert to the pre-1984 days to undermine the legitimacy of China's "one country, two systems" policy, but it can offer a more liberal interpretation of the Basic Law. In this sense, the press will make an important contribution to safeguarding freedom and other human rights.

Obviously, Hong Kong's press freedom is contingent on the extent to which the announced "one country, two systems" policy is faithfully implemented. Press freedom will have a better chance of survival if Hong Kong's judicial system remains relatively independent, if the press continues to compete in a vibrant market, and if media professionals resolve to marshal support and vigilantly guard against any arbitrary encroachments. Moreover, if Hong Kong's political economy is further integrated into the international order, then Beijing will have to think twice about tempering press freedom in Hong Kong. But even if all these conditions are fully met, no absolute guarantee can be provided. Singapore, for example, uses political power to bring the press to its knees despite the country's vigorous market system and high degree of integration into the international political economy.

THE POLITICAL ROLE OF THE PRESS

The Hong Kong press has always been a key link in the "boundary politics" between British colonial bureaucracy and Chinese civil society in the colony (see Chapter 1). In the administrative no-party state of Hong Kong, the colonial regime has achieved an elite–elite integration through cooptative absorption, but a lack of elite–mass integration severely deprives grass-roots participation. The Government Information Services monitors press opinion as one of the government's multifaceted policy inputs or a semiorganizational intelligence and brain trust, but it has little to do with democracy.

The political role of the press has been heightened by the political transition. Prior to the embarkation of the first round of Sino-British talks, the Hong Kong government advocated its "tripod of consents" whereby Britain, China, and Hong Kong should come to the negotiating table. China claimed to represent the Hong Kong compatriots and would deal with Britain alone. Both Britain and China claimed that they would consult the people of Hong Kong, but they did nothing but marshall respective press support to play what was called "public opinion cards." Since the Hong Kong people were denied the right to participate in the Sino-British negotiations, the role of the media as a political forum became particularly crucial during the transition. Opinion leaders and organized groups can express their views through the media. While the effectiveness of public opinion so expressed may be doubtful, at least the public has a site to air their concerns.

No regime is more aware of the importance of public opinion or more aggressive about influencing it than China. Public opinion in China is represented by the Communist Party which is, by definition, the vanguard of the proletariat. Public opinion is party opinion. It is one thing for China to control the media for internal consumption, quite another to spread falsehood in Hong Kong. Beijing's proclamation of no student deaths in the Tiananmen suppression served to undermine Hong Kong's already low level of confidence in China. Meanwhile, there is a widespread apprehension that illiberal colonial ordinances may fall into China's abuse after 1997, so a mounting public pressure has been exerted to change such laws.

While China influences Hong Kong, Hong Kong, though geographically insignificant, does offer a "model" for China. The Hong Kong press is better informed than China's official mouthpieces, so the mainland people learn about themselves often through information "exported to Hong Kong and reimported back to China." The Hong Kong press attacked China's radical Cultural Revolution and inspired the re-formist leaders to reemerge. Deng Xiaoping drew his economic reform plan—especially the special economic zones in South China—in partial emulation of the colony, vowing to "create several Hong Kongs" on the mainland and setting off a flurry of activities to "learn from the Hong Kong experience."[27] On the other hand, the colony has been made a convenient scapegoat in China's various campaigns, accused of inciting "spiritual pollution" and "bourgeois liberalization" in China. After all, Chinese leaders long to borrow Hong Kong's economic experience without its concomitant press freedom and bourgeois thought.[28]

Some of the most influential political magazines in the Chinese-speaking world, such as the *Seventies Monthly* and *Cheng Ming Monthly*, were originally published in Hong Kong with funding from the leftist circle. But the downfall of the Gang of Four made them turn more self-reflective about their editorial policy and more critical of Beijing. Hav-ing briefly been admitted in China, they were banned in 1979.[29] None of the Hong Kong newspapers were circulated in China before the 1980s; later, Hong Kong's Communist papers and such English publications as the *South China Morning Post* became available in China's major ho-tels. *Ming Pao* could be read by the cadres and the intellectuals.

In the era of economic reform, China has not been successful in attempts to prohibit people in south China from watching Hong Kong television across the border. Journalists in south China complained that unless the authorities gave them a freer hand, they could not compete successfully with their Hong Kong colleagues.[30] Guangzhou developed a Pearl Economic Radio Station—patterned after Hong Kong's com-mercial stations—so popular as to spark a chain-like diffusion of the new radio format to other parts of China.[31] Hong Kong's press freedom is a source of envy and inspiration for Chinese journalists and a spring of irritation for their rulers.[32]

Despite the Tiananmen crackdown, China's "reform and open" policy will continue. And it seems unlikely that China will be able to attain economic liberalization without putting up with its attendant po-litical and press liberalization. At this writing, almost two years after China's marshal law tanks rolled into Tiananmen, the hard-liners seem to be riding high. But China cannot revert to isolation even under al-ready severe foreign sanctions. Therefore we hold tempered optimism about Hong Kong's press freedom in the long run, but given the unpre-dictable turns China's power struggle might take we are also very wary of the difficult time that may lie ahead for the Hong Kong press in shorter and medium terms.

HOW TYPICAL?

This case study, like any others, is open to criticism for its particularity. As Selznick has succinctly concluded his acclaimed study of cooptation:

> Theoretical inquiry, when it is centered on a particular historical structure or event, is always hazardous. This is due to the continuous tension between concern for a full grasp and interpretation of the materials under investigation as history, and special concern for the induction of abstract and general relations. Abstractions deal harshly with "the facts," choosing such emphases and highlighting such characteristics as may seem factitious, or at least distorted, to those who have a stake in an historically well-rounded apprehension of the events themselves.[33]

Particularity has its own merits. But what appears to be a unique case may serve to illuminate a special condition of a more general model; it may also elucidate the complexity of theoretical interactions and hence contribute to the formulation of a more general model.

The shift of journalistic paradigms takes place at various paces and under diverse conditions, so comparative studies will prove useful. Political transition has taken place, though unevenly, in Eastern Europe, the Soviet Union, Spain, and throughout Latin America. It is beyond the scope of this project to develop a theoretical model that clarifies the conditions and processes of the relationship between the press and power in the transition, although the typology offered in Chapter 2 (see Table 2–1) is illuminating. We shall illustrate with paradigm shifts in South Korea and Taiwan amid rapid democratization processes, which are equally impressive in their own ways.

In South Korea, since military dictatorship gave way to multiparty democracy in 1987, the dominant party-state has had to share power with opposition parties and various social movement groups. The implications for the press are profound:

- The scope of political discourse in the press has widened; what used to be taboo subjects, such as unification with North Korea, are now openly discussed. South Korea has actively sought to expand ties with Communist countries, both to enrich trade opportunities and to outsmart North Korea diplomatically. The South Korean government has to walk a fine line between openness to the Communist world and what might be perceived as reckless and radical moves to promote South-North unification.

- The press was tamed by the dictatorial Chun regime which ordered the closing of newspapers he abhorred, forced proprietors to dismiss 900 of his journalist critics overnight, and then bribed and favored the obedient ones. The press, now reflecting the growing political pluralism, voices diverse views and has to stand on its own feet in market competition rather than draw on political subsidies. While the organized church publishes a politically conservative newspaper, the radical, nationalistic, antiestablishment and anti-U.S. *Hangarae Shimbun* also appears to have taken root.
- The once marginalized opposition parties are now routinely covered. The regime seeks to coopt, rather than coerce, journalists who, in the meantime, have organized unions and demanded greater control over editorial policy.[34]

Similarly, Taiwan lifted in 1987 the 38-year-old martial law that had been imposed since the KMT took refuge in Taiwan. Opposition parties were legalized, and the press ban was repealed. The impact of this sociopolitical reconfiguration is deeply felt by the press:

- A long-term guardian of ideological orthodoxy, the press is now sharply divided on the issue of whether Taiwan should seek unification with China or seek secession to form a "new and independent country"—an issue that had sent many people to jail. Taboos are broken loose.
- Under a press ban for almost 40 years, Taiwan had fixed the total number of newspapers at 31, each allowed to publish a fixed number of pages at one location only. Since 1988, tens of newspapers and magazines have mushroomed, each with more clearly demarcated press ideology. But because barriers to market entry have proved to be much more formidable than previously assumed, many newspapers have folded quickly after they appeared.
- Internal resources of the press have been redeployed to meet exterternal competition, thus emphasizing social conflicts, social movements, and the activities of opposition parties. Most interestingly, mainland China has been entangled as a battleground for the Taiwanese media, which dispatched reporters to reveal the mystery of "the motherland" to the 21 million people on the island.

These cases—Hong Kong, South Korea, Taiwan, and others—offer promise for more thoughtful comparisons, in light of the typology developed in Chapter 2 that explores the interaction between paradigm shifts and sociopolitical formations. Hong Kong fits the example of cooptation (where the power structure delivers high reward but low punishment to the press), whereas Taiwan and South Korea were characteristic of the incorporation category (where the power structures delivers high reward and high punishment to the press).

As we generalize, their major contrasts cannot be overlooked. First, while absorption of Hong Kong into China's centralized power extends over a decade, the speed with which Taiwan and South Korea underwent democratization and instituted multiparty systems (despite long incubation) was rapid. Second, in view of China's threats, the vigorously "free" Hong Kong press has to occasionally exercise self-censorship and say what is perceived to be permissible. Its counterparts in Taiwan and South Korea celebrate their hard-won press freedom, with self-censorship growing out of fashion. Their governments have increasingly replaced incorporation (high reward, high punishment) with cooptation (high reward, low punishment) in dealing with the press. The demand for editorial control—such as direct election of editors and participation in policy making—by South Korea's radicalized journalist unions is unparalleled in Taiwan or Hong Kong.

A more full-fledged comparative study will have to explore some of the following problematics: How is a journalistic paradigm structured? What are its manifestations and determinants? What are the conditions, patterns, and mechanisms of shifts in journalistic paradigms? What are the factors that prompt the state to use cooptation, inducement, suppression, or coercion? How do different types of power transition engender paradigm shifts? What are the political and organizational boundaries of the press's relative autonomy and its ideological discourse?

Notes

CHAPTER 1

1. Hong Kong is one of the world's premier financial centers, boasting a per capita gross domestic product of about US$10,939 in 1990, which came within striking distance of its colonial master, Britain, and surpassed its future master, China, by twenty-sevenfold.

2. Article III of the Treaty of Nanking (1842) contains the following:

> It being obviously necessary and desirable that British subjects should have some port whereat they may careen and refit their ships, when required, and keep stores for that purpose, His Majesty the Emperor of China cedes to her Majesty the Queen of Great Britain, etc., the Island of Hong Kong, to be possessed in perpetuity by Her Britannic Majesty, Her Heirs and Successors, and to be governed by such Laws and Regulations as Her Majesty the Queen of Great Britain, etc., shall see fit to direct.

The terms of the Convention of Peking, 1860, are as follows:

> With a view to the maintenance of law and order in and about the harbour of Hong Kong, His Imperial Majesty the Emperor of China agrees to cede to Her Majesty the Queen of Great Britain and Ireland, and to Her Heirs and Successors, to have and to hold as a dependency of Her Britannic Majesty's Colony of Hong Kong, that portion of the township of Kowloon, in the province of Kwangtung.

3. A document signed at Peking on June 9, 1898, which came into force on July 1, 1898, reads as follows: ". . . the limits of British territory shall be enlarged under lease to the extent indicated generally on the annexed map . . . the terms of the lease shall be ninety-nine years." The justification for the extension, according to the document, lay in the bald statement that "an extension of Hong Kong territory is necessary for the proper defence and protection of the Colony."

4. Norman J. Miners, *The Government and Politics in Hong Kong* (Hong Kong: Oxford University Press, 1977), p. 16.

5. Premier Zhou set three ground rules in 1956: (1) that Hong Kong should not be operated as an anti-China military base, referring to the U.S. Seventh Fleet; (2) that Hong Kong should not conduct subversive activities against China, referring to Taiwanese spies; and (3) that China's personnel should be safe-

guarded. Xuan Yuan-lo, *Looking Closely at Xinhua* (Hong Kong: Mirror, 1987), pp. 34–35.

6. *Contemporary Weekly*, 6 January 1990, pp. 34–35.

7. Miners, *Government and Politics*, p. 178.

8. Alvin Rabushka, *Hong Kong: A Study in Economic Freedom* (Chicago: University of Chicago Graduate School of Business, 1979), p. 25. These earnings are calculated from a variety of sources including exports to Hong Kong, economic operations (banks, warehouses, cinemas, etc.), remittances sent to mainland Chinese by people in Hong Kong and overseas, and from using Hong Kong as a redistribution center for Chinese-made goods.

9. Y. C. Jao, "Hong Kong's Role in Financing China's Modernization," in A. J. Youngson, ed., *China and Hong Kong: The Economic Nexus* (Hong Kong: Oxford University Press, 1984).

10. Peter Harris, *Hong Kong: A Study in Bureaucratic Politics* (Hong Kong: Heinenmann Asia, 1978) pp. 165–166.

11. Lau Siu-Kai, *Society and Politics in Hong Kong* (Hong Kong: Chinese University Press, 1981), p. 11.

12. Miners, *Government and Politics*, p. 241.

13. *Hong Kong Hansard* (Hong Kong: Government Printer, 1950), p. 41.

14. China did not recognize this theory when it refused to allow the Hong Kong government to represent Hong Kong people as a member in the negotiations, insisting that it could only participate as a member of the British team.

15. Harris, *Bureaucratic Politics*, p. 175.

16. Based on the tripod of consents, the Hong Kong government wished to participate in the Sino-British negotiations over Hong Kong's future. China flatly rejected its legitimacy to represent Hong Kong people, insisting that the colonial government could only be part of the British delegation rather than an entity of its own.

17. Harris, *Bureaucratic Politics*.

18. Ambrose Yeo-chi King, "Administrative Absorption of Politics in Hong Kong: Emphasis on the Grass Roots Level," *Asian Survey*, 15 (1975): pp. 422–439.

19. Lau, *Society and Politics*.

20. Miners, *Government and Politics*, p. 218.

21. Ibid.

22. Lin Youlan, *The History of Press Development in Hong Kong* (Taipei: World, 1977).

23. Lau, *Society and Politics*, pp. 17–20.

24. Robert E. Mitchell, "How Hong Kong Newspapers Have Responded to 15 Years of Rapid Social Change," *Asian Survey*, 9 (1969): pp. 673–678.

25. *Contemporary Weekly*, 6 January 1990, pp. 34–35.

26. James C. Y. Shen, *The Law and Mass Media in Hong Kong* (Hong Kong: Chinese University Press, 1972); Chin-Chuan Lee, "The Partisan Press in Hong Kong: Between British Colonial Rule and Chinese Politics" (Paper presented at the annual convention of the Association for Education in Journalism and Mass Communication, Memphis, 3–6 August 1985).

27. The Control of the Publication Ordinance was repealed in 1986, ending the safety deposit requirement for starting a new publication and canceling rules that restricted the import of publications and the publication of "agitating" materials. But the rule governing the publication of "false information" was amended and incorporated into the Public Order Ordinance. Under strong pressure from the press and the public, the government finally repealed this rule in 1988 as well.

28. *Ta Kung Pao, Wen Wei Pao,* and the *New Evening Post* were charged with reprinting an agitative editorial of the *People's Daily. Ta Kung Pao* was ordered suspended for six months, with its publisher Fei Yimin and editor Li Ziying found guilty. This harsh action provoked condemnation from Beijing and Guangdong. Finally *Ta Kung Pao,* in its eleventh day of suspension, was permitted to resume publication, while charges against the other two papers were dropped. In the 1967 riot, the Hong Kong government did not even bring these three major Communist papers to court actions. See Joseph Man Chan and Yau Sing-mo, "The Prospect of Press Freedom in Hong Kong: A Power Approach," *Ming Pao Monthly,* May 1987, pp. 11–12.

29. Daniel Bell, *The End of Ideology* (New York: Free Press, 1962).

30. Michael Schudson, *Discovering the News* (New York: Basic, 1978).

31. Herbert Gans, *Deciding What's News* (New York: Pantheon, 1979); Todd Gitlin, *The Whole World Is Watching* (Berkeley: University of California Press, 1980); Alvin Gouldner, *The Dialectic of Ideology and Technology* (New York: Oxford University Press, 1976); Stuart Hall, "Culture, the Media, and the 'Ideological Effect'," in James Curran, Michael Gurevitch, and Janet Woollacott, eds., *Mass Communication and Society* (Beverly Hills: Sage, 1977); R. K. Manoff and Michael Schudson, eds., *Reading the News* (New York: Pantheon, 1986); David Paletz and Robert M. Entman, *Media Power Politics* (New York: Free Press, 1981); Edward Said, *Covering Islam* (New York: Pantheon, 1981); Peter Schlesinger, *Putting "Reality" Together* (Beverly Hills: Sage, 1978); Gaye Tuchman, *Making News* (New York: Free Press, 1978); Edward Herman and Noam Chomsky, *Manufacturing Consent* (New York: Pantheon, 1988).

32. Frank Wilson, *French Political Parties Under the Fifth Republic* (New York: Praeger, 1982); J.W. Freiberg, *The French Press: Class, State, and Ideology* (New York: Praeger, 1981).

33. Colin Seymour-Ure, *The Political Impact of Mass Media* (Beverly Hills: Sage, 1974).

34. Harris, *Bureaucratic Politics.*

35. Lam Shui-Fong and Vicky Tam, "1977: Hong Kong in Transition," pamphlet (Minneapolis: Hong Kong China Observers, 1990).

36. J.S. Hoadley, "Political Participation of Hong Kong Chinese: Patterns and Trends," *Asian Survey,* 13 (1973): pp. 604–616.

37. Joseph Cheng, *Hong Kong: In Search of a Future* (Hong Kong: Oxford University Press, 1984).

38. There is no newspaper circulation auditing bureau in Hong Kong. The estimates of readership (not circulation) were made on the basis of data pro-

vided by Survey Research Hong Kong as of 1984 and included the following papers:

Ultraleftist: *Ta Kung Pao,* 47,000; *Wen Wei Po,* 54,000; *New Evening Post,* 75,000; *Ching Pao,* 47,000; *Hong Kong Commercial Daily,* 83,000.
Centrist: *Ming Pao,* 405,000; *Hong Kong Economic Journal,* 69,000; *Oriental Daily News,* 1,530,000; *Sing Pao,* 852,000; *Tin Tin Jih Pao,* 233,000 (sold in 1985 to Ho Sai-chu, a pro-China business man).
Rightist: *Hong Kong Daily News,* 319,000; *Sing Tao Jih Pao,* 219,000; *Wah Kiu Yat Pao,* 146,000; *Express Daily* (*Sing Tao's* sister paper), 138,000; *Sing Tao Evening News,* 180,000.
Ultrarightist: *Hong Kong Times,* 40,000 (estimated).

39. Disclosed by Lee Tse-chung in *Contemporary Weekly,* 13 January 1990, p. 19. Lee was fired as the publisher of *Wen Wei Pao* after the Tiananmen crackdown in 1989.
40. For details see Chapter 7.
41. Computed from *SRH Media Index 1989* (Hong Kong: Survey Research Hong Kong, 1989), Table New1B, General Report.
42. Hong Kong Government, *Kowloon Disturbance 1966, Report of Commission of Inquiry* (Hong Kong: Government Printer, 1967).
43. Miners, *Government and Politics.*
44. Lu Wen, "The Development of Xinhua's Hong Kong Branch," *Mirror Monthly,* 16 August 1987, pp. 82–97.
45. For more details, see Chapter 3. "A Special Topic: A Review of Xu Jiatun's Three Years in Hong Kong," *Pai Hsing Semimonthly,* no. 123, 1 July 1986, pp. 8–17; Yu Giwen, "The CCP's Work System in Hong Kong," *Nineties Monthly,* October 1985, pp. 56–59.
46. Long Sin, *A Shadow Government of Hong Kong* (Hong Kong: Haisan, 1985).

CHAPTER 2

1. "The Days That Shook Marcos Out of Power," *Far Eastern Economic Review,* 6 March 1986, pp. 18–19; "How the Rebels Won the Battle of the Air Waves," *Far Eastern Economic Review,* 6 March 1986, p. 20.
2. Youngchul Yoon, "Political Transition and Press Ideology in South Korea, 1980–1988" (Ph.D. diss., University of Minnesota, 1989), Chapter 2.
3. Raymond Williams, *Marxism and Literature* (New York: Oxford University Press, 1977).
4. Steven Lukes, "Power and Authority," in Tom Bottomore and Robert Nisbet, eds., *A History of Sociological Analysis* (New York: Basic, 1978), pp. 633–676; Philip Trounstine and Terry Christensen, *Movers and Shakers: The Study of Community Power* (New York: St. Martin's Press, 1982).

5. John Kenneth Galbraith, *The Anatomy of Power* (Boston: Houghton Mifflin, 1983).

6. Herbert Gans, *Deciding What's News* (New York: Pantheon, 1979) p. 81; Phillip Tichenor, George Donohue, and Clarice Olien, *The Press and Community Conflict* (Beverly Hills: Sage, 1980).

7. Graham Murdock and Peter Golding, "Capitalism, Communication, and Class Relations," in James Curran, Michael Gurevitch, and Janet Woollacott, eds., *Mass Communication and Society* (Beverly Hills: Sage, 1977); Graham Murdock, "Large Corporations and the Control of the Communications Industries," in Michael Gurevitch, Tony Bennett, James Curran, and Janet Woollacott, eds., *Culture, Society, and the Media* (New York: Methuen, 1982).

8. Louis Althusser, *Lenin and Philosophy and Other Essays* (London: New Left, 1971).

9. Williams, *Marxism and Literature;* Stuart Hall, "Culture, the Media, and the 'Ideological Effect,' " in Curran, Gurevitch, and Woollacott, *Mass Communication and Society*.

10. Todd Gitlin, *The Whole World Is Watching* (Berkeley: University of California Press, 1980).

11. Chin-Chuan Lee and Joseph Man Chan, "Journalistic Paradigms in Flux: The Press and Political Transition in Hong Kong," *Bulletin of Ethnology Academia Sinica*, no. 63 (Spring, 1987), p. 110.

12. Robert Dahl, *Who Governs* (New Haven: Yale University Press, 1961); Robert Dahl, "A Critique of the Ruling Elite Model," in Willis Hawley and Frederick Wirt, eds., *The Search for Community Power* (Englewood Cliffs: Prentice-Hall, 1974); Robert Nisbet, *Community and Power* (New York: Oxford University Press, 1953).

13. Fred Siebert, Theodore Peterson, and Wilbur Schramm, *Four Theories of the Press* (Urbana: University of Illinois Press, 1956).

14. For the British case, see George Boyce, "The Fourth Estate: The Reappraisal of a Concept," in George Boyce, James Curran, and Pauline Wingate, eds., *Newspaper History* (Beverly Hills: Sage, 1978); for the American case, see Dan Schiller, *Objectivity and the News: The Public and the Rise of Commercial Journalism* (Philadelphia: University of Pennsylvania Press, 1981).

15. Eddie Goldenberg, *Making the Paper* (Lexington, MA: Heath, 1975).

16. Gaye Tuchman, *Making News* (New York: Free Press, 1978); Mark Fishman, *Manufacturing the News* (Austin: University of Texas Press, 1980).

17. Leon Sigal, *Reporters and Officials* (Lexington, MA: Heath, 1973).

18. David Paletz, Peggey Reichert, and Barbara McIntyre, "How the Mass Media Support Local Government Authority," *Public Opinion Quarterly*, 35 (1971): pp. 80–92.

19. Harvey Molotch and Marilyn Lester, "Accident News: The Great Oil Spill as Local Occurrence and National Event," *American Journal of Sociology*, 81 (1975): pp. 235–260.

20. Clarice Olien, Phillip Tichenor, and George Donohue, "Use of the Press and the Power of a Group," *Sociology of Rural Life*, 4 (1981): pp. 1–2, 7.

21. Pamela Shoemaker, "Media Treatment of Deviant Political Groups," *Journalism Quarterly*, 61 (1984): pp. 66–75, 82.

22. Gans, *Deciding What's News*.

23. Philip Schlesinger, *Putting "Reality" Together* (Beverly Hills: Sage, 1978).

24. Edward Said, *Covering Islam* (New York: Pantheon, 1981).

25. For a comprehensive review, see Chin-Chuan Lee, "Mass Media: Of China, About China," in Chin-Chuan Lee, ed., *Voices of China: The Interplay of Politics and Journalism* (New York: Guilford Press, 1990), pp. 19–25; David L. Paletz and Robert M. Entman, *Media, Power, Politics* (New York: Free Press, 1981), pp. 213–233.

26. Edward S. Herman and Noam Chomsky, *Manufacturing Consent* (New York: Pantheon, 1988).

27. Tsan-kuo Chang, "Reporting U.S.–China Policy, 1950–1984," in Lee, ed., *Voices of China;* Tsan-kuo Chang, "The Impact of Presidential Statements on Press Editorials Regarding U.S. China Policy, 1950–1984," *Communication Research*, 16 (1989): pp. 486–509.

28. Josiane Jouet, "Review of Radical Communication Research: The Conceptual Limits," in Emile McAnany et al., eds., *Communication and Social Structure* (New York: Praeger, 1981); J. W. Frieberg, *The French Press: Class, State, and Ideology* (New York: Praeger, 1981).

29. Peter Dreier, "The Position of the Press in the U. S. Power Structure," *Social Problems*, 29 (1982): pp. 298–310.

30. Paletz and Entman, *Media, Power, Politics*, p. 13.

31. George Donohue, Clarice Olien, and Phillip Tichenor, "A 'Guard Dog' Conception of Mass Media" (Paper presented to the Association for Education in Journalism and Mass Communication, San Antonio, Texas, August 1987).

32. The article appeared in Andrew Arno and Wimal Dissanayake, eds., *The News Media in National and International Conflict* (Boulder, Colorado: Westview, 1984), pp. 183–202.

33. Thomas Kuhn, *The Structure of Scientific Revolutions*, 2nd ed. (Chicago: University of Chicago Press, 1970).

34. Margaret Masterman, "The Nature of a Paradigm," in Imre Lakatos and Alan Musgrave, eds., *Criticism and the Growth of Knowledge* (New York: Cambridge University Press, 1970).

35. Lakatos and Musgrave, ibid.

36. George Ritzer, *Sociology: A Multiple Paradigm Science* (Boston: Allyn and Beacon, 1975). Ritzer suggests a definition of paradigm that synthesizes Masterman's threefold typology:

A paradigm is a fundamental image of the subject matter within a science. It serves to define what should be studied, what questions should be asked, how they should be asked, and what rules should be followed in interpreting the answers obtained. The paradigm is the broadest unit of consensus within a science and serves to differentiate one scientific community (or subcommunity) from another. It subsumes, defines, and interrelates the exemplars, theories, and methods and instruments that exist within it. (p. 7)

37. Gans, *Deciding What's News.*
38. Lance Bennett, Lynn Gressett, and William Haltom, "Repairing the News: A Case Study of the News Paradigm," *Journal of Communication,* 35, no. 2 (1985): pp. 50–68.
39. Lee and Chan, "Journalistic Paradigms in Flux;" Chan and Lee, "Journalistic Paradigms on Civil Protests"; Joseph Man Chan and Chin-Chuan Lee, "Press Ideology and Organizational Control in Hong Kong," *Communication Research,* 15, no. 2 (1988): pp. 195–197. Presumably, a journalistic paradigm is composed of the following levels of specificity:

1. News values, defined as the journalist's specific dispositions (such as novelty, proximity, and cultural relevance) in deciding what is news.
2. News frames, or the angles by which journalists portray events. For example, in 1989, the Chinese media tried to attribute a spontaneous democracy movement to external causes. A news frame is organized by many "strips," such as attribution of external causes of a protest to foreign "agitation."

40. Gitlin, *World Is Watching;* Tuchman, *Making News;* Gans, *Deciding What's News;* David Altheide and Robert Snow, *Media Logic* (Beverly Hills: Sage, 1979). Gitlin defines news frames as "persistent patterns of cognition, interpretation, and presentation, of selection, emphasis, and exclusion, by which journalists routinely organize discourse, whether visual or verbal" (p. 7). Altheide and Snow view media logic as consisting of:

a form of communication; the process through which media present and transmit information. Elements of this form include the various media and the formats used by these media. Format consists, in part, of how the material is organized, the style in which it is presented, the focus or emphasis on particular characteristics of behavior and the grammar of media communication. Format becomes a framework or a perspective that is used to present as well as interpret phenomena. (p. 10)

William Gamson, in studying American media discourse about the Arab–Israel conflict, divides it into the "gestalt framing" and that which provides reasoning or justifications for positions. See William Gamson, "The Political Culture of the Arab–Israel Conflict," *Conflict Management and Peace Science,* 5 (1981): pp. 79–83.

41. Lee and Chan, "Journalistic Paradigms in Flux."
42. Daniel Hallin, *The "Uncensored War"* (New York: Oxford University Press, 1986); Gitlin, *World Is Watching;* Chan and Lee, "Shifting Journalistic Paradigms"; Yoon, *Political Transition.*

43. Herbert Fensterheim and M. E. Tresselt, "The Influence of Value System on the Perception of People," *Journal of Abnormal and Social Psychology*, 48 (1953): pp. 93–98.

44. Stuart Hall, "Deviance, Politics and the Media," in Paul Rock and Mary McIntosh, eds., *Deviance and Social Control* (London: Tavistock, 1974), p. 277.

45. Ibid.

46. Chan and Lee, "Journalistic Paradigms on Civil Protests," p. 188.

47. Ibid., p. 199.

48. Chin-Chuan Lee, "Partisan Press Coverage of Government News in Hong Kong," *Journalism Quarterly*, 62 (1985): pp. 770–776.

49. Chin-Chuan Lee and Yuet-lin Lee, "Constructing Partisan Realities by the Press: A Riot in Hong Kong" (Paper presented to the annual convention of the Midwest Political Science Association, Chicago, 19 April 1985).

50. For example, Joseph Man Chan and Chin-Chuan Lee, "Shifting Journalistic Paradigms: Editorial Stance and Political Transition in Hong Kong," *China Quarterly*, no. 117 (March 1989): pp. 97–117. This article forms the main part of Chapter 3 in this book.

51. Dennis Wrong, *Power: Its Forms, Bases, and Uses* (London: Blackwell, 1988), p. 43.

52. William Gamson, *Power and Discontent* (Homewood, IL: Dorsey, 1968); Antonio Gramsci, *Selections from the Prison Notebooks*, ed. and trans. Quintin Hoare and Geoffrey Nowell Smith (New York: International Publishers, 1971); Galbraith, *Anatomy of Power*. We are indebted to Youngchul Yoon for the development of this typology, see Yoon, *Political Transition*, Chapter 5.

53. Raymond Williams, *Television: Technology and Cultural Form* (New York: Schoken, 1975).

54. Lee, "Mass Media: Of China, About China."

55. Michael Schudson, *Discovering the News* (New York: Basic, 1978).

56. Robert K. Manoff and Michael Schudson, eds., *Reading the News* (New York: Pantheon, 1986).

57. Warren Breed, "Social Control in the Newsroom: A Functional Analysis," *Social Force*, 33 (1955): pp. 326–336.

58. Edward Epstein, *News from Nowhere* (New York: Vintage, 1973); Gans, *Deciding What's News;* Herbert Gans, *Popular Culture and High Culture* (New York: Basic, 1974).

59. Chin-Chuan Lee, "In Quest of an Alternative to Professional Journalism in the Third World" (Paper presented at the annual convention of the International Communication Association, San Francisco, 24–28 May 1984).

60. Colin Seymour-Ure, *The Political Impact of Mass Media* (Beverly Hills: Sage, 1974).

61. Breed, *Social Control;* Leon Sigal, *Reporters and Officials* (Lexington, MA: Heath, 1973); Lee Sigelman, "Reporting the News: An Organizational Analysis," *American Journal of Sociology*, 79 (1973): pp. 132–151.

62. Chan and Lee, "Press Ideology."

63. Galbraith, *Anatomy of Power.*

64. Kuhn, *Structure of Scientific Revolutions.*

65. Gitlin, *World Is Watching,* p. 273.

66. Ibid.

67. Hallin, *The "Uncensored War,"* pp. 116–117.

68. Gans, *Deciding What's News,* p. 290.

69. Schudson, *Discovering the News.*

70. Peter L. Berger and Thomas Luckmann, *The Social Construction of Reality* (New York: Anchor, 1967).

71. Gans, *Deciding What's News,* p. 54.

72. J. M. Pennings distinguishes three general interorganizational strategies to manage vertical and horizontal interdependencies and thus reduce uncertainty: forestalling, forecasting, and absorption. Forestalling is coping behavior that prevents or controls the emergence of unpredictable behaviors of other organizations. Forecasting is coping behavior that predicts or forecasts the behavior of interdependent organizations. Absorption is coping behavior that mitigates the negative consequences of other organizations. See J. M. Pennings, "Strategically Interdependent Organizations," in P. Nystrom and W. H. Starbuck, eds., *Handbook of Organizational Design,* vol. 1 (London: Oxford University Press, 1981).

73. Joseph Cheng, *Hong Kong: In Search of a Future* (Hong Kong: Oxford University Press, 1984).

74. Max Weber, *Economy and Society,* ed. Guenther Roth and Claus Wittich (Berkeley: University of California Press, 1969), pp. 33–38.

75. Philip Selznick, *TVA and the Grass Roots: A Study in the Sociology of Formal Organization* (Berkeley: University of California Press, 1949), p. 13. According to Hawley, the current literature on cooptation is predominantly definitional in nature. There is also a renewal of interest in cooptation in studies in organizational sociology and administration as evidenced by the increase in the frequency with which Selznick's TVA study has been cited between 1975–1979. Karen E. Hawley, "A Theory of an Outsider's and Insider's Decision to Participate in a Political Issue and Its Implication for the Process of Cooptation" (Ph.D. diss., University of Minnesota, 1980).

76. Selznick, ibid., p. 17. Besides formal cooptation, Selznick points out that informal cooptation occurs when a focal organization may have legitimacy in the eyes of the public at large but small interest groups threaten its formal authority. There is no broad-based opposition to the organization. The focal organization brings the outsiders into the policy-determining structure but it does not explicitly acknowledge (particularly in public) the establishment of any formal relationship with the group.

77. Jeffrey Pfeffer and Phillip Salancik, *The External Control of Organizations: A Resource Dependence Perspective* (New York: Harper and Row, 1978), p. 161.

78. Harold Lasswell, "The Structure and Function of Communication in Society," in Lyman Bryson, ed., *The Communication of Ideas* (New York: Harper and Row, 1948).

79. Howard E. Aldrich, *Organizations and Environments* (Englewood: Prentice-Hall, 1979).

80. Tuchman, *Making News.*

81. Kuhn, *Structure of Scientific Revolutions.*

82. For example, Lucian Pye, "Communication and Political Culture in China," *Asian Survey,* 18 (1978): pp. 221–246; Chin-Chuan Lee, *Media Imperialism Reconsidered* (Beverly Hills: Sage, 1980), pp. 203–237; Majid Tehranian, "Iran: Communication, Alienation, and Revolution," *Intermedia,* 7, no. 2 (1979): pp. 6–12.

83. Bennett, Gressett and Haltom, "Repairing the News."

84. Lee and Chan, "Journalistic Paradigms in Flux."

CHAPTER 3

1. John Kenneth Galbraith, *The Anatomy of Power* (Boston: Houghton Mifflin, 1983); Antonio Gramsci, *Notes from the Prison* (New York: International Publishers, 1971).

2. *Hong Kong Hansard,* 1975–76, pp. 43–45.

3. Ambrose Yeo-chi King, "Administrative Absorption of Politics in Hong Kong: Emphasis on the Grass Roots Level," *Asian Survey,* 15 (1975): pp. 422–439.

4. Government Information Services, *GIS* (Hong Kong: Government Printer, 1987).

5. *South China Morning Post,* 23 April 1981. On each occasion, the following are awarded:

    5 CBEs (Commander of the Order of the British Empire) and CMGs (Companion Order of St. Michael and St. George)

    5 OBEs (Officers of the Order of the British Empire)

    4 ISOs (Imperial Service Orders)

  10 MBEs (Members of the Order of the British Empire)

  20 BEMs (British Empire Medals)

  25 CPMs (Colonial Police Medals)

The list is prepared by the Governor and then goes to the Foreign and Commonwealth Office. The number put forward will have to be considered along with those on lists from other territories. Besides, up to 50 Badges of Honor are awarded locally on the authority of the Queen in an effort to recognize the contributions made by people holding essential jobs in the lower social stratum.

6. Lee Ming-kun, *Hong Kong's Politics and Society in Transition* (Hong Kong: Commercial, 1987).

7. *Kowloon Disturbances 1966, Report of Commission of Inquiry* (Hong Kong: Government Printer, 1967), pp. 126–131; Chin-Chuan Lee, "Partisan

Press Coverage of Government News in Hong Kong," *Journalism Quarterly,* 62 (1985): pp. 770–776.

8. It is no accident that former Governor Edward Youde declared in a press conference that in addition to the English-language newspapers, he read five Chinese newspapers including *Ming Pao, Hong Kong Economic Journal, Wen Wei Pao, Ta Kung Pao,* and the *Hong Kong Times.* (See Lu Keng, *The Era of Deng Xiaoping* [Hong Kong: Pai Hsing, 1990], p. 277.)

New Statesman of London disclosed in an investigative report that 11 pressure groups in Hong Kong, including the prestigious Hong Kong Observer, had come under secret government surveillance. Embarrassed by the revelation, the government denied any intention to infiltrate or neutralize these groups. (See *Hong Kong Standard,* 16 January 1981; Standing Committee on Pressure Groups, "Information Paper for Chief Secretary's Committee Monitoring of Pressure Group Activities," Home Affairs Branch, Hong Kong Government.) Activist foreign journalists working with disadvantaged groups have been denied visas or declared persona non grata.

9. Galbraith, *Anatomy of Power.*

10. Steven Lukes, *Power: A Radical View* (London: Macmillan, 1974).

11. Todd Gitlin, *The Whole World Is Watching* (Berkeley: University of California Press, 1980), p. 253.

12. Raymond Williams, *Marxism and Literature* (New York: Oxford University Press, 1977).

13. The GIS had a total of 167 information officers in 1982 (see *Pai Hsing,* 16 September 1982, p. 3), but has grown into a HK$17 million operation employing about 480 people as of 1990 (see Michael Bociurkiw, "In the Jaws of China," *South China Morning Post,* 25 February 1990).

14. Former GIS Director, Cheung Man-yee, acknowledged that certain government departments were quite bureaucratic, but she contended that the government as a whole had improved. (*Ming Pao,* 26 January 1985.)

15. "GIS Staff Are Official Reporters—An Interview with New GIS Director Cheung Man-yee," *Pai Hsing Semimonthly,* 1 January 1985, p. 16.

16. Bociurkiw, "In the Jaws of China," quoting Irene Yau.

17. Chang Kuo-sin, "GIS Chief and the Press," *Hong Kong Standard,* 25 January 1984.

18. *Pai Hsing Semimonthly,* 16 September 1982, p. 51.

19. "GIS Staff Are Government Reporters," *Pai Hsing Semimonthly,* 1 January 1985, p. 16.

20. Lee, "Partisan Press Coverage." Major categories of the press coverage include policy announcements (16%); government bidding, recruitment, and other administrative business news (15%); ceremonies, speeches, and visits (12%); government services and construction projects (11%); as well as explanations, replies, or clarifications of policy matters (11%).

21. Ibid.

22. Peter Tsao, ex-GIS director, remarked in an interview that the GIS would strive for accuracy and would not fabricate facts. He said, however, that

more "positive" news would promote social stability, noting that the GIS did not like to see excessive amounts of "negative" news that could damage public confidence in the Government (*Wah Kiu Yat Pao,* 12 February 1983).

23. "GIS Staff Are Official Reporters," *Pai Hsing Semimonthly.*

24. *Ming Pao,* 26 January 1985.

25. Kam Shu-fai, "Hong Kong Government and the News Media," *Pai Hsing Semimonthly,* 16 September 1982.

26. Government Information Services, *GIS.*

27. Reporters lauded the reorganized GIS for improving efficiency (see the *China Times Weekly,* 27 April 1983). One journalist said, "In the past, GIS officials usually gave nothing but an ambiguous answer at the end of the day. If you raised further questions, they would say sorry, they had to go home. Now they try to give an answer as soon as possible."

28. Cheung Man-yee, a respected director of Radio Television Hong Kong, was appointed by Tsao as head of the GIS's public relations unit. She subsequently succeeded Tsao to head the entire GIS.

29. Chan King-shuen, "On the Cold War between China and Britain," *Pai Hsing Semimonthly,* 16 September 1986.

30. *Hong Kong Economic Journal,* 30 December 1984, and 11 January 1985.

31. For example, *Ta Kung Pao,* 22 November 1985.

32. For example, the October 1985 issue of the *Nineties Monthly* regarded Xinhua as an alternative power center to the colonial regime.

33. Interview.

34. Interview.

35. Joseph Cheng, "Politics: The New Game in Town," *Asiaweek,* 21 July 1985, pp. 35–37; 19 July 1985, pp. 28–31; Lee Yee, "Challenging the Lame Duck," *Hong Kong Economic Journal,* 25 November 1985.

36. Government Information Services, *GIS;* Bociurkiw, "In the Jaws of China." The quotes were from Irene Yau, who succeeded Tsao, Cheung, and Chan to become the GIS director.

37. *Pai Hsing Semimonthly,* 16 February 1986.

38. *Sing Tao Jih Pao,* 29 March 1986.

39. Since 1987 it has been the case that reports are ready before officials reach their morning desks. The GIS has added a new publication called *What the Magazines Say,* summarizing opinions expressed in magazines. GIS reports also introduce more topics of special interest, such as public reactions to the Basic Law.

40. Government Information Services, *GIS.*

41. *Hong Kong Economic Journal,* 30 December 1984, and 11 January 1985. This opinion was expressed by Cheung Man-yee, who succeeded Peter Tsao to be the GIS director.

42. *Ming Pao,* 13 February 1986. This opinion was expressed by Chan Cho-tsak, who succeeded Cheung Man-yee as the GIS director.

43. Government Information Services, *GIS.*

44. See, for example, *Wah Kiu Yat Pao*, 26 November 1985. Former GIS directors Peter Tsao and Cheung Man-yee have both expressed such concern.

45. Thomas Hahn, head of the Association of Government Information Officers, reportedly said, "Our group as a whole distrusts the Chinese Communist government . . . It is obvious that they will like to have their own trustworthy people in the government information machinery." Bociurkiw, "In the Jaws of China."

46. Mao Zedong, "On Contradiction," in *Selected Works*, vol. 1, (Beijing: People's Press, 1966), pp. 274–312.

47. Chiu Hung-dah and Ren Xiaoqi, eds., *Negotiation Strategy of the Communist China* (Taipei: Lien-jing, 1985).

48. Emily Lau, "A Kind of Defection," *Far Eastern Economic Review*, 24 May 1990, p. 11; *Contemporary Weekly*, 9 December 1989, pp. 20–21; *Contemporary Weekly*, 13 January 1990.

49. *Cheng Ming Monthly*, September 1983.

50. Xuan Yuan-lo, *Looking Closely at Xinhua* (Hong Kong: Wide-angled Mirror, 1987), pp. 83–99. Our informants revealed that Xinhua threw at least 200 dinner parties a year.

51. See *Far Eastern Economic Review*, 4 January 1986.

52. Some sources report that Xinhua has increased the number of its staff to 1,000.

53. Anthony Giddens, *Central Problems in Social Theory* (Berkeley: University of California Press, 1979).

54. Communication studies have provided strong evidence for the "agenda-setting function" of the media: The media may not be successful in telling people what to think, but are stunningly powerful in telling people what to think *about*. Others speak of the media as "social constructors of reality." For a general survey, see Denis McQuail, *Mass Communication Theory* (London: Sage, 1987).

55. Quoted in Qi Xin [Lee Yee], "Analyzing the Xu Jiatun Affairs," *Nineties Monthly*, June 1990, p. 26. The interview was originally published in China's journal, *Comparative Social and Economic Systems*, vol. 1 (1988). Xu had a copy of that interview sent to Lee Yee, editor of the *Nineties Monthly* and his critic.

56. One such example of this is Xinhua's leak to *Sing Tao Jih Pao* that Xu Jiatun would assume Xinhua's directorship in Hong Kong.

57. *Hong Kong Economic Journal Monthly*, October 1984.

58. Long Sin, *The Shadow Government of Hong Kong* (Hong Kong: Hai-san, 1985).

59. Chan King-shuen, "An Insider's View of the Suppression of the *Seventies Monthly* and *Cheng Ming Monthly*," *Pai Hsing Semimonthly*, 16 August 1981; Yu Mang, "Pok Shaofu, Har Kung and Freedom of Speech in Hong Kong," *Cheng Ming Monthly*, October 1985.

60. Cheung Kit-fung, "Will It Be Possible to Maintain the Status Quo After 1997?" *Pai Hsing Semimonthly*, 1 January 1985.

61. Julia Leung, "China Gets a Better Press in Hong Kong," *Asian Wall Street Journal,* 7 January 1986.

62. Fei Yimin, the late publisher of *Ta Kung Pao,* was an NPC delegate. Media leaders who are current members of the CPPCC include Tsui Sze-man, publisher of the *Mirror Monthly;* Deacon Chiu, chairman of the Asian Television; and Ho Sai-chiu, publisher of *Tin Tin Daily News.*

63. Emily Lau, "Capitalist Delegates to People's Congress," *Far Eastern Economic Review,* 1 August 1985.

64. Ambrose King, "Hong Kong's Political Transition," *China Times Weekly* (New York), 3 November 1985, pp. 16–17.

65. "Reconsider Capitalism and Build Socialism Consciously," *Qiu Shi,* 1988, no. 5.

66. *Contemporary Weekly,* 13 January 1990.

67. Interview.

68. Interview.

69. *The Journalist,* 22 January 1990, p. 81.

70. Richard Solomon, "Chinese Political Negotiating Behavior," (Rand Corporation, 1983); Chiu and Ren, *Negotiation Strategy.*

71. *Hong Kong Economic Journal,* 15 May 1990. This figure was disclosed in an article aimed to "expose" Xu's wrongdoing and alleged corruption after his unauthorized departure for the United States. There was speculation that it was written by people close to his successor.

72. A local businessman explains, "They invite you to dinner. After a week, they invite you again—and then again. After many dinners, it's most difficult to say bad things about your host." (Julia Leung, "China Woos Hong Kong's Business Elite," *Asian Wall Street Journal,* 16 January 1988.)

73. *Cheng Ming Monthly,* October 1985.

74. Qi, "Analyzing the Xu Jiatun Affair."

75. *Pai Hsing Semimonthly,* 1 July 1986, p. 9.

76. Interview.

77. Leung, "China Gets a Better Press."

78. *Pai Hsing Semimonthly,* 1 July 1986, p. 9.

79. *Contemporary Weekly,* 13 January 1990, p. 12.

80. Joseph Cheng; interview with Lee; Minneapolis, Minn.: 16 April 1990.

81. Deng Xiaoping told a group of visiting Hong Kong leaders: "No matter what kind of dress one wears, no matter what position one holds, Chinese take pride in the Chinese as a people. Hong Kong people have this national pride too. Hong Kong people can run Hong Kong well; we must have this confidence." (*Selections from the Documents on the Question of Hong Kong* [Beijing: People's, 1985] p. 3.)

82. Evading a journalist's queries, Yao Guang, head of the Chinese team in the Sino-British negotiations, said: "We are compatriots. We are not afraid of hardship, neither are you, because we are all Chinese. Isn't that right?" (Tsang Wai Yin, *Days and Nights in Beijing* [Hong Kong: Publications Ltd., 1983], p. 67.)

83. "Heart to Heart in Peking Pantheon", Editorial, *South China Morning Post,* 12 April 1985.

84. Ibid.

85. "United Front in Hong Kong," *Asiaweek,* 2 November 1984; Leung, "China Gets a Better Press."

86. Interview.

87. *Ming Pao,* 9 January 1986.

88. Xu Jiatun tried to brief journalists once, but some journalists complained about being excluded while others broke the "off the record" promise, so briefing was not institutionalized. Informal contacts remained frequent.

CHAPTER 4

1. This conceptualization was first developed in Chin-Chuan Lee and Joseph Man Chan, "Journalistic Paradigms in Flux: The Press and Political Transition in Hong Kong," *Bulletin of the Institute of Ethnology Academia Sinica,* no. 63 (Spring 1987), pp. 109–131 (originally presented at the annual convention of the International Communication Association, Chicago, 22–26 August 1986, as well as at the conference on "Communication, Politics, and Culture in East Asia," University of Minnesota, May 8–9, 1986).

2. Joseph Galaskiewicz, "Interorganizational Relations," *Annual Review of Sociology,* 11 (1985): pp. 281–304.

3. Denis McQuail, *Mass Communication Theory* (Beverly Hills: Sage, 1983), p. 108.

4. Gaye Tuchman, *Making News* (New York: Free Press, 1978).

5. Lee Sigelman, "Reporting the News: An Organizational Analysis," *American Journal of Sociology,* 79 (1973): pp. 132–151.

6. Edward J. Epstein, *News from Nowhere* (New York: Vintage, 1973); Herbert J. Gans, *Deciding What's News* (New York: Pantheon, 1979); Philip Schlesinger, *Putting "Reality" Together* (Beverly Hills: Sage, 1978); Jeremy Tunstall, *Journalists At Work* (London: Constable, 1971).

7. Joseph Man Chan and Chin-Chuan Lee, "Press Ideology and Organization Control in Hong Kong," *Communication Research,* 15, no. 2 (1988): pp. 185–197.

8. Interview.

9. Interview.

10. Interview.

11. This title has been dropped from the mastheads of *Sing Tao Wan Pao* (evening), which is not sold in Taiwan, and from the Northern American editions of *Sing Tao Jih Pao.*

12. Soon after, Poon emigrated to Canada.

13. Pok Shaofu, "My Pillow Testifies to My Serene Sleep Every Night," *Ming Pao,* 27 January 1986.

14. Interview with Shum Choi-sang.

15. Emily Lau, "A Media Melting Pot of All Political Strips," *Far Eastern Economic Review*, 13 February 1986.

16. For example, on March 27, 1986 *Wah Kiu Yat Pao* carried a lead editorial headlined, "The Dictatorial Government Ought to Be Held Accountable to the People." This would have been unimaginable just a few years ago.

17. Louis Cha, "In Defense of Freedom of Speech," editorial, *Ming Pao*, 27 January 1986. Cha was reportedly so heart-stricken by Beijing's brutal suppression of the democracy movement in 1989 that he proposed to Murdoch a purchase of *Ming Pao*. But the deal did not come to fruition.

18. Interview.

19. Interview.

20. Ho Lai-kit, "Louis Cha: A Learned Boss," in Ho Lai-kit, *Ten Interviews* (Hong Kong: Culture Book House, 1977).

21. Ibid., p. 18.

22. Interview with Cha's aide. This disclosure was confirmed by Cha himself in an editorial (*Ming Pao*, 11 June 1989).

23. Editorial, *Ming Pao*, 29 January 1986.

24. Louis Cha, "On Press Freedom," *Ming Pao*, 21–23 March 1986.

25. Interview with a senior editor.

26. Interview.

27. Interview.

28. "United Front in Hong Kong," *Asiaweek*, 2 December 1984.

29. For example, "Hong Kong People Definitely Do Not Believe the Communist Party's Promises," editorial, *Hong Kong Times*, 16 April 1984; "Communists' Words Cannot Be Trusted," editorial, *Hong Kong Times*, 3 August 1984; "The Two Cutting Edges of the United Front Tactics by Local Communists," editorial, *Kung Sheung Yat Pao*, 16 September 1984; "Don't Eat the Sugar-coated Poison," editorial, *Hong Kong Times*, 12 January 1984; "'Hong Kong Administering Hong Kong' Is a Sugar-Coated Poison," editorial, *Kung Sheung Yat Pao*, 9 December 1982.

30. *Kung Sheung Yat Pao* did appear to make adjustment attempts, but the changes came too little, too late to save its own fate. For example, its reporters appeared at a reception party in 1983 in honor of Xu Jiatun as Xinhua's new director. The paper has covered Xinhua's activities and Sino-British negotiations more heavily but skeptically. Robert Ho, the publisher, explained that he feared a drastic shift would have lost old readers but gained few new ones. (For an interview with Ho, see *Hong Kong Economic Journal*, 9 May 1988.)

31. Lu Keng, *The Era of Deng Xiaoping* (Hong Kong: Pai Hsing, 1990), p. 277.

32. For example, Dr. Chang Ching-yu, Taiwan's former director of the Government Information Office, could not obtain a visa to officiate at the inauguration of a KMT propaganda office in Hong Kong.

33. KMT forces in Hong Kong included the Chinese Cultural Association, the Central News Agency, the *Hong Kong Times*, China Travel Agency (which is a quasi-consular office), Overseas Chinese Travel Agency (which grants Tai-

wan visas to overseas Chinese), Kowloon Chamber of Commerce, and a dozen private colleges whose credentials are recognized by Taiwan. See Huang Kang-sheng, *The Problem of Hong Kong's Existence* (Hong Kong: Buo-yee, 1987), p.31.

34. *Selections from the Document on the Question of Hong Kong* (Beijing: People's, 1985), p. 8. Xu Jiatun repeated the same message in an exclusive interview with Lu Keng (*Pai Hsing Semimonthly*, 1 February 1985).

35. Pok Shaofu, "Thank You, Mr. Xu Jiatun's Goodwill," *Newsdom Weekly*, 17 August 1985; Pok, "My Pillow Testifies"; Tong Chung-han, "Recent Activities of Pro-Taiwan Forces in Hong Kong," *Pai Hsing Semimonthly*, 16 November 1985.

36. Hong Kong is Taiwan's third largest export market, after the United States and Japan. Additionally, about 40% of Taiwan's exports pass through Hong Kong to Southeast Asia, the Middle East, and Western Europe. This is not to mention Hong Kong's political role. (See "The Choices Taiwan Has to Make in Face of the Hong Kong Problem," *Mirror Monthly*, August 1983.) Taiwan formed a special interministerial committee to oversee its Hong Kong policy, which aimed to absorb part of Hong Kong's investments. Taiwan has also decided to invest aggressively in Hong Kong to establish a stronghold.

37. Publisher Eddie Tseng said: "Beijing has said Hong Kong can exist under a 'one-country, two-systems' policy. We will stay to test this [policy] to see if they can accept our system. But we won't change to suit their palate, and we won't close down voluntarily." (See Emily Lau, "A Media Melting Pot of All Political Stripes," *Far Eastern Economic Review*, 13 February 1986, p. 29.)

38. Martin Lee, a member of China's Basic Law Drafting Committee and of Hong Kong's Legislative Council, often spoke in favor of establishing democratic process in Hong Kong and against the PRC's interference. The *Hong Kong Times* (for example, editorial, 10 April 1986) praised Lee for having the courage to speak the truth while chiding his colleagues for acting like Beijing's "rubber stamp." (see Huang, *Hong Kong's Existence*, pp. 26–28). Lee was openly attacked by Beijing for his role in supporting the 1989 student democracy movement in China.

39. Shi Yufei, "The *Hong Kong Times'* Quarrel in Taipei," *Nineties Monthly*, February 1985.

40. For example, "Stay Calm Amidst Changes, Unite and Self-help," editorial, *Hong Kong Times*, 27 September 1984.

41. Lee and Chan, "Journalistic Paradigms in Flux."

42. Interview.

43. *Hong Kong Times*, 20 December 1985.

44. According to Lee Tse-chung, when applying to the Hong Kong government for this advertising status, *Wen Wei Pao* was criticized by Wang Kuang, Xu Jiatun's predecessor as director of Xinhua, for conceding to the "two Chinas" policy because both *Sing Tao Jih Pao* and *Wah Kiu Yat Pao*, which enjoyed the same privilege, bear the "Republic of China" in their mastheads. See *Contemporary Weekly*, 13 January 1990, p. 19.

45. In the mid-1980s, a group of taxi drivers went on strike due to a

dispute over price increases. When they petitioned their grievances to Xinhua, Xinhua told them to go to the Hong Kong government instead.

46. Interview.

47. Lau, "A Media Melting Pot." One reporter said, "Sometimes we are told to ring up certain people for reactions, and when our reporters ring them, they read out prepared statements. These people have been briefed by Xinhua on what to say."

48. Ibid.

49. In Beijing, CNA is a separate organization from Xinhua News Agency; in Hong Kong, all China-related agencies, including the CNA, are supervised by Xinhua's Hong Kong branch.

50. Interview with a *Wen Wei Pao* executive, who said, "We have begun to realize that the management and business side of the paper counts more than the editorial side, because it is the managerial system, not the editorial content itself, that determines whether the paper will enjoy a high circulation."

51. *Wen Wei Pao* claimed in an editorial (6 January 1986) that it had found a new sense of hope in promoting Hong Kong's prosperity and in facilitating the political transition.

52. Interview.

53. Chan and Lee, "Press Ideology and Organizational Control."

54. Huge differences in pay scale exist within *Wen Wei Pao*. The Hong Kong cadres are paid according to the local standard; the Party members assigned to the paper from the mainland receive a living stipend and other benefits but must submit extra pay to the authorities; the non-Party members assigned from the mainland are paid by China's standard and receive rental exemption. See Lee Tse-chung, "Three Systems Within One Paper," *Contemporary Weekly*, 20 January 1990, p. 20.

55. Interview.

56. Interview.

57. *Wen Wei Pao* started covering horse racing in 1985, to be followed by *Ta Kung Pao* in its wake. Horse-racing coverage is, however, relatively insignificant compared to the vivid, prominent display of gossip about entertainment stars.

58. Interview.

59. Philip Selznick, *TVA and the Grass Roots: A Study in the Sociology of Formal Organization* (Berkeley: University of California Press, 1949), p. 13; Karen E. Hawley, "A Theory of an Outsider's and Insider's Decision to Participate in a Political Issue and Its Implication for the Process of Cooptation" (Ph.D. diss., University of Minnesota, 1980).

60. Joseph Cheng, *Hong Kong: In Search of a Future* (Hong Kong: Oxford University Press, 1984).

61. Max Weber, *Economy and Society*, ed. Gunther Roth and Claus Wittich (Berkeley: University of California Press, 1969), pp. 31–38.

62. For example, said the *Express*, a sister paper of the rightist *Sing Tao Jih Pao* (editorial, 4 October 1985): "Merits should be given to the Basic Law Consultative Committee whenever it deserves. To describe the Consultative

Committee in black and white terms is to show one's political bias. In light of trends in the political sphere, we can only aim lower for a betterment of the existing conditions through the Consultative Committee."

63. Sun Lung-chi, *The Deep Structure of the Chinese Culture* (Hong Kong: Lung-meng, 1983).

64. John Kenneth Galbraith, *The Anatomy of Power* (Boston: Houghton Mifflin, 1983); Steven Lukes, *Power: A Radical View* (London: MacMillan, 1974).

CHAPTER 5

1. Louis Cha, "The First of July, 1997," *Ming Pao,* 16 August 1983.

2. David Bonavia, *Hong Kong 1997* (Hong Kong: South China Morning Post, 1985).

3. In submitting to the National People's Congress Standing Committee for ratification, Foreign Minister Wu Xueqian specifically said on November 6, 1984:

The Taiwan question is different from the Hong Kong question in nature. But the "one country, two systems" concept will be applicable to resolving the Taiwan question. The resolution of the Hong Kong question has a profound impact on the Taiwan authorities and the Taiwan people, and will be conducive to early realization of national unification. (*Selected Documents on Hong Kong* [Beijing: People's Daily, 1985] p. 26.)

In the same vein, Deng said,

The resolution of the Hong Kong issue will directly affect the Taiwan issue. They should be able to accept the "one country, two systems" method. . . . This method means that I don't eat you up, and you don't eat me up. Isn't that good? A foreigner asked me recently if the Taiwan question was the same with Hong Kong, I told him [it would be] more generous. That is, besides that which [we use] to resolve the Hong Kong question will be applicable to Taiwan, [Taiwan] will be allowed to keep its own army. (Ibid., p. 11.)

President Chiang Ching-kuo of Taiwan charged that Communist China was attempting to "use threats and promise of gains to divide our solidarity and to blow our morale." The Government Information Office rejected the "one country, two systems" idea as Communist China's "tactical plot and rhetoric of the current phase to create a false impression of peaceful coexistence." That policy, it said, amounted to a recognition of Communist failure and thus the mainland regime had to temporarily tolerate a capitalistic Hong Kong in order to maintain prosperity. Insisting that Taiwan is different from Hong Kong, it said Taiwan would refuse to be reduced to a local government status. Taiwan offered a "three-nos" policy as a response: No dodging, no contacts, and no talks (See *Unveiling the CCP's "One Country, Two Systems" Conspiracy* [Taipei: Mainland China Materials, 1987].)

Despite official rhetoric, the late President Chiang decided to lift martial law in 1987 and adopted a policy that allowed people to visit the mainland. An estimated half million people visited the mainland in 1988 alone. Curbing the growing tide of U.S. trade protectionism, Taiwan's investment capital has flowed to the mainland (about $1 billion in 1990, to be doubled in 1991); the unofficial trade, via Hong Kong, between both sides of the Taiwan Strait has climbed to $2.5 billion per year. Taiwan, like Hong Kong, was outraged at Beijing's massacre of students in 1989. Again, blasting "Taiwan spies" for instigating the disturbance in Beijing, mainland China also wasted no time to reaffirm that its policy on Taiwan remained unchanged.

4. See Appendix VI for a fuller text of the Joint Declaration.

5. *South China Morning Post*, 23 June 1989.

6. "Continual Absence of Assuring News for the Hong Kong People," Editorial, *Sing Tao Jih Pao*, 4 December 1982.

7. "The Female Prime Minister Committed to Moral Responsibility with Iron Shoulders," editorial, *Sing Tao Jih Pao*, 29 September 1982.

8. For example: "Have Confidence in London's Promises," editorial, *Sing Tao Jih Pao*, 6 July 1983; "The Hong Kong Government Has Successfully Diverted a Disaster," editorial, *Sing Tao Jih Pao*, 28 September 1983.

9. "Hong Kong Has a Very Bright Future," editorial, *Sing Tao Jih Pao*, 30 September 1982.

10. "In the Aftermath of Initialing the Agreement on Hong Kong's Future," editorial, *Sing Tao Jih Pao*, 27 September 1984. *Sing Tao Jih Pao* showed its acquiescence to the political development immediately after Foreign Minister Howe announced in April 1984 Britain's decision to return Hong Kong to China ("The Three Main Points in Foreign Minister Howe's Announcement," editorial, *Sing Tao Jih Pao*, 8 December 1984).

11. "Revive the Confidence to Invest in Hong Kong," editorial, *Sing Tao Jih Pao*, 12 December 1984.

12. "The Last Day of a Year Again," editorial, *Sing Tao Jih Pao*, 12 December 1984.

13. "To Discuss with Ji Pengfei on Seven Issues," editorial, *Sing Tao Jih Pao*, 12 December 1985.

14. "Peng Zhen's Talk and Hong Kong's Future," editorial, *Wah Kiu Yat Pao*, 21 July 1982; "The History and Reality That Deserve Respect," editorial, *Wah Kiu Yat Pao*, 4 August 1982; "Looking at the Beijing–London–Hong Kong Relationship in a Broad and Long-term Perspective," editorial, *Wah Kiu Yat Pao*, 24 September 1982; "What Mrs. Thatcher Cannot Disclose at Will," editorial, *Wah Kiu Yat Pao*, 29 September 1982.

15. "Welcoming the British Prime Minister Mrs. Thatcher to Visit Hong Kong," editorial, *Wah Kiu Yat Pao*, 27 September 1982; "What Mrs. Thatcher Cannot Disclose," *Wah Kiu Yat Pao;* "Negotiation on Hong Kong's Future Advances into the Second Stage," editorial, *Wah Kiu Yat Pao*, 4 July 1983;

"Governor Youde: The Burden Is Heavy, the Road Is Long," editorial, *Wah Kiu Yat Pao*, 28 July 1983.

16. "The Right Directions for Negotiations on Hong Kong's Future," editorial, *Wah Kiu Yat Pao*, 26 May 1983.

17. "Some Principles for Negotiation over Hong Kong's Future," editorial, *Wah Kiu Yat Pao*, 3 January 1984; "Dangerous Arguments to Be Keenly Watched," editorial, *Wah Kiu Yat Pao*, 27 January 1984.

18. "The Date to Retake Hong Kong's Sovereignty Is Decided," editorial, *Wah Kiu Yat Pao*, 17 August 1983. An editorial that best illustrates *Wah Kiu Yat Pao's* tendency to speak indirectly for Beijing at this early stage is "The Concept and Outline of 'Hong Kong Special Administrative Region,' " editorial, 17 October 1983.

19. "Dangerous Arguments," *Wah Kiu Yat Pao*.

20. "Hong Kong People's Wish," editorial, *Wah Kiu Yat Pao*, 2 August 1984.

21. "The Righteousness of Nationalism," Miu Yu Column, *Oriental Daily News*, 5 February 1983; also, "Imperialism," 17 October 1983.

22. "Hong Kong Law Ruling Hong Kong," Miu Yu Column, *Oriental Daily News*, 24 June 1983.

23. "Negotiating the Future," Miu Yu Column, *Oriental Daily News*, 8 December 1983. Shortly after this, Miu Yu indicated that he had learned of the British decision to withdraw from Hong Kong ("See Who Changes First," *Oriental Daily News*, 25 January 1984).

24. "High Evaluation of Hong Kong People," Miu Yu Column, *Oriental Daily News*, 1 January 1984.

25. After the CCP consolidated its power in early 1950s, it launched a series of programs to nationalize the economy. In its transitional phase, the national bourgeoisie were promised "co-ownership," but this was finally swept away by the CCP's speedy measures to root out the private sector.

26. "The New Is Different from the Old," Miu Yu Column, *Oriental Daily News*, 6 April 1984.

27. "Twelve Points of Policy for Hong Kong," 28 April 1984.

28. For example, "Sino-British Accord," Miu Yu Column, *Oriental Daily News*, 2 August 1984; "Moral Responsibility," Miu Yu Column, *Oriental Daily News*, 13 September 1984; "Those Who Believe Will Be Saved," Miu Yu Column, *Oriental Daily News*, 30 April 1984; "Don't Be Afraid of Interference," Miu Yu Column, *Oriental Daily News*, 6 October 1984; "Rumors Feed on Rumors," Miu Yu Column, *Oriental Daily News*, 7 October 1984.

29. "How to Evaluate the Hong Kong Question," editorial, *Sing Pao*, 23 September 1983.

30. "Alleviate the 'Jardine Shock' Immediately," editorial, *Sing Pao*, 30 March 1984.

31. "Both the Agreement or the Joint Declaration Have Legal Binding Force," editorial, *Sing Pao*, 18 September 1984; "The Blueprint for a Smooth Transition," editorial, *Sing Pao*, 2 August 1984.

32. "All the Reactions to the Joint Declaration," editorial, *Sing Pao*, 29 September 1984.

33. "Actively Participate to Practice Civil Rights," editorial, *Sing Pao*, 28 September 1984.

34. "Competition for Lunar New Year Stalls Shows Confidence," editorial, *Sing Pao*, 7 January 1986.

35. "Three Requirements for an Arrangement on Hong Kong's Status," editorial, *Ming Pao*, 19 February 1981.

36. "A Strange Goose That Lays Golden Eggs," editorial, *Ming Pao*, 14 October 1982.

37. "Britain's Moral Responsibility towards Hong Kong," editorial, *Ming Pao*, 20 October 1982.

38. "Three Cards in the British Hand," editorial, *Ming Pao*, 4 July 1983.

39. " 'Same as Before'; Free Entry and Exit," editorial, *Ming Pao*, 25 November 1982.

40. "Horses Must Be Fed to Make It Work," editorial, *Ming Pao*, 7 July 1983.

41. "Ji Pengfei's Concrete Measures for 'Hong Kong Administered by Hong Kong People,' " editorial, *Ming Pao*, 15 October 1983.

42. See, e.g., "From '79 to '97," editorial, *Ming Pao*, 24 October 1983; "Making Use of Hong Kong Over a Long Time Rather Than Imposing Reforms," editorial, *Ming Pao*, 25 October 1983; "Fundamental Demands by China, Britain and Hong Kong," editorial, *Ming Pao*, 15 December 1983.

43. "Pledge and Guarantee of an International Nature," editorial, *Ming Pao*, 24 January 1984.

44. See "Deng Xiaoping Talked about the Confidence Problem of the Hong Kong People," editorial, *Ming Pao*, 27 June 1984; "How Policies on Hong Kong Are Made," editorial, *Ming Pao*, 11 August 1984.

45. Louis Cha, "An Innovation Applicable to the Whole World," *People's Daily*, 26 September 1984. Similar ideas were voiced earlier in a *Ming Pao* editorial entitled "A Model Applicable to the World," 29 June 1984.

46. "Confidence Is to Be Based on What Kind of Foundation?" editorial, *Ming Pao*, 2 July 1984.

47. "Welcoming the British Prime Minister to Visit Hong Kong," editorial, *Hong Kong Times*, 26 September 1982. Similar comments are reiterated in *Kung Sheung Yat Pao's* editorial, "The British Prime Minister Stands Firm on the Hong Kong Question," 5 November 1983.

48. "Comments on the Visit of the Intellectuals' Tour in Mainland China," editorial, *Kung Sheung Yat Pao*, 14 April 1983; "On the Question of 'Hong Kong's Sovereignty,' " editorial, *Kung Sheung Yat Pao*, 22 October 1982; " 'Nationalism' Dictates 'Autonomous Independence,' " editorial, *Kung Sheung Yat Pao*, 4 April 1983.

49. "Stay Calm Amidst Changes, Unite and Self-help," editorial, *Hong Kong Times*, 27 September 1984; "The Inglorious 'Initialization'," editorial, *Hong Kong Times*, 24 September 1984; "Hong Kong People Do Not Recognize the 'Joint Declaration,' " editorial, *Hong Kong Times*, 4 September 1984.

50. For example: "Hong Kong People Definitely Do Not Believe the Communist Party's Promises," editorial, *Hong Kong Times*, 16 April 1984; "Communists' Words Cannot Be Trusted," editorial, *Hong Kong Times*, 3 August

1984; "The Two Cutting Edges of Local Communists' United Front Tactics," editorial, *Kung Sheung Yat Pao*, 16 September 1984; "The So-called 'Hong Kong Model,'" editorial, *Hong Kong Times*, 24 December 1984.

51. "Don't Eat 'Sugar-Coated Poison,'" editorial, *Hong Kong Times*, 12 January 1974.

52. "'Hong Kong Administering Hong Kong' Is Sugar-coated Poison," editorial, *Kung Sheung Yat Pao*, 9 December 1982.

53. See editorials on the Joint Declaration: e.g. "Analyzing the 'Joint Declaration Draft,'" *Kung Sheung Yat Pao*, 27 September 1984; "Stay Calm Amidst Changes," *Hong Kong Times*. Editorials on the Basic Law: e.g. "Hong Kong People Have the Absolute Right in Making the 'Basic Law,'" *Kung Sheung Yat Pao*, 25 October 1984.

54. What began as a successional fight among the Times' staff evolved into a political fight. On one side are the hard-liners who asserted that they should fight against communism simply "for the sake of anticommunism". The opposing faction thought it was for "truth" that they fought communism. The major difference between these two approaches is that the first regards anticommunism as a permanent goal that is immutable, while the second asserts that anticommunism should be practiced in a "rational" way and should give "due regards" to changes within China. The controversy ended in an organizational reshuffling in which six staunch anti-Communist columnists were sacked and a page that was devoted to hard-line anticommunism was canceled. See Leung Min-kwun, "Anti-Communist Outpost in Chaos," *Nineties Monthly*, January 1985.

55. "Who Does Sir Youde Represent?" editorial, *Wen Wei Pao*, 9 July 1983.

56. "Check the Trend of Price Raises to Ensure the Public's Livelihood," editorial, *Wen Wei Pao*, 16 September 1983. Other exemplary editorials that raised serious doubts about the government's respect for public opinion include (1) "Has Public Opinion Ever Been Respected?" editorial, *Wen Wei Pao*, 5 September 1983; (2) "The Loud Calls for Preserving the Public's Livelihood," editorial, *Wen Wei Pao*, 19 September 1983; and (3) "How Constructive Can the 'Lubo Motion' Be?" editorial, *Ta Kung Pao*, 15 March 1984.

57. "An Aggressive and Solid Annual Report," editorial, *Wen Wei Pao*, 7 October 1984.

58. "Reviewing Hong Kong in Its First Year of Transition," editorial, *Wen Wei Pao*, 31 December 1986. This generally favorable review can also be contrasted with *Ta Kung Pao's* generally critical review two years earlier; "Reading Youde's Administrative Report," editorial, *Ta Kung Pao*, 16 October 1983.

59. "The Editor's Note," *Ta Kung Pao*, 27 February 1986.

60. Such characterizations of Hong Kong's prosperity were common in past ultraleftist newspapers' editorials. A more recent illustration can be found in *Ta Kung Pao's* short editorial, "High Land Price Policy Is Devastating," 4 December 1982.

61. "On District Council Election," editorial, *Wen Wei Pao*, 22 January 1985.

62. It should be noted that the paper was referring to an election at the district level, but not to an elected Legislative Council. The Hong Kong government tried to implement a limited electoral democracy in Hong Kong as part of its decolonization program, but had to withdraw the plan because of China's strong opposition.

63. Lance Bennett, Lynn Gressett, and William Haltom, "Repairing the News; A Case Study of the News Paradigm," *Journal of Communication, 35,* no. 2 (1985): pp. 50–68.

64. Todd Gitlin, *The Whole World Is Watching* (Berkeley: University of California Press, 1980); Chin-Chuan Lee and Joseph Man Chan, "Journalistic Paradigms in Flux: The Press and Political Transition in Hong Kong," *Bulletin of the Institute of Ethnology Academia Sinica,* no. 63 (Spring 1987): pp. 109–131.

65. The dates for all of the days of a week within each period were numbered and randomly chosen to make up a constructed week. The first "constructed week" included November 7, 1983 (Monday); January 3, 1985 (Tuesday); October 9, 1983 (Wednesday); March 3, 1983 (Thursday); April 6, 1984 (Friday); September 24, 1983 (Saturday); August 21, 1983 (Sunday). The second "constructed week" included January 6, 1986 (Monday); December 17, 1985 (Tuesday); February 5, 1986 (Wednesday); July 4, 1985 (Thursday); December 20, 1985 (Friday); January 4, 1986 (Saturday); December 1, 1985 (Sunday).

66. K. Krippendorf, *Content Analysis* (Beverly Hills: Sage, 1980), pp. 66–69.

67. In Chapter 6, we observe that after 1984 Hong Kong's politics is not a zero-sum game and the press can have friendship with both power centers. The evidence presented here serves to support this point. The colonial regime has experienced some declines and Xinhua has made impressive gains, which simply means that they have to *share* the limelight. Neither of them can dominate media attention any more.

CHAPTER 6

1. Timothy Luke, "Chernobyl: The Packaging of Transnational Ecological Disaster," *Critical Studies in Mass Communication,* 4 (1987): pp. 351–375.

2. The feasibility study was completed in 1980. In 1982, the Chinese government let Guangdong authorities go ahead with the nuclear project. After securing endorsement from the Hong Kong government in late 1983, the China Light & Power Company set up a subsidiary Hong Kong Nuclear Investment Company which, in turn, set up the Guangdong Nuclear Power Joint Venture Company with the Guangdong Nuclear Investment Company in early 1985. Seventy-five percent of the joint venture belongs to China and the rest to the Hong Kong counterpart.

3. Robert Delfs, "Finding the Energy," *Far Eastern Economic Review,* 29 August 1985, pp. 54–55.

4. Gamini Seneviratne, "Asia's Nuclear Family," *Far Eastern Economic*

Review, 15 May 1986, pp. 66–67; Louise Rosario, "Peking Gets Its Way," *Far Eastern Economic Review,* 22 January 1986, pp. 48–49.

5. In 1982, three interest groups—the Evergreen Society, the Christian Student Movement, and the Asian Information Center—formed the Joint Organization for the Concern of Nuclear Energy which had made some scantily noticed protests and demanded information about the plant.

6. "Respect Science, Value Expertise," editorial, *Ta Kung Pao,* 15 August 1986.

7. "Both Safety and Prosperity Are to Be Retained," editorial, *Wen Wei Pao,* 23 July 1986. "The Chernobyl Shadow Can Be Eliminated," editorial, *Ta Kung Pao,* 20 August 1986; "Nuclear Accident Leads to Nuclear Safety," editorial, *Wen Wei Pao,* 23 July 1986.

8. "Don't Pick Issues Outside the Safety Question," editorial, *Wen Wei Pao,* 23 July 1986.

9. "The Chernobyl Shadow," *Ta Kung Pao.*

10. "The Plan for the Daya Bay Nuclear Plant Remains Unchanged," editorial, *Ta Kung Pao,* 6 September 1986. The same viewpoint is shared by a *Wen Wei Pao* editorial, "Both Safety and Prosperity."

11. "Both Safety and Prosperity," *Wen Wei Pao.*

12. "Don't Pick Issues," *Wen Wei Pao.* "The Chernobyl Shadow," *Ta Kung Pao.* "Respect Safety and Public Opinion," editorial, *Wen Wei Pao,* 21 August 1986.

13. "The Chernobyl Shadow," *Ta Kung Pao.*

14. "The Chernobyl Shadow," *Ta Kung Pao;* "Treat the Inspection Report Seriously," editorial, *Ta Kung Pao,* 1 September 1986.

15. "Don't Pick Issues," *Wen Wei Pao;* "Plan for the Daya Bay Nuclear Plant," *Ta Kung Pao.*

16. "Respect Safety," *Wen Wei Pao.*

17. "Beijing and Hong Kong Have Fruitful Exchange," editorial, *Ta Kung Pao,* 22 September 1986.

18. Ibid.

19. "The Nuclear Energy Inspection Tour Is Essential," editorial, *Wen Wei Pao,* 16 August 1986. *Ta Kung Pao* shared similar views in its editorials: "Treat the Inspection Report Seriously," and "Beijing and Hong Kong have Fruitful Exchange."

20. "Fruitful Exchange," *Ta Kung Pao.*

21. "The 'Political Safety Coefficient' Needs to Be Calculated," editorial, *Ming Pao,* 21 June 1986. Also see "Chernobyl and Daya Bay," editorial, *Ming Pao,* 2 May 1986; "A Series of Errors Led to Disaster," editorial, *Ming Pao,* 22 August 1986.

22. "Concerning the Nuclear Safety Convent," editorial, *Ming Pao,* 28 September 1986; "Political and Economic Considerations," editorial, *Ming Pao,* 4 August 1986.

23. "1 Over 166," editorial, *Ming Pao,* 12 August 1986; "A Series of Errors," *Ming Pao;* "Li Peng Inspected Daya Bay Project," editorial, *Ming Pao,* 23 May 1986; "One Country, Two Systems or One Accident Ends All," editorial, *Ming Pao,* 26 June 1986; " 'Political Safety Coefficient,' " *Ming Pao.*

24. "The Daya Bay Nuclear Plant and Politics," editorial, *Ming Pao*, 5 August 1986.

25. For example: "One Country, Two Systems or One Accident," *Ming Pao;* "Unusual Economic Loss," editorial, *Ming Pao*, 25 July 1986; "Political and Economic Considerations," *Ming Pao;* "The Hong Kong Special Administrative Region Cannot Be Moved," editorial, *Ming Pao*, 11 September 1986.

26. "The Improbable Big Incident," editorial, *Ming Pao*, 30 July 1986.

27. E.g., "The Safety of the Daya Bay Nuclear Plant," editorial, *Ming Pao*, 20 May 1986; "Nuclear Plant and Politics," *Ming Pao*.

28. "The 'Fruits' of the Inspection Tour's Beijing Trip," editorial, *Ming Pao*, 23 September 1986.

29. "1 Over 166," *Ming Pao*.

30. For example, "The Report by the 'Public Relations' Team of Legco Members," editorial, *Ming Pao*, 31 August 1986; "The Legco Inspection Delegation's Stunt," editorial, *Ming Pao*, 28 August 1986.

31. "Inspection Delegation's Beijing Tour," *Ming Pao*. Also see "Whom Does the Inspection Delegation Represent?" editorial, *Ming Pao*, 4 September 1986.

32. "Safety Is the Crucial Question for the Nuclear Plant," editorial, *Sing Pao*, 17 August 1986; "Safety Ranks Higher Than Economic Benefits," editorial, *Sing Pao*, 15 September 1986; "The Inspection Tour Is Fruitful," editorial, *Sing Pao*, 7 August 1986.

33. "The Three Main Points of the Inspection Tour's Report," editorial, *Sing Pao*, 31 August 1986.

34. "Two Kinds of Opening Up for the Nuclear Plant Safety," editorial, *Sing Pao*, 12 May 1986.

35. "The Nuclear Power Exhibition and Nuclear Safety," editorial, *Sing Pao*, 13 September 1986.

36. "Economic Efficiency and Operative Personnel," editorial, *Sing Pao*, 2 September 1986.

37. "The Opinion to Stop Building the Nuclear Plant Directly Reached Beijing," editorial, *Sing Pao*, 13 August 1986.

38. "Safety Posed the Crucial Question for the Nuclear Plant," editorial, *Sing Pao*, 17 August 1986. The same idea is repeated in other editorials. For example, "Legislative Councillors to Tour France and U.S.A. to Study Nuclear Safety," 13 July 1986; "Cool Down the Summer Heat of Nuclear Power," 1 August 1986.

39. "Train People for Monitoring Nuclear Safety," editorial, *Sing Pao*, 22 September 1986.

40. For example, "Civic Education and Nuclear Power Education," editorial, *Sing Pao*, 5 August 1986; "The Achievements of the Nuclear Power Inspection Tour," editorial, *Sing Pao*, 7 August 1986.

41. "Quicken the Pace to Train Local Nuclear Experts," editorial, *Sing Pao*, 24 September 1986.

42. "Quicken the Pace," *Sing Pao*. This is also reiterated in: "Councillors to Tour France and U.S.A.," *Sing Pao;* and "Glad to See the Consensus on the Nuclear Power Question," *Sing Pao*, 16 October 1986.

43. "Be in Time for Monitoring the Nuclear Plant," editorial, *Sing Pao*, 6 September 1986.

44. "The Opinion to Stop the Nuclear Plant Reaches Beijing Directly," editorial, *Sing Pao*, 13 August 1986.

45. "Another New Development in the Nuclear Power Controversy," editorial, *Sing Pao*, 28 August 1986.

46. "The Nuclear Power Debate and Constitutional Change," editorial, *Sing Pao*, 23 August 1986.

47. For example, "Hong Kong People Are Concerned about the Nuclear Power Issue," editorial, *Sing Tao Jih Pao*, 25 June 1986; "Hong Kong People Cannot Afford the Price," editorial, *Wah Kiu Yat Pao*, 6 June 1986; "Is It Worthwhile to Run the Risk," editorial, *Wah Kiu Yat Pao*, 10 June 1986.

48. "Hong Kong People Cannot Afford," *Wah Kiu Yat Pao.*

49. "Nuclear Energy Is Not Worth the Price," *Wah Kiu Yat Pao*, 16 June 1986; "Respect the Hong Kong People's Anti-nuclear Opinion," editorial, *Sing Tao Jih Pao*, 16 July 1986.

50. "Hong Kong People Are Concerned," *Sing Tao Jih Pao.*

51. "Report on the Daya Bay Nuclear Power Plant," editorial, *Sing Tao Jih Pao*, 30 July 1986.

52. "Lack of Active Provision of Information about the Nuclear Plant," editorial, *Wah Kiu Yat Pao*, 30 June 1986; "The Anti-Nuclear [Movement] Needs a Cooling Period," editorial, *Wah Kiu Yat Pao*, 8 July 1986; "Provide as Much as Possible Information about the Nuclear Plant," editorial, *Wah Kiu Yat Pao*, 16 July 1986.

53. "Respect Hong Kong People's Opinion," *Sing Tao;* "Hong Kong People's Anti-nuclear Opinion," editorial, *Sing Tao Jih Pao*, 20 August 1986.

54. "The Ill Effects of 'Nuclear Energy Shock,' " editorial, *Sing Tao Jih Pao*, 24 September 1986.

55. "Neglect of Public Opinion Erodes Confidence," editorial, *Wah Kiu Yat Pao*, 29 August 1986.

56. "Be Rational in Dealing with the Nuclear Power Problem," editorial, *Sing Tao Jih Pao*, 27 August 1986.

57. Ibid.

58. "Beijing Has Opened the Door for Dialogue," editorial, *Wah Kiu Yat Pao*, 2 September 1986; "On the Nuclear Power Inspection Report," editorial, *Sing Tao Jih Pao*, 4 September 1986.

59. "The Constructive Two-edged Effects," editorial, *Wah Kiu Yat Pao*, 2 September 1986.

60. "Is the Dust Over the Nuclear Power Problem Settled?" editorial, *Hong Kong Times*, 26 September 1986. Also see "The Daya Bay Nuclear Power Plant Has Become a Burning Issue," editorial, *Hong Kong Times*, 25 June 1986.

61. "An Expression of Hong Kong Public Opinion," editorial, *Hong Kong Times*, 26 May 1986.

62. "Hong Kong Public's Keen Demand," editorial, *Hong Kong Times*, 15 July 1986; "Is the Dust Settled?" *Hong Kong Times.*

63. "Keen Demands," *Hong Kong Times.*

64. "Solving the Puzzle Over the Daya Bay Nuclear Power Plant," editorial, *Hong Kong Times*, 28 June 1986.

65. "Hong Kong Public Opinion," *Hong Kong Times*.

66. "The Fifth 'Persistence,' " editorial, *Hong Kong Times*, 23 September 1986; "Experience Breeds Wisdom," editorial, *Hong Kong Times*, 25 August 1986.

67. "Keen Demands," *Hong Kong Times;* "Plant Has Become a Burning Issue," *Hong Kong Times*.

68. "Hong Kong People Should Rely on Themselves For Blessing," editorial, *Hong Kong Times*, 31 July 1986.

69. For example, "The Hong Kong Special Administrative Region Cannot Be Moved," editorial, *Ming Pao*, 11 September 1986; "Nuclear Safety and Progress in the Political System," editorial, *Sing Pao*, 17 July 1986.

70. Herbert Simon, "The Carrot and Stick as Handmaidens of Persuasion in Conflict Situations," in Gerald Miller and Herbert Simon, eds., *Perspectives on Communication in Social Conflicts*. (Englewood, N.J.: Prentice Hall, 1974).

71. Louis Kriesberg, *Social Conflicts* (Englewood, N.J.: Prentice Hall, 1982).

CHAPTER 7

1. For comparative cases, see Daniel Hallin, *The Uncensored War* (New York: Oxford University Press, 1986); Youngchul Yoon, "Political Transition and Press ideology in South Korea" (Ph.D. diss., University of Minnesota, 1989); Osman Mohammed Araby, "The Press and Foreign Policy: A Comparative Study of the Role of the Elite Press in U.S. Foreign Policies in the Middle East" (Ph.D. diss., University of Minnesota, 1990).

2. The students listened to the Chinese-language broadcasts of the Voice of America and the British Broadcasting Corporation. They also read *Ta Kung Pao* and *Wen Wei Pao*, two leftist Hong Kong papers allowed to circulate in China. A VOA reporter was expelled from China in June, while many *Wen Wei Pao* reporters made it on to the government's "black list" after the massacre.

3. The *Herald* published an article critical of Deng for having fired Hu. The paper was confiscated and its editor, Qin Benli, was dismissed by Jiang Zemin, who was later promoted from his position as chief of the Communist Party in Shanghai to succeed Zhao Ziyang as general secretary of the CCP. See Hsiao Ching-chang and Yang Mei-rong, " 'Don't Force Us to Lie': the Case of the *World Economic Herald*," in Chin-Chuan Lee, ed., *Voices of China: The Interplay of Politics and Journalism* (New York: Guilford, 1990).

4. Interview.

5. "To Communicate with and to Forgive One Another," editorial, *Wen Wei Pao*, 24 April 1989.

6. "Creating a Good Atmosphere for Dialogue," editorial, *Wen Wei Pao*, 28 April 1989; "To Communicate with and Forgive," *Wen Wei Pao*.

7. See for example: "Communicate and Compromise to Maintain Stability," editorial, *Ta Kung Pao*, 26 April 1989.

8. As quoted and interpreted by a *Wen Wei Pao* editorial entitled "Solve the Problems by Democratic and Legal Means," 5 May 1989. Similar views are expressed by *Ta Kung Pao* in a signed commentary with the same title published on the same day.

9. "Struggle for Democracy, Root Out Corruption," editorial, *Wen Wei Pao*, 16 May 1989.

10. "Following Public Opinion Is the Basis of Politics," editorial, *Ta Kung Pao*, 18 May 1989.

11. "The Heart Pains and the Head Aches," editorial, *Wen Wei Pao*, 21 May 1989.

12. "The Million People's March Is Exhilarating," editorial, *Ta Kung Pao*, 22 May 1989.

13. Shi Junyu, "Public Opinion Is the Key Determinant of Events," *Ta Kung Pao*, 23 May 1989. Shi Junyu, "1.1 Billion People Shouted the Same Slogan," *Ta Kung Pao*, 24 May 1989.

14. "Oppose State Usurpers, the Li–Yang clique," editorial, *Wen Wei Pao*, 5 June 1989.

15. "Arise All People, Punish National Power Snatchers," editorial, *Wen Wei Pao*, 7 June 1989.

16. Ibid.

17. "Our Hope Rests with the People," staff commentator, *Ta Kung Pao*, 5 June 1989.

18. For example: Shi Junyu, "Chaos Fermenting in Shanghai and Other Cities," *Ta Kung Pao*, 8 June 1989; Shi Junyu, "The Degeneration of the Frozen Sino-American Relationship?" *Ta Kung Pao*, 15 June 1989; Shi Junyu, "Cheng Tok-bun Talked about the Loss Resulting from the Disturbance," *Ta Kung Pao*, 16 June 1989.

19. Interview with Kam Yiu-yu.

20. Interview with a *Ta Kung Pao* editor, 30 June 1989.

21. It was significant that Kam Yiu-yu, former editor-in-chief of *Wen Wei Pao*, and Tsui Sze-man, publisher of the pro-Beijing *Mirror Monthly*, accepted an invitation to participate in a discussion hosted by the KMT-linked *Newsdom Weekly*. Kam said that as a young revolutionary he was arrested by the KMT police in Shanghai but never did he encounter tanks and machine guns as did the young students in Tiananmen. Tsui said that he has changed his position from being an unconditional supporter of the Communist Party to being a conditional supporter, and now perhaps to being its unconditional opponent (*Newsdom Weekly*, 11 July 1989, p. 5). Publisher Lee Tse-chung, 78, broke into tears on television, vowing not to follow China's atrocious policy blindly (*Wen Wei Pao*, 5 June 1989, p. 6).

22. "If we had continued to toe the official line, people would have burned our papers," Kam Yiu-yu of *Wen Wei Pao* said emphatically in a personal interview, "How were we going to survive in Hong Kong?"

23. Interview with a Xinhua official.

24. Interview.

25. Premier Li branded the five Communist papers in Hong Kong as tak-

ing an "anti-revolutionary, anti-party" path, and vowed to put them, especially *Wen Wei Pao* and *Ta Kung Pao,* back under Beijing's control. Guangdong residents, who have regular access to Hong Kong media, received intensive "reeducation." Guangdong media had to rebut Hong Kong's "rumors." Reporters and editors were ordered to take political learning sessions twice a week, studying the text of Deng's June 9 talk (*Hong Kong Standard,* 23 June 1989).

26. Julia Leung, "Hong Kong Newspaper Risks China's Ire," *Asian Wall Street Journal,* 5 July 1989, p. 1.

27. Ibid. Both *Wen Wei Pao* and *Ta Kung Pao* were allowed to circulate inside China, so they were brought to Tiananmen Square daily. They boosted the students' morale by informing them of the support they received at home and abroad.

28. Leung, "Newspaper Risks China's Ire."

29. Interview.

30. Three staff members of *Ta Kung Pao,* "Our Grievance and Our Hope: Whither Is the Leftist Press?" *Hong Kong Economic Journal,* 12 July 1989, p. 25. Urging the Hong Kong journalistic community to exert pressure on the Communist press, the article strongly criticized *Ta Kung Pao*'s Yang as an "opportunist" and praised *Wen Wei Pao*'s Li as a man of principle. *Ta Kung Pao* angrily issued a letter of protest, flatly denouncing the article as unfounded.

31. "The Aftermath of June 4 in *Wen Wei Pao,*" *Ming Pao,* 15 July 1989, p.2.

32. "Xinhua in the Aftermath of June 4," *Contemporary Weekly,* No. 1, 25 November 1989, p. 14. This weekly is published by Lee Tse-chung and other former editorial staff members of *Wen Wei Pao.*

33. Joseph Man Chan and Chin-Chuan Lee, "Shifting Journalistic Paradigms: Editorial Stance and Political Transition in Hong Kong," *China Quarterly,* no. 117, March 1989, pp. 97–117.

34. "What Is Freedom of the Press?" editorial, *Ming Pao,* 29 January 1986.

35. Quoted in the *China Times,* 12 December 1988.

36. Ibid. Cha said: "I worked for the Communist-controlled *Ta Kung Pao* for 12 years. I have fought against the Communist Party for 20 years. I have worked on the Basic Law Drafting Committee for three years. I am confident that not many people know better than I do about the Communist Party's policy and its working style."

37. "The Mourning Activities of Chinese Students," editorial, *Ming Pao,* 19 April 1989.

38. "Several Events That Occurred in the Last Ten Days," editorial, *Ming Pao,* 26 April 1989.

39. "Beijing Decided to Crack Down on the Student Movement," editorial, *Ming Pao,* 27 April 1989.

40. "The Laudable April 27 Movement," editorial, *Ming Pao,* 28 April 1989.

41. "Press Freedom in Modern Society," editorial, *Ming Pao,* 2 May 1989.

42. For example: "Celebrate the May Fourth, Speak for the People," edi-

torial, *Ming Pao*, 5 May 1989; "Zhao Ziyang Talked about the 'Heart of Political Reforms,' " editorial, *Ming Pao*, 12 May 1989.

43. "Deng Xiaoping Is the Flag-Carrier of Reform," editorial, *Ming Pao*, 17 May 1989.

44. "Let's Ask Deng Xiaoping to Lead the Patriotic Student Movement," editorial, *Ming Pao*, 18 May 1989.

45. "Painfully Regret with Aching Hearts," editorial, *Ming Pao*, 21 May 1989.

46. "Can the People Accept That?" editorial, *Ming Pao*, 26 May 1989.

47. "All State Power Belongs to the People, No Individual Can Have Privilege," editorial, *Ming Pao*, 22 May 1989; "A Fool Acts Only to Hurt Himself," editorial, *Ming Pao*, 24 May 1989.

48. "What Caused the Outburst of Anger Among the People?" editorial, *Ming Pao*, 25 May 1989; "People's Moral Bravery Has Been Aroused," editorial, *Ming Pao*, 28 May 1989.

49. "Ignore Public Opinion, Fear No Bloodshed," editorial, *Ming Pao*, 5 June 1989.

50. "The Trends of China's Political Situation," editorial, *Ming Pao*, 7 June 1989.

51. Louis Cha, "You Youngsters Have a Lot of Time Ahead," editorial, *Ming Pao*, 11 June 1989. The *Japan Times* (19 June 1989, p. 17) translated this editorial into English with a new title—"Faith in China's Leaders Shattered by the Carnage."

52. "Provide a Safety Exit for the Hong Kong People," editorial, *Ming Pao*, 20 June 1989.

53. Hsu Ching-yun, "These Leaders Have Gone Mad," *The Journalist*, 12 June 1989.

54. Cha, "You Youngsters."

55. Ibid.

56. "Reform National Politics, Strengthen Hong Kong's Safety," editorial, *Oriental Daily News*, 22 May 1989.

57. "To Influence the Mainland Is to Help Oneself," editorial, *Oriental Daily News*, 23 May 1989.

58. "Democracy Being the Highest Ideal, Merchants Talk about Politics," editorial, *Oriental Daily News*, 24 May 1989.

59. "To Transform Grief and Anger into Energy, Be United to Struggle for Democracy," editorial, *Oriental Daily News*, 6 June 1989.

60. "A Question Over the Mourning of Hu Yaobang," editorial, *Sing Pao*, 17 April 1989.

61. "Mourning Hu Activities and the Democracy Movement," editorial, *Sing Pao*, 19 April 1989.

62. "Careful Management Is Better Than Violent Crackdown," editorial, *Sing Pao*, 21 April 1989.

63. "Distinguish the Student Movement from Factors of Disturbance," editorial, *Sing Pao*, 27 April 1989.

64. For example: "Keep Cool and Restrained, Communicate and Coop-

erate," editorial, *Sing Pao*, 28 April 1989; "Safeguard Human Rights Before Dialogues," editorial, *Sing Pao*, 29 April 1989; "Avoid Triviality and Quickly Start Genuine Dialogues," editorial, *Sing Pao*, 1 May 1989.

65. "Publishing [Deng's] Speech Will Open Up Dialogue," editorial, *Sing Pao*, 19 May 1989.

66. "Hong Kong People Should Keep Calm during This Big Leap Backward," editorial, *Sing Pao*, 21 May 1989.

67. "A Clearing Up of the Severe Situation Is Anticipated," editorial, *Sing Pao*, 23 May 1989.

68. "Restrain in Struggle for Freedom, Oppose Ruthless Rule," editorial, *Sing Pao*, 7 June 1989.

69. "Everybody Should Shoulder His Responsibility at This Critical Juncture," editorial, *Sing Pao*, 6 June 1989.

70. "The Implications of Deng Xiaoping's Appearance," editorial, *Sing Pao*, 10 June 1989.

71. "The Mainland Situation Has Little Influence on Hong Kong," editorial, *Wah Kiu Yat Pao*, 22 April 1989.

72. "The Seventieth Anniversary of the May Fourth Movement," editorial, *Wah Kiu Yat Pao*, 4 May 1989.

73. "How Hong Kong People Evaluate the Mainland Student Movement," editorial, *Wah Kiu Yat Pao*, 9 May 1989.

74. "The Supporting Activities of the Hong Kong Students," editorial, *Wah Kiu Yat Pao*, 18 May 1989.

75. "Be United to Rescue the Chaotic Situation," editorial, *Wah Kiu Yat Pao*, 29 May 1989.

76. "Intense Foreign Reactions to Beijing's Bloody Crackdown," editorial, *Wah Kiu Yat Pao*, 7 June 1989; "Mourning the Dead Beijing Residents," editorial, *Wah Kiu Yat Pao*, 5 June 1989.

77. "Beijing Must Stabilize the Situation," editorial, *Sing Tao Jih Pao*, 22 April 1989.

78. "The Mainland Students' Mourning Activities," editorial, *Sing Tao Jih Pao*, 25 April 1989.

79. "Why the Student Movement Cannot Grow," editorial, *Sing Tao Jih Pao*, 27 April 1989.

80. "The Chinese Communist Party's Conditional Dialogue," editorial, *Sing Tao Jih Pao*, 29 April 1989.

81. "Suppressing the Student Movement Is Unpopular," editorial, *Sing Tao Jih Pao*, 22 May 1989.

82. "Everyone Is Responsible for the Rise and Fall of China," editorial, *Sing Tao Jih Pao*, 23 May 1989.

83. "The Situation Is Difficult to Control," editorial, *Sing Tao Jih Pao*, 6 June 1989.

84. "People's Army Shot the People," editorial, *Sing Tao Jih Pao*, 4 June 1989.

85. "Calm the People's Anger, Pay for the Blood," editorial, *Sing Tao Jih Pao*, 7 June 1989.

86. "Commenting Again on Mainland Students' Democracy Movement," editorial, *Hong Kong Times,* 21 April 1989.

87. "The Chinese Communist Party Is Ready to Suppress the Students' Democracy Movement," editorial, *Hong Kong Times,* 27 May 1989.

88. "The Spirit of Democracy and Science Will Be Transmitted from Generation to Generation," editorial, *Hong Kong Times,* 4 May 1989.

89. "The Mainland Student Movement Has Developed to Be an All- People Movement," editorial, *Hong Kong Times,* 19 May 1989; "Ignorant and Crazy, Tears and Blood Blending," editorial, *Hong Kong Times,* 21 May 1989.

90. "Zhao Ziyang Stepped Down and Communist Troops Moved In," editorial, *Hong Kong Times,* 20 May 1989. "If Deng [Xiaoping], Li [Peng] and Yang [Shangkun] Are Not Fired, People's Anguish Will Not Be Soothed," editorial, *Hong Kong Times,* 25 May 1989.

91. "Democracy Shall Win! Brutal Rule Will Fall!" editorial, *Hong Kong Times,* 5 June 1989.

92. Walter Lippmann, *Public Opinion* (New York: Macmillan, 1922).

93. See note 1.

94. A publisher of a mass-oriented paper was quoted as saying, "After all, China news can boost circulation!" The publisher asked his staff to sensationalize the reportage to increase sales. Most Hong Kong papers were financially frugal and ill-staffed for covering this event. Half of the Hong Kong reporters sent to cover the story were professionally inexperienced, with only one to two years of work history; some even visited Beijing for the first time. Other reporters decided to "eyewitness" the making of history in Beijing at their own expenses. (See Sixty-four Hong Kong Reporters, *The People Won't Forget* [Hong Kong: Journalists Association, 1989] p. 333, 335.)

95. Ibid., pp. 330–334. News about Deng's death and Li's losing power were admittedly planted by an angry Chinese student who had just returned to the United States from a trip to China.

96. Social Research Hong Kong has been monitoring the people's confidence in Hong Kong's political and economic futures since 1985. In a survey done in the week after the imposition of martial law in Beijing, the political confidence index (assuming the 1985 index as 100) dropped by ten percentage points from the survey in January 1989, reaching an all-time low at 85%. The trend of declining confidence is reported in *Ming Pao,* 16 June 1989.

97. Chris Yeung, "Locals Warned Not to Meddle with Regime," *South China Morning Post,* 23 June 1989.

98. "Xinhua in the Aftermath of June 4," *Contemporary Weekly,* no. 1, 25 November 1989, pp. 14–17. Many of these books were written by pro-Zhao reformist intellectuals who have been arrested or are in exile. The leftist Joint Union Bookstore was ordered to take *People Won't Forget,* by 64 Hong Kong reporters, from the shelves. As of September 1990, however, some books banned by Beijing were still sold under the counter in leftist bookstores. Books by mainland writers not approved by the authorities were still published; in some cases the publication date has been altered to pre–June 4, 1989. See Emily Lau, "Media's Red Barons," *Far Eastern Economic Review,* 27 September 1990, p. 24.

99. "Xinhua in the Aftermath," *Contemporary Weekly.*

CHAPTER 8

1. Craig R. Whitney, "Britain Standing by Pledge Ceding Hong Kong to China" *New York Times,* 7 June 1989, p. 8.

2. Emily Lau, "Backroom Betrayal," *Far Eastern Economic Review,* 1 March 1990, pp. 14–15.

3. As one Thatcher minister explained it, the thinking behind ruling out immigration was that a cold, overpopulated island of 57 million people was no place for a sudden influx of Chinese from the tropics (see Whitney, "Britain Standing by Pledge"). An editorial by the *New York Times* (9 June 1989) commented: "The notion that Britain would be swamped by a huge influx from Hong Kong defies reason and experience. Certainty about passport rights would almost surely induce most Hong Kong residents to wait and test China's intentions, not join a panicky exodus."

4. For an example of such criticisms, an editorial by the *New York Times* (9 June 1989) commented:

> Is there no roar left in the old British lion? After the bloodletting in China, Prime Minister Thatcher's equivocation over Hong Kong seems spineless, even shameful. Adding insult, Foreign Secretary Geoffrey Howe now declares that Britain "could not easily contemplate" admitting 3.5 million Chinese holders of British passports because that might double the ethnic minority population.
>
> No other democracy has ever forced its passport holders to live under Communist rule. Sir Geoffrey's justification for this surrender of people and principle is downright appalling.
>
> Though she professes "utter revulsion" over China's killing of civilians, Mrs. Thatcher says Britain will nevertheless abide by an agreement made five years ago and hand over Hong Kong to China in 1997. It's hard to see why China deserves such an assurance.

5. Emily Lau, "Elites Take All," *Far Eastern Economic Review,* 19 April 1990.

6. Lau Shi-wai, "The Real Intentions of the British," commentary, *Ta Kung Pao,* 11 October 1989; Lo Chin-kin, "A Cool Analysis of the British Nationality Bill," *Ming Pao Monthly,* May 1990.

7. Harry Harding, *China's Second Revolution: Reform After Mao* (Washington: Brookings Institution, 1987); Chin-Chuan Lee, "Mass Media: Of China, About China," in Chin-Chuan Lee, ed., *Voices of China: The Interplay of Politics and Journalism* (New York: Guilford, 1990).

8. For a legal discussion, see David A. Jones, Jr., "A Leg to Stand on? Post-1997 Hong Kong Court as a Constraint on PRC Abridgement of Individual Rights and Local Autonomy," *Yale Journal of International Law,* 12, no. 2 (1987): pp. 250–293.

9. Emily Lau, "Media's Red Barons," *Far Eastern Economic Review,* 27 September 1990, p. 27.

10. "Xinhua's Management of the Situation after June 4," *Contemporary Weekly,* 25 November 1989, pp. 14–15.

11. Xu Jiatun was instructed by Zhao Ziyang to downplay the movement and not to impair Deng's image. After June 4, Ji Pengfei berated Xu for failing to control anti-Beijing activities in Hong Kong. Xu explained that any repressive actions then could have backfired under such circumstances. See *Contemporary Weekly,* 16 December 1989, p. 5; and Wai Ming, "Xu Jiatun Protects Cadres in Hong Kong," *Contemporary Weekly,* 20 January 1990, p. 4.

12. To cover events in China, reporters have to secure entry permits from Xinhua and their activities should not go beyond the itineraries spelled out in the application. Upon arrival in China, they must apply for a "reporter card" from the Chinese Journalists Association. They could neither gather information during personal travels nor interview institutions, units, and individuals by telephone while in China.

13. Ngai Yum-cho, "Hong Kong File," *Nineties Monthly,* September 1989, pp. 50–51.

14. "To Rise Again from the 'Ruins of Confidence,' " *Contemporary Weekly,* 25 November 1989.

15. According to our journalist informants, Xinhua arranged a special group trip to Beijing in December 1989, consisting of journalists from various media organizations. Previously, a similar invitation was declined by the Journalist Executives Association, for fear of having to pay tribute to the martial law soldiers and shake hands with Li Peng.

16. For example, *World Journal* (New York), 17 May 1990, p. 32.

17. Qi Xin [Lee Yee], "Analyzing the Xu Jiatun Affair," *Nineties Monthly,* June 1990, pp. 24–27. The *People's Daily* (overseas edition), *Wen Wei Pao,* and *Ta Kung Pao* did not report this event.

18. Emily Lau, "A Kind of Defection," *Far Eastern Economic Review,* 24 May 1990.

19. Huang Miao, "Beijing Tightens Its Reins over Hong Kong after the Ex-Director 'Escaped,' " *Contemporary Weekly,* 19 May 1990, pp. 10–11.

20. Chu Yihong, "Beijing Makes Plan to Take Over Hong Kong," *Hong Kong Economic Journal,* 8 August 1990.

21. Emily Lau, "Big Brother's Blacklist," *Far Eastern Economic Review,* 27 September 1990, p. 25.

22. Interview.

23. Liu Yuan-tu, "The Second Wave of the Hong Kong Emigrants," *Nineties Monthly,* June 1987, pp. 48–49; Ng. F. Y. and Choy H, "The Overflow of People and Capital," *Hong Kong Economic Journal Monthly,* 154 (1990): pp. 19–22.

24. Joseph Cheng; interview with Lee; Minneapolis, Minn.; 16 April 1990.

25. This survey interviewed half of all the working journalists in 25 print and broadcast organizations in Hong Kong, yielding a response rate of 75% out of a sample of 692. Sports writers, entertainment reporters, photojournalists, and freelance writers were excluded from the survey. The principal investigators are Joseph Man Chan, Paul Lee, and Chin-Chuan Lee. The data are being analyzed.

26. Lee, "Mass Media."

27. Kwok Wai-fung, "China's Research on Hong Kong and Macao Has Entered the Stage of Learning," *Ta Kung Pao*, 24 August 1988.

28. Shi Hua, "Communist China's Allergy to Hong Kong Publications," *Nineties Monthly*, March 1990, pp. 110–111.

29. Lee Yee, "What Kind of Press is Beneficial to China?" *Seventies Monthly*, August 1979. Since 1979 China has banned the importation of *Seventies Monthly* (later renamed *Nineties Monthly*), *Cheng Ming (Contending) Monthly, Dong Xiang (Trend), Wide-angled Mirror*, and *Mirror Monthly*. The publishers of the latter two are members of China's Political Consultative Conference, whereas the first three publications had been strongly pro-China. After the Tiananmen incident, *Pai Hsing Semimonthly* and *Contemporary Weekly* (a magazine published by the purged publisher of *Wen Wei Pao*, Lee Tse-chung) were added to the embargo list that barred their journalists from going to Beijing to cover the Basic Law Drafting Committee's last conference. See Shi, "Communist China's Allergy."

30. The Research Office of the China News Publication Bureau, "A Summary of Survey Results of Opinions on the Proposed Press Law," 15 December 1988. These journalists complained to a team led by Hu Jiwei responsible for drafting a press law. Hu supported Zhao Ziyang in the 1989 Tiananmen power struggle, and the press law is put on hold.

31. "A Special Collection of Articles on the Pearl Economic Radio," *Journal of Chinese Radio and Television*, no.7, 8 June 1988. We also interviewed Ng Chi-sum, a Hong Kong journalist who has researched on the Pearl Economic Radio station for a documentary.

32. Liu Binyan, a leading Chinese journalist in exile, said that if there were not for the Hong Kong press (and to some extent, the Taiwan press) to exert pressure on Beijing, China's human rights violation would have been even worse than now because (quoting Mao's words) "they [the leaders] could close the door and beat dogs."

33. Philip Selznick, *TVA and the Grass Roots: A Study in the Sociology of Formal Organization* (Berkeley: University of California Press, 1949), p. 250.

34. Youngchul Yoon, "Political Transition and Press Ideology in South Korea, 1980–1988" (Ph.D. diss., University of Minnesota, 1989).

Appendix I

Notes on Methodology

CHAPTERS 3 AND 4

Methodologically these two chapters are based on a qualitative study which, as Todd Gitlin notes, "'teases out' those determining but hidden assumptions which in their unique ordering remain opaque to quantitative content analysis." (See his *The Whole World Is Watching,* University of California Press, 1980, pp. 303–305 for an exposition on qualitative methodology.) First, we scrutinized archival materials at the Government Information Services library as well as the Hong Kong Collections of the University of Hong Kong and the Chinese University of Hong Kong. Newspaper clippings, magazine articles, and memoirs were thoroughly surveyed. More important, we interviewed a total of 54 journalists, government officials, Xinhua cadres, and media critics and analysts, as follows:

Ultraleftist: *Ta Kung Pao, Wen Wei Pao*	6
Centrist: *Ming Pao, Sing Pao, The Oriental Daily News, Hong Kong Economic Journal*	13
Rightist: *Sing Tao Jih Pao, Wah Kiu Yat Pao*	9
Ultrarightist: *The Hong Kong Times*	3
Broadcast journalists (TV and radio)	6
Magazine journalists	3
Columnists, media critics or analysts	6
Government officials	2
Xinhua officials	6

Interviewing a random sample was neither feasible nor advisable, for the roster of journalists was judiciously guarded and we were better served by selected informants. We first approached our press acquaintances, who then led our way to other informants in a "snow-balling" fashion. Only three rejections were encountered for want of personal ties.

Our press informants were evenly divided in organizational rank: high (equal to or above deputy editor-in-chief), medium (editor), and low (reporter) with the top priority going to reporters on the China beat. An average of three interviews per paper were ascertained. Other nonpress sources were interviewed for corroboration and enrichment of our interpretation. A broad interview guideline was developed but was modified to fit specific situations. This interview guideline covers five parts.

About editorial and reportorial policies: (1) How would you characterize the editorial and reportorial policies of your newspaper since the "1997" issue? (2) In what form do these policies exist? Who made them? Under what conditions were they made? How do they correspond to the stages in which the "1997" issue unfolds? (3) What are the critical issues on the "1997" question? How have these policies affected the news coverage and editorial on each issue? (4) How have the editorial/reportorial policies of other newspapers changed since the inception of the "1997" issue?

About organizational changes: (1) What organizational changes (strategic choices, beat structure, personnel turnover, etc.) has your newspaper undergone since the inception of the "1997" issue? What account for such changes?

About relations with the two power centers: (1) What are the patterns of interaction between your newspaper and Xinhua (New China News Agency)/GIS (Government Information Services)? Have these relations undergone some changes? Why? (2) Through what channels does Xinhua/GIS interact with your newspaper?

About intermedia competition: (1) How does your newspaper take competition with other newspaper and television? What do you compete about? How does intermedia competition affect your newspaper's coverage of the two power centers?

About journalists' expectation: Are you satisfied with the press performance in the last three years? What do you think of the future of press freedom in Hong Kong? What are your career plans?

We guarded against the "self-fulfilling prophecy" in interpreting interview materials and against the unwitting tendency to dismiss evidence counter to hypotheses. We accepted the corroborated facts, eliminated what appeared to be self-propaganda and verified discrepant accounts with additional sources. To enhance interpretative rigor, we cross-compared (1) documents with the interviews, (2) interviews *within* and *between* different ideological strata of the press, and (3) the accounts by journalists of contending political persuasions.

CHAPTER 5

We intensively examined 1,131 editorials carried by nine papers between September 1982 and February 1986. Table A-1 sums up the distribution of editorials analyzed. Our examination proceeded with hypotheses that emerged from our previous work and from "soaking" in the press materials. Since day-to-day newspaper editorials tend to be repetitive over a given time, we identified the text and quotes in accordance with the criteria of (1) political significance, (2) ability to represent the mode of the recurring themes, and (3) ability to preserve the subtlety of the latent and contextual meaning structure that signifies the change of themes, tones, and phrases over time.

A number of comparative check points have been made to guard against the likely though unwitting tendency to disregard unsupportive evidence. First, using the date of the signing of the Sino-British Joint Declaration (September

TABLE A-1. Distribution of Editorials Analyzed (1982–1986)

Political stand	Newspaper	Number of editorials
Ultraleftist	*Wen Wei Pao*	85
	Ta Kung Pao	55
Centrist	*Ming Pao*	310
	Sing Pao	60
	Oriental Daily News	121
Rightist	*Sing Tao Jih Pao*	114
	Wah Kiu Yat Pao	62
Ultrarightist	*Hong Kong Times*	96
	Kung Sheung Yat Pao	229
		$N = 1,132$

1984) as a watershed point, we scrutinized the editorial paradigms *before* and *after* this monumental event. Second, we cross-compared the shift of editorial paradigms by nine papers organized into four ideological strata. To enrich analytical depth and to maintain a critical eye on the materials, we examined the differences that existed both *between* and *within* the strata. Finally, this thorough reading of the editorials was undertaken in conjunction with interviews with journalists, government officials, and Xinhua cadres, and a study of published documents, journalist's memoirs, and magazines.

TABLE A-2. Distribution of Editorials Analyzed (1986)

Political stand	Newspaper	Number of editorials
Ultraleftist	*Wen Wei Pao*	2
	Ta Kung Pao	4
Centrist	*Ming Pao*	33
	Sing Pao	35
	Oriental Daily News	0
Rightist	*Sing Tao Jih Pao*	14
	Wah Kiu Yat Pao	17
Ultrarightist	*Hong Kong Times*	14
		$N = 119$

CHAPTER 6

We examined a total of 119 editorials published by 8 papers between April 26 and October 10, 1986. The major issues addressed were: the nuclear plant safety, economic costs and benefits, evaluation of public opinion, attitude toward the Hong Kong government, attitude toward the Chinese government, and attitude toward the relations between Hong Kong and China. Table A-2 gives the breakdown of editorials by papers.

CHAPTER 7

We intensively examined 252 editorials carried by eight newspapers between April 15 and June 20, 1989 (a total of 65 days). Table A-3 sums up the distribution of editorials analyzed.

TABLE A-3. Distribution of Editorials Analyzed (1989)

Political stand	Newspaper	Number of editorials
Ultraleftist	*Wen Wei Pao*	16
	Ta Kung Pao	28[a]
Centrist	*Ming Pao*	51
	Sing Pao	48
	Oriental Daily News	10
Rightist	*Sing Tao Jih Pao*	40
	Wah Kiu Yat Pao	22
Ultrarightist	*Hong Kong Times*	39
		$N = 254$

[a]Including 5 editorials, 1 staff commentary, and 22 signed commentaries or "surrogate editorials."

Appendix II

Glossary of Major Chinese Names

To the extent we know, we try to follow the ways in which the Chinese individuals choose to spell their own names in English. As a consequence, they are madly inconsistent: the Cantonese vs. the Mandarin, the Wade-Giles system vs. Pinyin, and Christian names vs. Romanized names. For people in Hong Kong and Taiwan, the given name is often hyphenated; for people in mainland China, the given name is not hyphenated. But in all cases, the Chinese custom dictates that the family name (usually shorter) precedes the given name (for example, Xu Jiatun). Western custom is followed for those with a Christian given name (for example, Martin Lee). Since there is no perfect solution to this chaos, we provide Chinese characters and a brief sketch for the frequently cited names to facilitate name identification:

Ann, Tse-kai (安子介): CBE, OBE, JP*; member, Legislative Council; member, Executive Council; member, Basic Law Drafting Committee; member, Chinese People's Political Consultative Committee.

Aw, Boon Haw (胡文虎): founder, *Sing Tao Jih Pao;* father of Sally Aw.

Aw, Sally (胡　仙): publisher, *Sing Tao Jih Pao.*

Cha, Chi-ming (查濟民): member, Basic Law Drafting Committee; member, National People's Congress; member, Chinese People's Political Consultative Conference.

Cha, Louis (查良鏞): OBE; publisher, *Ming Pao;* quit the Basic Law Drafting and Consultative Committees after the June 4, 1989, massacre in Tiananmen.

Chan, Cho-tsak (陳祖澤): former director, Government Information Services.

Chang, Wan Fung (張雲楓): deputy editor-in-chief, *Wen Wei Pao;* member, Basic Law Consultative Committee.

Chen, Bojian (陳伯堅): deputy director, *Wen Wei Pao.*

Chen, Zihuei (陳志輝): head of the KMT organization in Hong Kong.

Cheng, Graham (鄭正訓): JP; member, Basic Law Drafting Committee.

Cheung, Man-yee (張敏儀): director of the Government Information Services during the Sino-British negotiations.

---

* CBE = Commander of the Order of the British Empire; OBE = Officer of the Order of the British Empire; MBE = Member of the Order of the British Empire; JP = Justice of Peace.

Chiang, Ching-kuo (蔣 經 國): successor of his father, Chiang Kai-shek; the late President of the Republic of China (Taiwan) until his death in 1987.

Chiang, Kai-shek (蔣 介 石): the late President of the Republic of China.

Chiu, Deacon (邱 德 根): JP, board chairman, Asia Television.

Deng, Xiaoping (鄧 小 平): most powerful man in China after Mao died; chairman of the Central Military Commission until late 1989.

Fei, Yiming (費 彝 民): the late publisher of *Ta Kung Pao;* member, National People's Congress; member, Chinese People's Political Consultative Conference; member, Basic Law Drafting Committee.

Fok, Ying Tong (霍 英 東): a business tycoon; member, Basic Law Drafting Committee; member, National People's Congress; member, Chinese People's Political Consultative Conference.

Har, Kung (哈 公): a satirist.

Ho, George (何 佐 治): OBE, JP; director, Commercial Radio.

Ho, Man-fat (何 文 法): publisher, *Sing Pao Daily News;* member, Basic Law Consultative Committee.

Ho, Robert (何 鴻 毅): son and successor of Ho Shih-li as publisher of *Kung Sheung Daily News.*

Ho, Sai-chu (何 世 柱): MBE, JP; publisher, *Tin Tin Daily News;* member, Chinese People's Political Consultative Conference.

Ho, Shih-li (何 世 禮): son and successor of Ho Tung; Chiang Kai-shek's former deputy defense minister.

Ho, Ting Kwan (何 庭 鈞): assistant general manager, TV Broadcasts Ltd.; member, Basic Law Consultative Committee.

Ho, Tung (何 東): founder, *Kung Sheung Daily News.*

Hu, Chu-jen (胡 菊 人): editor, *Pai Hsing Semimonthly;* member, Basic Law Consultative Committee.

Hu, Yaobang (胡 耀 邦): the deposed reformist CCP general secretary, the mourning of whose death triggered the massive student protest movement in 1989.

Huang, Rayson (黃 麗 松): CBE; member, Legislative Council; former vice-chancellor, University of Hong Kong; member, Basic Law Drafting Committee.

Ji, Pengfei (姬 鵬 飛): former chairman, Office of Hong Kong and Macao Affairs, State Council, China.

Jiang, Zemin (江 澤 民): promoted to be the CCP general secretary after the June 4, 1989, uprising in Tiananmen.

Jiang, Qing (江 青): Mao's widow.

Kam, Yiu-yu (金 堯 如): former editor-in-chief of *Wen Wei Pao.*

Kok, Kwong (釋 覺 光): a Buddhist leader; member, Basic Law Drafting Committee.

Kwong, Peter (鄺 廣 傑): an Anglican bishop; member, Basic Law Drafting Committee but quit after June 4, 1989.

Lam, Shan-muk (林 山 木): publisher, *Hong Kong Economic Journal.*

Lau, Wong Fat (劉 皇 發): MBE, JP; member, Legislative Council; member, Basic Law Drafting Committee.

Lee, Martin (李柱銘): JP; an outspoken critic of China who was stripped of his duty as a member of the Basic Law Drafting Committee in 1989 due to his staunch support of the pro-democracy students in China; member, Legislative Council.

Lee, Tse-chung (李子誦): fired by Xinhua as publisher of *Wen Wei Pao* due to his support of the 1989 Chinese democracy movement.

Lee, Yee (李　怡): publisher of the *Nineties Monthly* which was originally pro-China but fell into disfavor with Beijing.

Li, Chuwen (李儲文): deputy director, *Ta Kung Pao;* member, Chinese People's Political Consultative Conference.

Li, David (李國寶): JP; banker; member, Legislative Council; member, Basic Law Drafting Committee.

Li, Ka Shing (李嘉誠): JP; a real-estate tycoon; member, Basic Law Drafting Committee.

Li, Peng (李　鵬): hardline premier of China who imposed martial law in Beijing to suppress the 1989 pro-democracy movement.

Li, Simon (李福善): member, Basic Law Drafting Committee.

Liu, Yiu Chu (廖瑤珠): lawyer; member, Basic Law Drafting Committee; member, National People's Congress.

Lu, Keng (陸　鏗): publisher, *Pai Hsing Semimonthly.*

Ma, Lin (馬　臨): CBE, JP; former vice-chancellor, Chinese University of Hong Kong; member, Basic Law Drafting Committee.

Ma, Sik-chun (馬惜珍): publisher of the *Oriental Daily News,* taking refuge in Taiwan on charge of drug trafficking.

Mao, Zedong (毛澤東): founder of the People's Republic.

Miu, Yu (繆　雨): a columnist for the *Oriental Daily News.*

Pao, Yue Kong (包玉剛): Sir, CBE, JP; a shipping, real-estate, banking and air-transportation tycoon; member, Basic Law Drafting Committee.

Peng, Zhen (彭　眞): former chairman, National People's Congress.

Pok, Shaofu (卜少夫): publisher of the pro-KMT *Newsdom* weekly.

Poon, Chun-leung (潘振良): former editor, *Sing Tao Evening News;* member, Basic Law Consultative Committee.

Pun, Chiu-yin (潘朝彥): assistant general manager, Commercial Radio; member, Basic Law Consultative Committee.

Qin, Benli (欽本立): the deposed editor of the *World Economic Journal* in Shanghai.

Shaw, Run Run (邵逸夫): CBE; board chairman, TV Broadcasts Ltd.; board chairman, the Shaw Brothers, the largest motion picture empire in Southeast Asia.

Shi, Junyu (施君玉): a columnist of *Ta Kung Pao.*

Shum, Choi-sang (岑才生): OBE, JP; publisher, *Wah Kiu Daily News;* member, Basic Law Consultative Committee.

Szeto, Wah (司徒華): an outspoken critic of China, stripped of his duty as a member of the Basic Law Drafting Committee due to his support of the 1989 pro-democracy movement in China; member of the Legislative Council.

Tam, Wai Chu (譚惠珠): lawyer; member, Legislative Council; member, Executive Council; member, Basic Law Drafting Committee.

Tam, Yu Chung (譚耀宗): pro-China labor union leader; member, Legislative Council; member, Basic Law Drafting Committee.

Tsao, Peter (曹廣榮): former director, Government Information Services.

Tseng, Eddie (曾恩波): the late publisher of the *Hong Kong Times*.

Tsui, Sze-man (徐四民): publisher, *Mirror* monthly; member, Chinese People's Political Consultative Conference.

Wang, Ting-zhi (王亭之): a columnist.

Wong, Po Yan (黃保欣): CBE, OBE; member, Legislative Council; member, Basic Law Drafting Committee.

Wong, Wai-sing (黃維城): secretary, Asia Television; member, Basic Law Consultative Committee.

Wong, Yat-huen (黃日暄): program officer, Radio & Television Hong Kong; member, Basic Law Consultative Committee.

Wu, Raymond (鄔維庸): JP; member, Basic Law Drafting Committee.

Wu, Xueqian (吳學謙): former foreign minister of China.

Xu, Jiatun (許家屯): former director, Xinhua News Agency's Hong Kong Branch.

Yang, Qi (楊　奇): publisher, *Ta Kung Pao*.

Yang, Shangkun (楊尚昆): hardline President of China.

Yuan, Mu (袁　木): hardline State Council spokesman of China.

Yung, Sanford (容永道): member, Basic Law Drafting Committee; member, Chinese People's Political Consultative Conference.

Zhao, Ziyang (趙紫陽): the deposed CCP general secretary in the 1989 pro-democracy movement.

Zhou, Enlai (周恩來): the late premier of the People's Republic and a main architect of China's foreign policy.

Appendix III

Names of Chinese Publications

Cheng Ming (*Contending*): leftist-turned-independent political monthly specializing in China and promoting reforms in China.

Ching Pao (*The Sparkling Daily*): minor Communist-controlled newspaper.

Contemporary Weekly: political magazine started by Lee Tse-chung after he was fired as publisher of *Wen Wei Pao* in 1989.

Hong Kong Commercial Daily: newly published commercial paper.

Hong Kong Daily News: a rightist newspaper.

Hong Kong Economic Journal: highly independent centrist publication.

Hong Kong Times: the organ of the KMT in Hong Kong.

Kung Sheung Daily News (Yat Pao) (*The Industrial and Commercial Daily*): staunch anti-Communist paper; closed in 1984.

Ming Pao (*The Enlightenment Daily*): the most influential centrist paper with a wide intellectual readership. Louis Cha is the publisher.

Mirror Monthly: pro-Beijing journal.

New Evening Post: Communist-controlled paper.

Newsdom Weekly: pro-Taiwan journal owned by Pok Shaofu.

Nineties Monthly: leftist-turned-independent political journal, previously known as the *Seventies Monthly*.

Oriental Daily News: apolitical mass-oriented paper with highest circulation.

Pai Hsing (or Pai Shing) Semimonthly (*People*): independent, somewhat right-of-the-center publication.

Sing Pao Daily News (*The Success Daily*): apolitical mass-oriented paper.

Sing Tao Jih Pao (*The Star-Island Daily*): one of the oldest Hong Kong newspapers with a rightist orientation. Sally Aw is the publisher.

Ta Kung Pao (*The Impartial Daily*): major Communist-controlled paper.

Tin Tin Daily News (Yat Pao) (*The Everyday Daily*): paper of minor importance owned by a pro-Beijing business man.

Wah Kiu Yat Pao (*The Overseas Chinese Daily*): one of the oldest papers in Hong Kong with a rightist orientation.

Wen Wei Pao (Po) (*The Literary Gazette*): major Communist organ.

Wide-Angled Mirror: centrist monthly.

Appendix IV

Sino-British Joint Declaration

JOINT DECLARATION OF THE GOVERNMENT OF THE UNITED KINGDOM OF GREAT BRITAIN AND NORTHERN IRELAND AND THE GOVERNMENT OF THE PEOPLE'S REPUBLIC OF CHINA ON THE QUESTION OF HONG KONG

The Government of the United Kingdom of Great Britain and Northern Ireland and the Government of the People's Republic of China have reviewed with satisfaction the friendly relations existing between the two Governments and peoples in recent years and agreed that a proper negotiated settlement of the question of Hong Kong, which is left over from the past, is conducive to the maintenance of the prosperity and stability of Hong Kong and to the further strengthening and development of the relations between the two countries on a new basis. To this end, they have, after talks between the delegations of the two Governments, agreed to declare as follows:

1. The Government of the People's Republic of China declares that to recover the Hong Kong area (including Hong Kong Island, Kowloon and the New Territories, hereinafter referred to as Hong Kong) is the common aspiration of the entire Chinese people, and that it has decided to resume the exercise of sovereignty over Hong Kong with effect from 1 July 1997.

2. The Government of the United Kingdom declares that it will restore Hong Kong to the People's Republic of China with effect from 1 July 1997.

3. The Government of the People's Republic of China declares that the basic policies of the People's Republic of China regarding Hong Kong are as follows:

   (1) Upholding national unity and territorial integrity and taking account of the history of Hong Kong and its realities, the People's Republic of China has decided to establish, in accordance with the provisions of Article 31 of the Constitution of the People's Republic of China, a Hong Kong Special Administrative Region upon resuming the exercise of sovereignty over Hong Kong.

   (2) The Hong Kong Special Administrative Region will be directly under the authority of the Central People's Government of the People's Republic of China. The Hong Kong Special Administrative

Region will enjoy a high degree of autonomy, except in foreign and defence affairs which are the responsibilities of the Central People's Government.

(3) The Hong Kong Special Administrative Region will be vested with executive, legislative and independent judicial power, including that of final adjudication. The laws currently in force in Hong Kong will remain basically unchanged.

(4) The Government of the Hong Kong Special Administrative Region will be composed of local inhabitants. The chief executive will be appointed by the Central People's Government on the basis of the results of elections or consultations to be held locally. Principal officials will be nominated by the chief executive of the Hong Kong Special Administrative Region for appointment by the Central People's Government. Chinese and foreign nationals previously working in the public and police services in the government departments of Hong Kong may remain in employment. British and other foreign nationals may also be employed to serve as advisers or hold certain public posts in government departments of the Hong Kong Special Administrative Region.

(5) The current social and economic systems in Hong Kong will remain unchanged, and so will the life-style. Rights and freedoms, including those of the person, of speech, of the press, of assembly, of association, of travel, of movement, of correspondence, of strike, of choice of occupation, of academic research and of religious belief will be ensured by law in the Hong Kong Special Administrative Region. Private property, ownership of enterprises, legitimate right of inheritance and foreign investment will be protected by law.

(6) The Hong Kong Special Administrative Region will retain the status of a free port and a separate customs territory.

(7) The Hong Kong Special Administrative Region will retain the status of an international financial centre, and its markets for foreign exchange, gold, securities and futures will continue. There will be free flow of capital. The Hong Kong dollar will continue to circulate and remain freely convertible.

(8) The Hong Kong Special Administrative Region will have independent finances. The Central People's Government will not levy taxes on the Hong Kong Special Administrative Region.

(9) The Hong Kong Special Administrative Region may establish mutually beneficial economic relations with the United Kingdom and other countries, whose economic interests in Hong Kong will be given due regard.

(10) Using the name of "Hong Kong, China", the Hong Kong Special Administrative Region may on its own maintain and develop economic and cultural relations and conclude relevant agreements with states, regions and relevant international organisations.

The Government of the Hong Kong Special Administrative Region may on its own issue travel documents for entry into and exit from Hong Kong.

(11) The maintenance of public order in the Hong Kong Special Administrative Region will be the responsibility of the Government of the Hong Kong Special Administrative Region.

(12) The above-stated basic policies of the People's Republic of China regarding Hong Kong and the elaboration of them in Annex I to this Joint Declaration will be stipulated, in a Basic Law of the Hong Kong Special Administrative Region of the People's Republic of China, by the National People's Congress of the People's Republic of China, and they will remain unchanged for 50 years.

4. The Government of the United Kingdom and the Government of the People's Republic of China declare that, during the transitional period between the date of the entry into force of this Joint Declaration and 30 June 1997, the Government of the United Kingdom will be responsible for the administration of Hong Kong with the object of maintaining and preserving its economic prosperity and social stability; and that the Government of the People's Republic of China will give its cooperation in this connection.

5. The Government of the United Kingdom and the Government of the People's Republic of China declare that, in order to ensure a smooth transfer of government in 1997, and with a view to the effective implementation of this Joint Declaration, a Sino-British Joint Liaison Group will be set up when this Joint Declaration enters into force; and that it will be established and will function in accordance with the provisions of Annex II to this Joint Declaration.

6. The Government of the United Kingdom and the Government of the People's Republic of China declare that land leases in Hong Kong and other related matters will be dealt with in accordance with the provisions of Annex III to this Joint Declaration.

7. The Government of the United Kingdom and the Government of the People's Republic of China agree to implement the preceding declarations and the Annexes to this Joint Declaration.

8. This Joint Declaration is subject to ratification and shall enter into force on the date of the exchange of instruments of ratification, which shall take place in Beijing before 30 June 1985. This Joint Declaration and its Annexes shall be equally binding.

Done in duplicate at Beijing on   1984 in the English and Chinese languages, both texts being equally authentic.

For the
Government of the United Kingdom
of Great Britain and Northern Ireland

For the
Government of the
People's Republic of China

Appendix V

Hong Kong Basic Law

The Basic Law of the Hong Kong Special Administrative Region of the People's Republic of China was adopted at the third session of the seventh National People's Congress of the People's Republic of China on April 4, 1990 and shall take effect as of July 1, 1997.

The Basic Law contains:

Chapter I. General principles (Articles 1–11)

Chapter II. Relationship between the central authorities and the Hong Kong Special Administrative Region (Articles 12–23)

Chapter III. Fundamental rights and duties of the residents (Articles 14–18)

Chapter IV. Political structure (Articles 43–104)

Chapter V. Economy (Articles 105–135)

Chapter VI. Education, science, culture, sports, religion, labor and social services (Articles 136–149)

Chapter VII. External affairs (Articles 150–157)

Chapter VIII. Interpretation and amendment of the Basic Law (Articles 158–159)

Chapter IX. Supplementary provisions (Article 160)

The text of the preamble, Chapter I, and Chapter II reads as follows:

PREAMBLE

Hong Kong has been part of the territory of China since ancient times; it was occupied by Britain after the Opium War in 1840. On 19 December 1984, the Chinese and British Governments signed the Joint Declaration on the Question of Hong Kong, affirming that the Government of the People's Republic of China will resume the exercise of sovereignty over Hong Kong with effect from 1 July 1997, thus fulfilling the long-cherished common aspiration of the Chinese people for the recovery of Hong Kong.

Upholding national unity and territorial integrity, maintaining the prosperity and stability of Hong Kong, and taking account of its history and realities, the People's Republic of China has decided that upon China's resumption of the exercise of sovereignty over Hong Kong, a Hong Kong Special Administrative Region will be established in accordance with the provisions of Article 31 of the Constitution of the People's Republic of China, and that under the principle of "one country, two systems", the socialist system and policies will not be practised in Hong Kong. The basic policies of the People's Republic of China regarding Hong Kong have been elaborated by the Chinese Government in the Sino-British Joint Declaration.

In accordance with the Constitution of the People's Republic of China, the National People's Congress hereby enacts the Basic Law of the Hong Kong Special Administrative Region of the People's Republic of China, prescribing the systems to be practised in the Hong Kong Special Administrative Region, in order to ensure the implementation of the basic policies of the People's Republic of China regarding Hong Kong.

CHAPTER I: GENERAL PRINCIPLES

Article 1

The Hong Kong Special Administrative Region is an inalienable part of the People's Republic of China.

Article 2

The National People's Congress authorizes the Hong Kong Special Administrative Region to exercise a high degree of autonomy and enjoy executive, legislative and independent judicial power, including that of final adjudication, in accordance with the provisions of this Law.

Article 3

The executive authorities and legislature of the Hong Kong Special Administrative Region shall be composed of permanent residents of Hong Kong in accordance with the relevant provisions of this Law.

Article 4

The Hong Kong Special Administrative Region shall safeguard the rights and freedoms of the residents of the Hong Kong Special Administrative Region and of other persons in the Region in accordance with law.

Article 5

The socialist system and policies shall not be practised in the Hong Kong Special Administrative Region, and the previous capitalist system and way of life shall remain unchanged for 50 years.

Article 6

The Hong Kong Special Administrative Region shall protect the right of private ownership of property in accordance with law.

Article 7

The land and natural resources within the Hong Kong Special Administrative Region shall be State property. The Government of the Hong Kong Special Administrative Region shall be responsible for their management, use and development and for their lease or grant to individuals, legal persons or organizations for use or development. The revenues derived therefrom shall be exclusively at the disposal of the government of the Region.

Article 8

The laws previously in force in Hong Kong, that is, the common law, rules of equity, ordinances, subordinate legislation and customary law shall be maintained, except for any that contravene this Law, and subject to any amendment by the legislature of the Hong Kong Special Administrative Region.

Article 9

In addition to the Chinese language, English may also be used as an official language by the executive authorities, legislature and judiciary of the Hong Kong Special Administrative Region.

Article 10

Apart from displaying the national flag and national emblem of the People's Republic of China, the Hong Kong Special Administrative Region may also use a regional flag and regional emblem.

The regional flag of the Hong Kong Special Administrative Region is a red flag with a bauhinia highlighted by five star-tipped stamens.

The regional emblem of the Hong Kong Special Administrative Region is a bauhinia in the centre highlighted by five star-tipped stamens and encircled by the words "Hong Kong Special Administrative Region of the People's Republic of China" in Chinese and "HONG KONG" in English.

Article 11

In accordance with Article 31 of the Constitution of the People's Republic of China, the systems and policies practised in the Hong Kong Special Administrative Region, including the social and economic systems, the system for safeguarding the fundamental rights and freedoms of its residents, the executive, legislative and judicial systems, and the relevant policies, shall be based on the provisions of this Law.

No law enacted by the legislature of the Hong Kong Special Administrative Region shall contravene this Law.

CHAPTER II: RELATIONSHIP BETWEEN THE CENTRAL AUTHORITIES AND THE HONG KONG SPECIAL ADMINISTRATIVE REGION

Article 12

The Hong Kong Special Administrative Region shall be a local administrative region of the People's Republic of China, which shall enjoy a high degree of autonomy and come directly under the Central People's Government.

Article 13

The Central People's Government shall be responsible for the foreign affairs relating to the Hong Kong Special Administrative Region.

The Ministry of Foreign Affairs of the People's Republic of China shall establish an office in Hong Kong to deal with foreign affairs.

The Central People's Government authorizes the Hong Kong Special Administrative Region to conduct relevant external affairs on its own in accordance with this Law.

Article 14

The Central People's Government shall be responsible for the defence of the Hong Kong Special Administrative Region.

The Government of the Hong Kong Special Administrative Region shall be responsible for the maintenance of public order in the Region.

Military forces stationed by the Central People's Government in the Hong Kong Special Administrative Region for defence shall not interfere in the local affairs of the Region. The Government of the Hong Kong Special Administrative Region may, when necessary, ask the Central People's Government for assistance from the garrison in the maintenance of public order and in disaster relief.

In addition to abiding by national laws, members of the garrison shall abide by the laws of the Hong Kong Special Administrative Region.

Expenditure for the garrison shall be borne by the Central People's Government.

Article 15

The Central People's Government shall appoint the Chief Executive and the principal officials of the executive authorities of the Hong Kong Special Administrative Region in accordance with the provisions of Chapter IV of this Law.

Article 16

The Hong Kong Special Administrative Region shall be vested with executive power. It shall, on its own, conduct the administrative affairs of the Region in accordance with the relevant provisions of this Law.

Article 17

The Hong Kong Special Administrative Region shall be vested with legislative power.

Laws enacted by the legislature of the Hong Kong Special Administrative Region must be reported to the Standing Committee of the National People's Congress for the record. The reporting for record shall not affect the entry into force of such laws.

If the Standing Committee of the National People's Congress, after consulting the Committee for the Basic Law of the Hong Kong Special Administrative Region under it, considers that any law enacted by the legislature of the Region is not in conformity with the provisions of this Law regarding affairs within the responsibility of the Central Authorities or regarding the relationship between the Central Authorities and the Region, the Standing Committee may return the law in question but shall not amend it. Any law returned by the Standing Committee of the National People's Congress shall immediately be invalidated. This invalidation shall not have retroactive effect, unless otherwise provided for in the laws of the Region.

Article 18

The laws in force in the Hong Kong Special Administrative Region shall be this Law, the laws previously in force in Hong Kong as provided for in Article 8 of this Law, and the laws enacted by the legislature of the Region.

National laws shall not be applied in the Hong Kong Special Administrative Region except for those listed in Annex III to this Law. The laws listed therein shall be applied locally by way of promulgation or legislation by the Region.

The Standing Committee of the National People's Congress may add to or delete from the list of laws in Annex III after consulting its Committee for the Basic Law of the Hong Kong Special Administrative Region and the government of the Region. Laws listed in Annex III to this Law shall be confined to those relating to defence and foreign affairs as well as other matters outside the limits of the autonomy of the Region as specified by this Law.

In the event that the Standing Committee of the National People's Congress decides to declare a state of war or, by reason of turmoil within the Hong Kong Special Administrative Region which endangers national unity or security and is beyond the control of the government of the Region, decides that the Region is in a state of emergency, the Central People's Government may issue an order applying the relevant national laws in the Region.

Article 19

The Hong Kong Special Administrative Region shall be vested with independent judicial power, including that of final adjudication.

The courts of the Hong Kong Special Administrative Region shall have jurisdiction over all cases in the Region, except that the restrictions on their jurisdiction imposed by the legal system and principles previously in force in Hong Kong shall be maintained.

The courts of the Hong Kong Special Administrative Region shall have no jurisdiction over acts of state such as defence and foreign affairs. The courts of the Region shall obtain a certificate from the Chief Executive on questions of fact concerning acts of state such as defence and foreign affairs whenever such questions arise in the adjudication of cases. This certificate shall be binding on the courts. Before issuing such a certificate, the Chief Executive shall obtain a certifying document from the Central People's Government.

Article 20

The Hong Kong Special Administrative Region may enjoy other powers granted to it by the National People's Congress, the Standing Committee of the National People's Congress or the Central People's Government.

Article 21

Chinese citizens who are residents of the Hong Kong Special Administrative Region shall be entitled to participate in the management of state affairs according to law.

In accordance with the assigned number of seats and the selection method specified by the National People's Congress, the Chinese citizens among the residents of the Hong Kong Special Administrative Region shall locally elect deputies of the Region to the National People's Congress to participate in the work of the highest organ of state power.

Article 22

No department of the Central People's Government and no province, autonomous region, or municipality directly under the Central Government may interfere in the affairs which the Hong Kong Special Administrative Region administers on its own in accordance with this Law.

If there is a need for departments of the Central Government, or for provinces, autonomous regions, or municipalities directly under the Central Government to set up offices in the Hong Kong Special Administrative Region, they must obtain the consent of the government of the Region and the approval of the Central People's Government.

All offices set up in the Hong Kong Special Administrative Region by departments of the Central Government, or by provinces, autonomous regions, or municipalities directly under the Central Government, and the personnel of these offices shall abide by the laws of the Region.

For entry into the Hong Kong Special Administrative Region, people from other parts of China must apply for approval. Among them, the number of persons who enter the Region for the purpose of settlement shall be determined by the competent authorities of the Central People's Government after consulting the government of the Region.

The Hong Kong Special Administrative Region may establish an office in Beijing.

Article 23

The Hong Kong Special Administrative Region shall enact laws on its own to prohibit any act of treason, secession, sedition, subversion against the Central People's Government, or theft of state secrets, to prohibit foreign political organizations or bodies from conducting political activities in the Region, and to prohibit political organizations or bodies of the Region from establishing ties with foreign political organizations or bodies.

Appendix VI

Chronology
of Events

Included are events that bear direct or indirect relevance to the relations between China and Hong Kong, China and Britain, and Britain and Hong Kong. More detailed accounts are taken of periods between 1982 and 1984 (regarding Sino-British negotiations) and of 1989 (regarding Beijing's democracy movement) to provide contexts for the analysis in the text.

1949

October 1: The People's Republic of China is founded.

1950

May 5: The Foreign Ministry of China protests to Britain, in vain, over the restrictions imposed by the Hong Kong government on Chinese immigration to the colony.

1963

March 8: The *People's Daily* reiterates that the status quo of Hong Kong would be maintained until "historical conditions are ripe."

1967

May 12: Riots erupt in Hong Kong as part of China's Cultural Revolution.

1972

February 12: Premier Zhou Enlai reveals that the issue of Hong Kong will be resolved by agreement at the opportune time.

March 10: China submits a memorandum to the United Nations Special Committee on Colonialism, asking that Hong Kong and Macao be taken off the list of colonies.

1973

April 17: Agence France Presse reports that Beijing wants to set up a "representative organ" in Hong Kong.

May 21: Informed sources reveal that China's request to set up a "representative organ" will be rejected.

1978

December 18: The Chinese foreign trade minister, Li Qiang, tells Hong Kong reporters that 1997 is still a long way off.

1979

March 24–April 4: Vice-premier Deng Xiaoping tells the visiting governor of Hong Kong, Sir Murray MacLehose, that investors in Hong Kong should "put their hearts at ease."

May 7: China's assistant foreign minister, Song Zhiguang, indicates that Hong Kong will be settled in an appropriate way when the lease expires.

October 7: Premier Hua Guofeng says that the question of Hong Kong will be solved through negotiations and that the interests of investors will be protected.

December 11: First Party secretary of Guangdong Province, Xi Zhongxun, says in Macao that Hong Kong and Macao are "special regions" of China.

1980

July 30: The British government releases the white paper on the British Nationality Bill which denies British subjects registered in Hong Kong the right of abode in the United Kingdom when Hong Kong ceases to be a British colony.

1981

April 1: British foreign secretary, Lord Carrington, says that Deng Xiaoping has assured that the investors' interests will be protected before and after 1997.

September 30: Ye Jiangying, chairman of the Standing Committee of the National People's Congress, issues a nine-point plan for peaceful reunification with Taiwan, which would make Taiwan an autonomous Special Administrative Region.

1982

April 6: Deng Xiaoping tells former British Prime Minister Edward Heath that China will let the Hong Kong people govern themselves after the recovery of sovereignty and that China's new Constitution will allow the establishment of Special Administrative Regions.

May 21: Deng Xiaoping receives Fok Ying Tong, a Hong Kong billionaire.

May 23: Premier Zhao Ziyang, who succeeds Hua Guofeng, meets with Lee Ka-shing, a real-estate tycoon from Hong Kong.

June 1: Deng Xiaoping receives Dr. Rayson Huang, vice-chancellor of the University of Hong Kong.

June 15: Deng receives Fei Yimin (publisher of *Ta Kung Pao*) and other pro-China leaders from Hong Kong and Macao.

July 16: Peng Zhen, vice-chairman of the Standing Committee of the National People's Congress, urges the compatriots in Taiwan, Hong Kong, and Macao to study Article 31 in the new constitution that provides the establishment of Special Administrative Regions.

September 22: British Prime Minister Margaret Thatcher arrives in Beijing for negotiations. (Between September 1982 and June 1983, Britain hopes that it will be allowed to continue administering Hong Kong after its return to China. This hope proves unrealistic.)

September 23: Zhao Ziyang explicitly states that China will recover Hong Kong's sovereignty.

September 24: Deng Xiaoping and Margaret Thatcher agree to enter diplomatic negotiations over Hong Kong's future. Xinhua News Agency says that the Chinese government's position on the recovery of the whole of Hong Kong is "unequivocal and known to all."

September 25: Thatcher asserts that the treaties governing the status of Hong Kong, which China does not recognize, can only be altered but not abrogated.

September 27: Arguing that a country (China) that does not abide by an international treaty (the Treaty of Nanjing) will not stand by another, Thatcher promises that Britain will consult the Hong Kong people in Sino-British negotiations. Both the stock market and the Hong Kong dollar plummet.

September 30: A Chinese foreign ministry spokesman says China does not recognize the unequal treaties.

October 1: Xinhua disputes Thatcher's claims about Britain's moral responsibility to the people of Hong Kong.

October 11: Confirming its differences with China, Britain states that its aim is to preserve Hong Kong's stability and prosperity in a way acceptable to the Parliament and the people of Hong Kong.

November 1: Xi Zhongxun, vice-chairman of the Standing Committee of the National People's Congress, says that a scheme will be developed to maintain Hong Kong's stability and prosperity beyond 1997. Liao Chengzhi, head of the State Council's Hong Kong and Macao Office, says that Hong Kong will continue to function as a free port and financial center.

December 4: The National People's Congress of China promulgates a new constitution, Article 31 of which provides for the establishment of Special Administrative Regions.

1983

February 10: Foreign Minister Wu Xueqian reveals that Sino-British negotiations have not gone beyond procedural matters to substantive issues.

April 5: About 140 Hong Kong and Macao prominent residents are appointed to sit on the national or provincial People's Congresses and the Chinese People's Political Consultative Conference.

April 11: Liao Chengzhi reportedly reveals that Hong Kong will have its own mini-constitution after 1997.

May 12: Liao Chengzhi states that China will not accept Hong Kong as an independent party in Sino-British negotiations. Rather, members from Hong Kong will be treated as part of the British delegation.

June 6: Zhao Ziyang reports to the Sixth National People's Congress that "China will recover Hong Kong's sovereignty at a suitable time and will take appropriate measures to maintain the prosperity of Hong Kong."

June 10: Liao Chengzhi dies. Ji Pengfei becomes head of the Hong Kong and Macao Office.

June 16: Peter Rees, British chief secretary of the treasury, renews Britain's commitment to securing a Sino-British agreement acceptable to Hong Kong people.

June 17: Xu Jiatun, the newly appointed director of the Xinhua Branch in Hong Kong, states that Chinese sovereignty over Hong Kong shall not be negotiable.

June 22: The Queen of England states that the British government "will continue talks with China with the aim of reaching a solution acceptable to this Parliament, to China and to the people of Hong Kong."

June 24: Sir Edward Youde, governor of Hong Kong, indicates that he will join the Sino-British negotiations when the time is appropriate.

June 25: Deng Xiaoping promises that China will not change its policy toward Hong Kong.

July 30: Xu Jiatun, a member of the CCP central committee, becomes the highest-ranking official to head the Hong Kong branch of Xinhua News Agency.

July 1: Beijing and London jointly announce that the second phase of talks on Hong Kong's future will begin in Beijing on July 12.

July 7: Sir Edward Youde declares that he represents the people of Hong Kong in the negotiations.

July 8: The Chinese foreign ministry indicates that Sir Youde will be regarded only as a member of the British negotiation team, not as a representative of Hong Kong.

July 12–13: First round of the phase-two negotiations takes place, characterized as "useful and constructive."

July 25–26: Second round of the phase-two negotiations takes place, described as "useful."

July 29: A group of post-secondary student union activists return from Beijing with more information about China's blueprint for the future Hong Kong.

August 2–3: Third round of negotiations. No progress is made.

August 15: Hu Yaobang, general secretary of the Chinese Communist Party, proclaims that China will take back Hong Kong on July 1, 1997.

September 16: Xinhua criticizes the Hong Kong government for fanning public opinion to demand a British presence in Hong Kong beyond 1997.

September 21: Foreign Minister Wu Xueqian attributes stagnation of the negotiations to Britain's rigid attitudes.

September 22–23: Fourth round of negotiations takes place. No progress is indicated. Xinhua repudiates British claims that Hong Kong's prosperity is owed to British rule. Prime Minister Thatcher says in London that the uncertainty gives rise to Hong Kong's major financial and political turmoils.

September 24: The Hong Kong dollar plummets to a record low and the value of gold rises to a record high.

September 28: Richard Luce, British minister of state for foreign and commonwealth affairs with special responsibility for Hong Kong, arrives in Hong Kong, noting that China's criticism of Britain is worrisome and not conducive to the negotiations. Luce pledges that Britain will heed the will of Hong Kong people.

September 30: Ji Pengfei confirms that if an agreement is not reached by September 1984, China will unilaterally declare its plan to take over Hong Kong.

October 3: The spokesman of China's Foreign Ministry criticizes remarks by Thatcher and Luce.

October 4: Xinhua criticizes Thatcher's remarks.

October 6: The *People's Daily* criticizes Luce's remarks.

October 10: The *People's Daily* urges the British government to be more realistic and to shed its colonial attitudes.

October 15: Hong Kong's financial secretary, Sir John Bremridge, announces that the Hong Kong dollar would be pegged at HK$7.8 to US$1, effective from October 17.

October 19–20: Fifth round of negotiations takes place, described as "useful and constructive."

October 21: Sir Edward Youde discloses that Sino-British informal contacts will be held.

November 14–15: Sixth round of talks takes place, described as "useful and constructive." Informal contacts between both sides continue.

November 15: Ji Pengfei pledges that Hong Kong's systems will remain unchanged for fifty years beyond 1997.

November 24: Hu Yaobang pledges that China will guarantee the safety of all foreign investors in Hong Kong.

December 3: Peng Zhen, chairman of the Standing Committee of the National People's Congress, argues that keeping Hong Kong's capitalism intact after 1997 will be constitutional.

December 7–8: Seventh round of talks takes place, described as "useful and constructive."

1984

January 7: Ji Pengfei reportedly has revealed that China intends to have a tripartite legislature for the future Hong Kong comprising pro-China, pro-British, and neutral members.

January 13: Thousands of rioters loot main Kowloon streets in the evening, taking advantage of a strike by taxi drivers against the government. Xu Jiatun delivers his first formal speech to the University of Hong Kong, noting that Hong Kong as a highly developed capitalist society will count on intellectuals for leadership.

January 17: Ji Pengfei details China's blueprint for Hong Kong after 1997. Zhao Ziyang addresses the question of Hong Kong at the Canadian House of Commons and the Senate. Margaret Thatcher discusses the issue of Hong Kong with Sir Edward Youde and executive councillors.

January 25–26: Eighth round of talks takes place, described as "useful and constructive."

February 22–23: Ninth round of talks takes place, described as "useful and constructive."

February 24: Xu Jiatun hosts a banquet for Chinese unofficial members of Hong Kong's Executive and Legislative Councils. The Legislative Council passes unanimously a motion that the Sino-British agreement, before its finalization, should be openly debated. *Wen Wei Pao* criticizes that motion as a British plot.

February 25: Chief secretary of Hong Kong, Sir Philip Haddon-Cave, announces measures to foster democratization on the regional and district levels.

February 28: Richard Luce, British minister for foreign and commonwealth affairs with special responsibility for Hong Kong, reiterates that the Sino-British agreement will have to be acceptable to the British and the Chinese governments and to the Hong Kong people.

March 8: Twenty-one civil organizations in Hong Kong urge that the contents of the Sino-British negotiations be published.

March 14: The Legislative Council of Hong Kong resolves that any proposal for Hong Kong will be debated in the Council.

March 16–17: Tenth round of negotiations takes place, described as "useful and constructive."

March 26–27: Eleventh round of talks takes place, described as "useful and constructive."

March 28: Jardine Matheson, the oldest and one of the most influential corporations in Hong Kong, announces its plan to relocate in Bermuda.

April 11–12: Twelfth round of negotiations takes place, described as "useful and constructive."

April 15–18: British Foreign Secretary, Sir Geoffrey Howe, ends his visit to China. A Sino-British joint communiqué indicates that progress is being made toward an agreement acceptable to both sides.

April 18–20: Sir Howe states in Hong Kong that it is unrealistic "to think of an agreement that provides for British administration in Hong Kong after 1997."

April 21: Ji Pengfei says that KMT personnel and institutions will be allowed to remain in Hong Kong after 1997.

April 27–28: Thirteenth round of negotiations takes place, described as "useful and constructive."

May 9–10: Fourteenth round of negotiations takes place, described as "useful and constructive."

May 17: The British House of Commons debates the issue of Hong Kong.

May 25: When asked at a press conference to confirm the promise made earlier by Huang Hua (vice-chairman of the National People's Congress) and Geng Biao (defense minister) that China will not station the Liberation Army in Hong Kong after 1997, Deng replies, "Nonsense!"

May 30–31: Fifteenth round of negotiations takes place, described as "useful and constructive." It is agreed that a task group will be set up to expedite the negotiation process.

June 12–13: Sixteenth round of negotiations takes place, described as "useful and constructive."

June 23: Deng Xiaoping meets senior members of the Executive and Legislative

Councils, stating that there are only two parties (China and Britain, but not Hong Kong) in the Sino-British negotiations.

June 25: Senior members of the Executive and Legislative Councils return to Hong Kong and pledge their support to China's recovery of Hong Kong.

June 27–28: Seventeenth round of negotiations takes place, described as "useful and constructive."

July 11–12: Eighteenth round of negotiations takes place, described as "useful and constructive."

July 18: The governor of Hong Kong announces the green paper on the development of representative government, which proposes to gradually increase unofficial and elective members of the Executive and Legislative Councils. China reacts negatively.

July 19: Sir Geoffrey Howe announces that an office will be set up to assess Hong Kong's public reaction to the Sino-British agreement.

July 24–25: Nineteenth round of negotiations takes place, described as "useful and constructive."

July 31: Deng Xiaoping informs Howe in Beijing that the solution of the Hong Kong issue will set an exemplar of conflict resolution in history.

August 1: Sir Geoffrey Howe declares in Hong Kong that the Sino-British Joint Liaison Group will operate until 2000.

August 8–9: Twentieth round of negotiations takes place, described as "useful and constructive."

August 21–22: Twenty-first round of negotiations takes place, described as "useful and constructive."

September 5–6: Twenty-second round of negotiations takes place, described as "useful and constructive."

September 22: Britain and China announce that the negotiations have resulted in a final agreement.

September 26: Britain and China initial the Sino-British Joint Declaration in Beijing. Taiwan does not recognize the Joint Declaration.

October 15: The Legislative Council of Hong Kong debates over the Sino-British Joint Declaration.

November 14: The Standing Committee of the Chinese National People's Congress endorses the draft Sino-British Joint Declaration.

November 21: The Hong Kong government releases the white paper on the development of representative government.

December 6: The British House of Commons passes the Sino-British Joint Declaration.

December 20: Zhao Ziyang and Margaret Thatcher sign the Sino-British Joint Declaration in Beijing. Deng Xiaoping tells Thatcher that China will faithfully implement the Joint Declaration.

1985

February 24: The Hong Kong and Macao Office is elevated to the ministry level in the PRC's State Council.

March 7: About 40% of the registered voters turn out for the first district election in Hong Kong.

April 28: The government of Taiwan announces that it will not interfere with indirect trade between China and Taiwan.

May 27: The political transition of Hong Kong officially begins with the exchange of approval statements for the Joint Declaration between Britain and China.

June 12: The Sino-British Joint Declaration is registered at the United Nations.

June 18: The Standing Committee of the National People's Congress approves the name list of the Basic Law Drafting Committee which comprises members from China and those from Hong Kong.

July 1: The Sino-British Joint Declaration takes effect.

July 1–5: The Basic Law Drafting Committee holds the first meeting in Beijing.

July 17: The Hong Kong members of the Basic Law Drafting Committee set up a subcommittee to draft a constitution for the Basic Law Consultative Committee, a body that is designed to advise the Drafting Committee.

July 22: The first Sino-British Joint Liaison Group holds its first meeting.

August 20: The constitution of the Basic Law Consultative Committee is preliminarily approved.

September 25: The Legislative Council of Hong Kong holds the first indirect election.

October 17: The British government publishes the white paper on the Nationality Bill which denies British subjects registered in Hong Kong the right of abode in England.

November 21: Xu Jiatun, Director of Xinhua, accuses Britain of deviating from the Sino-British Joint Declaration in pursuing direct district elections.

December 21: The Basic Law Consultative Committee holds its founding general meeting. Ji Pengfei, Head of the Hong Kong and Macao Office, visits Hong Kong.

1986

January 4: Lu Ping, secretariat of the Hong Kong and Macao Office, leads a delegation of experts to Hong Kong to solicit opinion on the Basic Law.

January 20: Chinese Foreign Minister Wu Xueqian holds talks with British foreign minister.

March 6: Elections for the Urban Council and Metropolitan Council are held in Hong Kong.

April 18–22: At its second plenary session, the Basic Law Drafting Committee decides on the structure of the Basic Law and forms five special subject subgroups.

April 21: Deng Xiaoping vows that the "four cardinal principles" will not apply in Hong Kong. These principles refer to adherence to Marxist–Leninist–Maoist thought, socialism, Communist leadership, and proletarian dictatorship.

July 4: Hong Kong Nuclear Investment Company and Guangdong Nuclear Power Joint Venture brief the Legislative and Executive Councils of Hong Kong on a nuclear power plant to be built at Daya Bay.

July 13: Civil groups form a Joint Conference for the Shelving of Daya Bay Nuclear Plant and start a campaign to solicit signatures.

July 16: The Legislative Council of Hong Kong debates over the plans to build the Daya Bay Nuclear Power Plant.

July 17: China announces four measures to ensure nuclear safety at Daya Bay.

July 19: The Nuclear Safety Bureau of China reveals that it will cooperate with France in assessing the safety of the nuclear plant at Daya Bay.

August 2: The Legislative Council of Hong Kong sends a delegation abroad to investigate matters of nuclear safety.

August 17: Antinuclear forces in Hong Kong send a delegation to petition Beijing to stop or relocate the Daya Bay Plant.

September 23: The contract is signed in Beijing for building the Daya Bay Plant.

October 8: Chiang Ching-kuo, president of Taiwan, discloses to visiting *Washington Post* Publisher Katherine Graham that the 37-year-old martial law will be repealed.

October 14: Hu Yaobang, Deng Xiaoping, and Zhao Ziyang meet Queen Elizabeth II respectively.

October 21: Queen Elizabeth II visits Hong Kong.

October 28: Taiwan's first opposition Democratic Progressive Party is formed.

November 2: The democratic groups in Hong Kong hold a rally to demand direct election and autonomous rule.

November 29–December 2: The Basic Law Drafting Committee holds its third plenary session.

December 5: Sir Edward Youde dies in Beijing.

December 9: Students in the Chinese cities of Wuhan and Hefei march to demand greater democracy.

December 12: Big character posters appearing in Beijing University call upon the students to march for democracy.

1987

January 1: Three thousand students march in Beijing for democracy.

January 12: President and Vice-president of China Technology University are sacked for their alleged involvement in the students' democracy movement.

January 13: Deng Xiaoping emphasizes the importance of campaigning against bourgeois liberalization.

January 16: Hu Yaobang resigns as general secretary of the CCP due in part to his reluctance to crack down on the student movement. Premier Zhao Ziyang becomes acting general secretary.

January 24: Liu Binyan, Fang Lizhi, and Wang Ruowang are expelled from the CCP.

January 29: Zhao Ziyang sets the limits of the campaign against bourgeois liberalization.

March 31: Zhao Ziyang assures that the campaign against bourgeois liberalization will not spill over into Hong Kong and Macao.

April 9: Sir David Wilson becomes governor of Hong Kong.

April 13–17: The Basic Law Drafting Committee holds its fourth plenary session.

April 16: Deng Xiaoping informs the Basic Law Drafting Committee that universal suffrage is not appropriate for Hong Kong.

April 22: Wu Xueqian discusses Hong Kong affairs with Sir Geoffrey Howe in Bangkok.

June 18: Li Hou, deputy director of the Hong Kong and Macao Office, declares opposition to holding direct elections in Hong Kong in 1988.

July 15: Taiwan lifts martial law.

August 22–26: The Basic Law Drafting Committee holds its fifth plenary session.

September 23: Sir David Wilson visits Beijing to hold political review for 1988 and discusses the implementation of the Sino-British Joint Declaration with Chinese officials.

September 27: About 10,000 Hong Kong citizens hold a rally to support direction election in 1988.

October 19: The world stock market crashes.

October 20: The Joint Hong Kong Stock Market suspends trading for four days.

October 26: Sir Geoffrey Howe meets Sir David Wilson. The Hong Kong Stock Market reopens and the Hang Sang Index plummets.

November 1: The 13th Congress of the CCP closes in Beijing. Zhao Ziyang becomes general secretary and Deng Xiaoping remains as head of the Military Commission.

November 24: Li Peng succeeds Zhao Ziyang as premier.

December 12–16: The Basic Law Drafting Committee holds its sixth plenary session.

1988

January 13: Li Teng-huei becomes Taiwan's president, following the death of Chiang Ching-kuo.

February 10: The Hong Kong government releases the white paper on the Development of Representative Government which rules out direct elections.

April 24–28: The seventh plenary session of the Basic Law Drafting Committee ends with the release of "Draft Basic Law for the Solicitation of Opinions."

November 2: Sir David Wilson visits Beijing.

December 3: The Basic Law Drafting Committee's political system subcommittee approves the "mainstream resolution" in Guangzhou. The resolution, drafted by Louis Cha (publisher of *Ming Pao*), calls for postponement of direct elections of executive officials until 2012, or 15 years after China's takeover of Hong Kong. Prodemocracy groups in Hong Kong hold a 795-hour-long hunger strike protesting against the passage of that resolution.

1989

January 9–15: At its eighth plenary session, the Basic Law Drafting Committee submits the draft Basic Law to the Standing Committee of the National People's Congress of the PRC in Beijing.

February 15: The Standing Committee of National People's Congress resolves to publish the draft of the Basic Law. The Basic Law Consultative Committee begins its consultative work.

February 16: Thirty-three leading intellectuals in Beijing petition the Chinese authorities in an open letter to release Wei Jingsheng and other dissidents.

February 26: Professor Fang Lizhi, a leading dissident intellectual, is barred from attending a banquet hosted by the visiting President Bush in Beijing.

March 16: Forty-three Chinese intellectuals write a joint letter, asking the Beijing authorities to release the imprisoned dissidents.

April 3: Big character posters in Beijing University demand that the campus be a special democratic zone.

April 15: Hu Yaobang dies in Beijing.

April 17: Students march to mourn Hu Yaobang in Beijing.

April 20: Students are beaten and driven off the Xinhua Gate by the police.

April 21: An estimated 60,000 students hold an overnight sit-in at Tiananmen Square.

April 23: The students' petition letter is rejected by the Beijing authorities.

April 23: The Beijing Provisional Intercollegiate Autonomous Student Union is established.

April 24: Students boycott classes in Beijing.

April 26: The *People's Daily* labels the student movement as a "disturbance," a euphemism for justifying the crackdown that is to follow.

April 27: One million Beijing citizens support the marching students.

May 3: Yuan Mu, spokesman of China's State Council, rejects the conditions set by students for a government–student dialogue.

May 4: A day of special significance in modern Chinese history. One May 4, 1919, students in Beijing protested against the warlord government for kow-towing to the Japanese aggressor. The "May Fourth Movement" also ushered in ideas of democracy and science. On May 4, 1989, students and journalists march in Beijing to demand greater press freedom; students march in Hong Kong to support them. Zhao Ziyang states that he does not view the student movement as a "disturbance" because it calls for internal reform rather than an overthrow of the Party.

May 13: Students begin hunger strike in Tiananmen Square.

May 15: Students fast outside Xinhua's headquarters in Hong Kong to show their solidarity with students in Beijing.

May 17: One million citizens, soldiers and cadres march in Beijing to support the students.

May 19: Zhao Ziyang, in what is to be his final public appearance, visits the hunger strikers in Tiananmen Square.

May 20: Li Peng imposes martial law in parts of Beijing. Citizens and students block military units and vehicles from entering the city. About 40,000 people march in Hong Kong despite a typhoon.

May 21: One million people march in Hong Kong to support students in Beijing. Intellectuals and journalists in Beijing march to demand the resignation of Premier Li Peng.

May 27: Tens of thousands in Hong Kong attend a popular concert, raising US$1 million to support students in Beijing.

May 28: Two million overseas Chinese march to show solidarity with students in Beijing.

June 4: The Chinese troops, with tanks and machine guns, force their way into Tiananmen Square and crush the student movement.

June 9: Deng Xiaoping breaks his silence to reemerge on television, announcing that the "disturbance" has been suppressed.

June 19: Hong Kong's senior legislative and executive councillors visit London to demand the right of abode for Hong Kong-born citizens.

June 22: Ji Pengfei remarks that China's "one country, two systems" policy will remain valid but Hong Kong must not be used as an anti-China base.

June 24: Jiang Zemin replaces Zhao Ziyang as general secretary of the CCP.

June 27: The business and industrial sectors of Hong Kong demand that the United Kingdom grant the right of abode in England to the people of Hong Kong.

July 2: Sir Geoffrey Howe visits the colony, where citizens march to demand the right of abode in England.

July 8: Xu Jiatun, director of Xinhua's Hong Kong branch, urges Hong Kong people to stabilize Hong Kong.

July 15: Xinhua strips Lee Tse-chung of his post as publisher of *Wen Wei Pao*.

July 21: The *People's Daily* criticizes Hong Kong citizens for supporting the Beijing movement.

August 11: The *Outlook Weekly*, a magazine that reflects China's foreign policy views, criticizes the Hong Kong Alliance in Support of Patriotic Democratic Movement in China for engaging in anti-Communist activities.

August 25: The Prince of Wales cancels his impending visit to China.

August 26: The Chinese representative of the Sino-British Liaison Group accuses the British of enhancing the differences between the two countries.

September 23: The police confront demonstrators outside Xinhua's national day banquet in Hong Kong.

October 5: To punish Hong Kong for its role in supporting the Chinese students, China ceases to accept illegal mainland immigrants sent back by the Hong Kong police.

October 18: The Chinese Foreign Ministry accuses Britain of attempting to "internationalize" the issue of Hong Kong.

October 19: Prime Minister Thatcher discusses Hong Kong's confidence crisis in the Commonwealth Congress.

October 24: China resumes acceptance of illegal immigrants returned by Hong Kong.

November 19: China decides to amend the Basic Law draft, specifying that Hong Kong not be used as a base to subvert China.

December 20: Britain announces plans to grant the right of abode in the United Kingdom to about 50,000 Hong Kong families.

December 25: Xinhua New Agency accuses Shum Kin-fun, a leader of the Hong Kong Alliance in Support of Patriotic Democratic Movement in China, of helping movement leaders flee from China.

1990

January 1: About 10,000 Hong Kong citizens march for democracy in China. Xu Jiatun retires. Zhou Nan, deputy foreign minister of China, replaces Xu.

January 10: Governor Sir David Wilson visits Beijing.

February 12–17: The ninth plenary session of the Basic Law Drafting Committee ends with the release of the final draft of the Basic Law which will be submitted to the National People's Congress for approval. The final draft is considered to be even more conservative than Louis Cha's "mainstream resolution," prompting several thousands of students to march in Hong Kong.

April 4: The National People's Congress approves the Basic Law of the Hong Kong Special Administrative Region of the People's Republic of China.

Early May: Xu Jiatun departed for the United States without Beijing's authorization, for fear of recrimination by China's hardline leaders.

Bibliography

I. ENGLISH-LANGUAGE SOURCES

Aldrich, Howard E. *Organizations and Environments*. Englewood, N.J.: Prentice-Hall, 1979.

Aldrich, Howard, and Jeffrey Pfeffer. "Environments of Organizations." *Annual Review of Sociology*, 1976:79–105.

Altheide, David, and Robert Snow. *Media Logic*. Beverly Hills: Sage, 1979.

Althusser, Louis. *Lenin and Philosophy and other Essays*. London: New Left, 1971.

Araby, Osman Mohammed. "The Press and Foreign Policy: A Comparative Study of the Role of the Elite Press in U.S. Foreign Policies in the Middle East." Ph.D. diss., University of Minnesota, 1990.

Bagdikian, Ben H. *The Media Monopoly*. Boston: Beacon, 1983.

Bell, Daniel. *The End of Ideology*. New York: Free Press, 1962.

Bennett, Lance. *The Politics of Illusion*. New York: Longman, 1983.

Bennett, Lance, Lynn Gressett, and William Haltom. "Repairing the News: A Case Study of the News Paradigm." *Journal of Communication*, 35, 2 (1985):50–68.

Berger, Peter L., and Thomas Luckmann. *The Social Construction of Reality*. New York: Anchor, 1967.

Bociurkiw, Michael. "In the Jaws of China." *South China Morning Post*, February 25, 1990.

Bonavia, David. *Hong Kong 1997*. Hong Kong: South China Morning Post, 1985.

Boyce, George. "The Fourth Estate: The Reappraisal of a Concept." In George Boyce, James Curran, and Pauline Wingate, eds., *Newspaper History*. Beverly Hills: Sage, 1978.

Breed, Warren. "Social Control in the Newsroom: A Functional Analysis." *Social Force*, 33 (1955):326–336.

Burns, John P. "The Structure of Communist Party Control in Hong Kong." *Asian Survey*, 30, 8 (1990):748–765.

Chan, Joseph Man, and Chin-Chuan Lee. "Journalistic Paradigms on Civil Protests: A Case Study in Hong Kong." In Andrew Arno and Wimal Dissanayake, eds., *The News Media in National and International Conflict*. Boulder, Colorado: Westview Press, 1984.

———. "Press Ideology and Organization Control in Hong Kong." *Communication Research*, 15, 2 (1988):185–197.

————. "Shifting Journalistic Paradigms: Editorial Stance and Political Transition in Hong Kong." *China Quarterly*, no. 117 (March 1989):97–117.

Chan, Ming K., and Tuen-yu Lau. "Dilemma of the Communist Press in a Pluralistic Society." *Asian Survey*, 30, 8 (1990):731–747.

Chang, Joanne. "China's Hong Kong Victory: A Study of the PRC's Negotiating Style." Paper presented at the Asian Studies Association Annual Convention, San Francisco, March 25, 1988.

Chang, Kuo-sin. "GIS Chief and the Press." *Hong Kong Standard*, January 25, 1984.

Chang, Tsan-kuo. "The Impact of Presidential Statements on Press Editorials Regarding U.S. China Policy, 1950–1984." *Communiction Research*, 16 (1989): 486–509.

————. "Reporting U.S.-China Policy, 1950–1984." In *Voices of China. See* Lee, ed., 1990.

Cheng, Joseph. *Hong Kong: In Search of a Future.* Hong Kong: Oxford University Press, 1984.

————. "Politics: The New Game in Town." *Asiaweek*, July 12, 1985: 35–37; July 19, 1985: 28–31.

Ching, Frank. *Hong Kong and China: For Better or For Worse.* New York: China Council of the Asia Society and the Foreign Policy Association, 1985.

Chomsky, Noam, and Edward Herman. *After the Cataclysm: Postwar Indochina and the Reconstruction of Imperial Ideology.* Boston: South End Press, 1979.

Dahl, Robert. *Who Governs.* New Haven: Yale University Press, 1961.

————. "A Critique of the Ruling Elite Model." In Willis Hawley and Frederick Wirt, eds., *The Search for Community Power.* Englewood Cliffs: Prentice Hall, 1974.

Delfs, Robert. "Finding the Energy." *Far Easten Economic Review*, May 15, 1986: 54–55.

Donohue, George, Clarice Olien, and Phillip Tichenor. "A 'Guard Dog' Conception of Mass Media." Paper presented to the Association for Education in Journalism and Mass Communication, San Antonio, Texas, August 1987.

Dreier, Peter. "The Position of the Press in the U.S. Power Structure." *Social Problems*, 29 (1982): 298–310.

Epstein, Edward Jay. *News from Nowhere.* New York: Vintage, 1973.

Fan, Shuh Ching. *The Population of Hong Kong.* Hong Kong: Swindon, 1974.

Fensterheim, Herbert, and M.E. Tresselt. "The Influence of Value System on the Perception of People." *Journal of Abnormal and Social Psychology*, 48 (1953):93–98.

Fishman, Mark. *Manufacturing the News.* Austin: University of Texas Press, 1980.

Freiberg, J. W. *The French Press: Class, State, and Ideology.* New York: Praeger, 1981.

Galaskiewicz, Joseph. "Interorganizational Relations." *Annual Review of Sociology*, 11 (1985):281–304.

Galbraith, John K. *The Anatomy of Power.* Boston: Houghton Mifflin, 1983.

Gamson, William. *Power and Discontent.* Homewood, Ill.: Dorsey, 1968.

————. "The Political Culture of Arab–Israel Conflict." *Conflict Management and Peace Science,* 5 (1981):79–93.

Gans, Herbert. *Deciding What's News.* New York: Pantheon, 1979.

————. *Popular Culture and High Culture.* New York: Basic, 1974.

Giddens, Anthony. *Central Problems in Social Theory.* Berkeley: University of California Press, 1979.

Gitlin, Todd. *The Whole World Is Watching.* Berkeley: University of California Press, 1980.

Goldenberg, Eddie. *Making the Papers.* Lexington, Mass.: Lexington Books, 1975.

Gouldner, Alvin. *The Dialectic of Ideology and Technology.* New York: Oxford University Press, 1976.

Gramsci, Antonio. *Selections from the Prison Notebooks,* edited and translated by Quintin Hoare and Geoffrey Nowell Smith. New York: International Publishers, 1971.

Hall, Stuart. "Watching the Box." *New Society,* no. 411 (August 13, 1970):295–296.

————. "Deviance, Politics and the Media." In Paul Rock and Mary McIntosh, eds., *Deviance and Social Control.* London: Tavistock, 1974.

————. "Culture, the Media, and the 'Ideological Effect.'" In James Curran, Michael Gurevitch, and Janet Woollacott, eds., *Mass Communication and Society.* Beverly Hills: Sage, 1977.

————. "The Rediscovery of 'Ideology': Return of the Repressed in Media Studies." In Michael Gurevitch, Tony Bennett, James Curran, and Janet Woollacott, eds., *Culture, Society, and the Media.* New York: Methuen, 1982.

Hallin, Daniel. *The "Uncensored War": The Media and Vietnam.* New York: Oxford University Press, 1986.

Harris, Peter. *Hong Kong: A Study in Bureaucratic Politics.* Hong Kong: Heinemann Asia, 1978.

Hawley, Karen E. "A Theory of an Outsider's and Insider's Decision to Participate in a Political Issue and its Implication for the Process of Cooptation." Ph.D. diss., University of Minnesota, 1980.

Herman, Edward S., and Noam Chomsky. *Manufacturing Consent.* New York: Pantheon, 1988.

Hoadley, J. S. "Political Participation of Hong Kong Chinese Patterns and Trends." *Asian Survey,* 13 (1973):604–616.

Hong Kong Annual Report, 1986. Hong Kong: Government Printer.

Hong Kong Annual Report, 1985. Hong Kong: Government Printer.

Hong Kong Annual Report, 1980. Hong Kong: Government Printer.

Hong Kong Government. *Kowloon Disturbances 1966, Report of Commission of Inquiry.* Hong Kong: Government Printer, 1967.

Hong Kong Government Information Services. *GIS.* Hong Kong: Government Printer, 1987.

Jao, Y. C. "Hong Kong's Role in Financing China's Modernization." In A. J.

Youngson, ed., *China and Hong Kong: The Economic Nexus.* Hong Kong: Oxford University Press, 1984.

Jones, David A., Jr. "A Leg to Stand On? Post-1997 Hong Kong Courts as a Constraint on PRC Abridgment of Individual Rights and Local Autonomy." *Yale Journal of International Law,* 12, 2 (1987):250–293.

Jouet, Josiane. "Review of Radical Communication Research: The Conceptual Limits." In Emile McAnany et al., eds., *Communication and Social Structure.* New York: Praeger, 1981.

Harding, Harry. *China's Second Revolution: Reform After Mao.* Washington, D.C.: Brookings Institution, 1987.

Hsiao, Ching-chang, and Mei-rong Yang. "'Don't Force Us to Lie:' The Case of the *World Economic Herald.*" In *Voices of China. See* Lee, ed., 1990.

King, Ambrose Y. C. "Administrative Absorption of Politics in Hong Kong: Emphasis on the Grass Roots Level." *Asian Survey,* 15 (1975):422–439.

King, Ambrose Y. C., and Rance P. L. Lee, eds., *Social Life and Development in Hong Kong.* Hong Kong: Chinese University Press, 1981.

Kriesberg, Louis. *Social Conflicts.* Englewood, N.J.: Prentice-Hall, 1982.

Krippendorf, K. *Content Analysis.* Beverly Hills: Sage, 1980.

Kuan, Hsin-chi, and Siu-Kai Lau. "Mass Media and Politics in Hong Kong." Occasional paper, no. 28. Center for Hong Kong Studies, Chinese University of Hong Kong, 1988.

Kuhn, Thomas. *The Structure of Scientific Revolutions.* Chicago: University of Chicago Press, 1962 (1st ed.); 1970 (2nd ed.).

———. *The Essential Tension.* Chicago: University of Chicago Press, 1977.

Lakatos, Imre, and Alan Musgrave. *Criticism and the Growth of Knowledge.* Cambridge: Cambridge University Press, 1970.

Lam, Shui-Fong, and Vicky Tam. "1997: Hong Kong in Transition." pamphlet. Minneapolis: Hong Kong China Observers, 1990.

Lasswell, Harold. "The Structure and Function of Communication in Society." In Lyman Bryson, ed., *The Communication of Ideas.* New York: Harper and Row, 1948.

Lau, Emily. "Threats to Press Freedom from Outside—and Within." *Far Eastern Economic Review,* October 25, 1984: 54–56.

———. "Capitalist Delegates to People's Congress." *Far Eastern Economic Review,* August 1, 1985.

———. "A Media Melting Pot of All Political Stripes." *Far Eastern Economic Review,* February 13, 1986.

———. "Backroom Betrayal." *Far Eastern Economic Review,* March 1, 1990: 14–15.

———. "Elites Take All." *Far Eastern Economic Review,* April 19, 1990.

———. "A Kind of Defection." *Far Eastern Economic Review,* May 24, 1990.

———. "Media's Red Barons." *Far Eastern Economic Review,* September 27, 1990.

Lau, Siu-kai. *The Government and Politics in Hong Kong.* Hong Kong: Chinese University Press, 1982.

Lee, Chin-Chuan. *Media Imperialism Reconsidered.* Beverly Hills: Sage, 1980.

——. "In Quest of an Alternative to Professional Journalism in the Third World." Paper presented at the annual convention of the International Communication Association, San Francisco, May 24–28, 1984.

——. "Partisan Press Coverage of Government News in Hong Kong." *Journalism Quarterly*, 62 (1985):770–776.

——. "The Partisan Press in Hong Kong: Between Colonial Rule and Chinese Politics." Paper presented at the annual convention of the Association for Education in Journalism and Mass Communicaton, Memphis, August 3–6, 1985.

——. "Mass Media: Of China, About China." In *Voices of China. See* Lee, ed., 1990.

——, ed. *Voices of China: The Interplay of Politics and Journalism.* New York: Guilford, 1990.

Lee, Chin-Chuan, and Yuet-lin Lee. "Constructing Partisan Realities by the Press: A Riot in Hong Kong." Paper presented to the Midwest Political Science Association convention, Chicago, April 19, 1985.

Lee, Chin-Chuan, and Joseph Man Chan. "Journalistic Paradigms in Flux: The Press and Political Transition in Hong Kong." *Bulletin of Ethnology Academia Sinica*, 63 (1987):109–131.

——. "The Hong Kong Press in China's Orbit: Thunder of Tiananmen." In *Voices of China. See* Lee, ed., 1990.

——. "Government Management of the Press in Hong Kong," *Gazette*, 46 (1990):125–139.

——. "The Hong Kong Press Coverage of the Tiananmen Protests," *Gazette*, 46 (1990):175–195.

Leung, Julia. "China Gets a Better Press in Hong Kong." *Asian Wall Street Journal*, January 7, 1986.

——. "China Woos Hong Kong's Business Elite." *Asian Wall Street Journal*, January 16, 1989.

——. "Hong Kong Newspaper Risks China's Ire." *Asian Wall Street Journal*, July 5, 1989, p. 1.

Lippmann, Walter. *Public Opinion*. New York: Macmillan, 1922.

Luke, Timothy. "Chernobyl: The Packaging of Transnational Ecological Disaster." *Critical Studies in Mass Communication*, 4 (1987):351–375.

Lukes, Steven. "Power and Authority." In Tom Bottomore and Robert Nisbet, eds., *A History of Sociological Analysis,*. New York: Basic, 1978.

——. *Power: A Radical View*. London: Macmillan, 1974.

Manoff, R. K., and Michael Schudson, eds. *Reading the News*. New York: Pantheon, 1986.

Masterman, Margaret. "The Nature of a Paradigm." In Imre Lakatos and Alan Musgrave, eds., *Criticism and the Growth of Knowledge*. Cambridge: Cambridge University Press, 1970.

McQuail, Denis. *Mass Communication Theory*. Beverly Hills: Sage, 1983.

Miners, Norman J. *The Government and Politics of Hong Kong*. Hong Kong: Oxford University Press, 1977.

Mitchell, Robert E. "How Hong Kong Newspapers Have Responded to 15 Years of Rapid Social Change." *Asian Survey*, 9 (1969):673–678.

Molotch, Harvey, and Marilyn Lester. "Accident News: The Great Oil Spill as Local Occurrence and National Event." *American Journal of Sociology*, 81 (1975):235–260.

Murdock, Graham. "Large Corporations and the Control of the Communications Industries." In *Culture, Society and the Media. See* Hall 1982.

Murdock, Graham, and Peter Golding. "Capitalism, Communication and Class Relations." In *Mass Communication and Society. See* Hall 1977.

Nisbet, Robert. *Community and Power*. New York: Oxford University Press, 1953.

Olien, Clarice, George Donohue, and Philip Tichenor. "Use of the Press and the Power of a Group." *Sociology of Rural Life*, 4 (1981):1–2,7.

Paletz, David, Peggey Reichert, and Barbara McIntyre. "How the Mass Media Support Local Government Authority." *Public Opinion Quarterly*, 35 (1971):80–92.

Paletz, David, and Robert M. Entman. *Media Power Politics*. New York: Free Press, 1981.

Pennings, J. M. "Strategically Interdependent Organizations." In P. Nystrom and W. H. Starbuck, eds., *Handbook of Organizational Design*. Vol. 1. London: Oxford University Press, 1981.

Pfeffer, Jeffrey, and Phillip Salancik. *The External Control of Organizations: A Resource Dependence Perspective*. New York: Harper and Row, 1978.

Pye, Lucian. "Communication and Political Culture in China." *Asian Survey*, 18 (1978):221–246.

Rabushka, Alvin. *Hong Kong: A Study in Economic Freedom*. Chicago: University of Chicago, Graduate School of Business, 1979.

Ritzer, George. *Sociology: A Multiple Paradigm Science*. Boston: Allyn and Bacon Press, 1975.

Rosario, de Louise. "Peking Gets Its Way." *Far Eastern Economic Review*, January 22, 1986: 48–49.

Said, Edward. *Covering Islam*. New York: Pantheon, 1981.

Schiller, Dan. *Objectivity and the News: The Public and the Rise of Commercial Journalism*. Philadelphia: University of Pennsylvania Press, 1981.

Schlesinger, Peter. *Putting "Reality" Together*. Beverly Hills: Sage, 1978.

Schudson, Michael. *Discovering the News*. New York: Basic, 1978.

Selznick, Philip. *TVA and the Grass Roots: A Study in the Sociology of Formal Organization*. Berkeley: University of California Press, 1949.

Seneviratne, Gamini. "Asia's Nuclear Family." *Far Eastern Economic Review*, May 15, 1986: 66–67.

Seymour-Ure, Colin. *The Political Impact of Mass Media*. Beverly Hills: Sage, 1974.

Shen, James. *The Law and Mass Media in Hong Kong*. Hong Kong: Chinese University Press, 1972.

Shoemaker, Pamela. "Media Treatment of Deviant Political Groups." *Journalism Quarterly*, 61 (1984):66–75,82.

Siebert, Fred, Theodore Peterson, and Wilbur Schramm. *Four Theories of the Press*. Urbana: University of Illinois Press, 1956.

Sigal, Leon. *Reporters and Officials: The Organization and Politics of Newsmaking*. Lexington, Mass.: Lexington Books, 1973.

Sigelman, Lee. "Reporting the News: An Organizational Analysis." *American Journal of Sociology*, 79 (1973):132–151.

Simon, Herbert. "The Carrot and Stick as Handmaidens of Persuasion in Conflict Situations." In Gerald Miller and Herbert Simon, eds., *Perspectives on Communication in Social Conflicts*. Englewood, N.J.: Prentice-Hall, 1974.

Sinclair, Kelvin, ed. *Who's Who in Hong Kong*. 4th ed. Hong Kong: Aisanet Information Services, 1988.

Solomon, Richard. "Chinese Political Negotiating Behavior." Unpublished paper. Los Angeles: Rand Corporation, 1983.

Tehranian, Majid. "Iran: Communication, Alienation and Revolution." *Intermedia*, 7, 2 (1979):6–12.

Ting, Lee-Hsia Hsu. *Government Control of the Press in Modern China, 1900–1949*. Cambridge: Harvard University Press, 1974.

Tichenor, Philip, George Donohue, and Clarice Olien. *The Press and Community Conflict*. Beverley Hills: Sage, 1980.

Trounstine, Philip, and Terry Christensen. *Movers and Shakers: The Study of Community Power*. New York: St. Martin's Press, 1982.

Tuchman, Gaye. *Making News*. New York: Free Press, 1978.

Tunstall, Jeremy. *Journalists at Work*. London: Constable, 1971.

"United Front in Hong Kong." *Asiaweek*, December 2, 1984: 22–23.

Weber, Max. *Economy and Society*. Ed. Guenther Roth and Claus Wittich. Berkeley: University of California Press, 1969.

Wesley-Smith, Peter. *An Introduction to the Hong Kong Legal System*. Hong Kong: Oxford University Press, 1987.

Williams, Raymond. *Marxism and Literature*. New York: Oxford University Press, 1977.

Wilson, Frank. *French Political Parties Under the Fifth Republic*. New York: Praeger, 1982.

World Bank. *World Development 1989*. New York: Oxford University Press, 1989.

Wrong, Dennis. *Power: Its Forms, Bases, and Uses*. London: Blackwell, 1988.

Yeung, Chris. "Locals Warned Not to Meddle with Regime." *South China Morning Post*, June 23, 1989.

Yoon, Youngchul. "Political Tranisition and Press Ideology in South Korea, 1980–1988." Ph.D. diss., University of Minnesota, 1989.

II. SELECTED CHINESE-LANGUAGE SOURCES

"An Inside Report on Xu Jiatun's Forced Departure." *Contemporary Weekly*, no. 25 (May 19, 1990): 3–11.

"A Review of Xu Jiatun's Three Years in Hong Kong." *Pai Hsing Semimonthly,* 123 (July 1, 1986): 8–17.

Cha, Louis. *On Hong Kong's Future.* Hong Kong: Ming Pao, 1984.

———. "The First of July, 1997," *Ming Pao,* August 16, 1983.

———. "An Innovation Applicable to the Whole World." *People's Daily,* September 26, 1984.

———. "On Press Freedom." *Ming Pao,* March 21–23, 1986.

Chan, Hung-ngai. *Hong Kong's Legal System and the Basic Law.* Hong Kong: Wide-angled Mirror, 1986.

Chan, Joseph Man, and Yau Shing-mo. "The Power Bases of Hong Kong's Press Freedom." *Ming Pao Monthly,* May 1987: 10–14.

Chan, King-shuen. "Insiders' View of the Suppression on the Seventies and Chang Ming." *Pai Hsing Semimonthly,* August 16, 1981: 3–4.

———. "On the Cold War Between China and Britain." *Pai Hsing Semimothly,* September 16, 1983.

Cheng, Joseph, ed. *A Collection of Essays on Hong Kong's Economy, Politics, and Society.* Hong Kong: Going Fine, 1984.

Cheung, Bing-Leung. "The Pratical and Political Implications of the Establishment of Management Councils by the Hong Kong Government." *Ming Pao Monthly,* February 1988: 37–41.

Cheung, Kit-fung. "Is It Possible to Maintain the Status Quo Beyond 1997?" *Pai Hsing Semimonthly,* January 1, 1985: 9–11.

Chiang, Susie. "While Both Sing the Democratic Tune, They Differ on the Pace." *China Times,* December 20, 1988.

———. "The CCP Is Purging Hong Kong's Leftist Media." *China Times,* June 24, 1989: 3.

Chiu, Hung-dah, and Ren Xiaoqi, eds. *Negotiation Strategy of Communist China.* Taipei: Lien-jing, 1985.

Chu, Yihong. "Beijing Makes Plan to Take Over Hong Kong." *Hong Kong Economic Journal,* August 8, 1990.

Ho, Lai-kit. "Louis Cha: A Learned Boss." In *Ten Interviews.* Hong Kong: Culture Book House, 1977.

Hong Kong and China: Historical Documents. Vol. 1. Hong Kong: Wide-angled Mirror, 1984.

Hsu, Ching-yun. "These Leaders Have Gone Mad." *The Journalist,* June 12, 1989.

Huang, Kang-sheng. *The Problem of Hong Kong's Existence.* Hong Kong: Buoyee, 1987.

Huang, Miao. "Beijing Tightens its Reins over Hong Kong after the Ex-Director 'Escaped.' " *Contemporary Weekly,* May 19, 1990, pp. 10–11.

Kam, Shu-fai. "Hong Kong Government and the News Media." *Pai Hsing Semimonthly,* September 16, 1982: 50–53.

King, Ambrose Y. C. "Hong Kong's Political Change in Transition." *China Times Weekly* (New York), 36 (November 3–19, 1985): 16–17.

Kwok, Wai-fung. "China's Research on Hong Kong and Macao Has Entered the Stage of Learning." *Ta Kung Pao,* August 24, 1988.

Lam, Sam-muk. *The Question of Hong Kong's Future: Conception and Reality.* Hong Kong: Hong Kong Economic Journal, 1984.

Lau, Emily. "How Do the News Media Face 1997?" *Nineties Monthly,* September 1984: 62–67.

Lee, Chin-Chuan. *Politics of Journalism, Journalism of Politics.* Taipei: Yuan-sheng, 1987.

———. "Hong Kong's Power Transition and Mass Media." *Pai Hsing Semi-monthly,* March 16, 1986.

Lee, Ming-kun. *Hong Kong Politics and Society in Transition.* Hong Kong: Commercial, 1987.

Lee, Tse-chung. "Three Systems Within One Paper." *Contemporary Weekly,* January 20, 1990: 20.

Lee, Yee. *Hong Kong's Negotiation and China's Future.* Hong Kong: Going Fine, 1985.

———. "Challenging the Lame Duck." *Hong Kong Economic Journal,* November 25, 1985.

———. "Why Is the Voice of Criticism Reduced?" *Hong Kong Economic Journal,* March 31, 1986.

———. "What Kind of Press Is Beneficial to China?" *Seventies Monthly,* August 1979.

Leung, Min-kwun. "Anti-communism Outpost in Choas." *Nineties Monthly,* January 1985.

Lin, Youlan. *The History of Press Development in Hong Kong.* Taipei: World, 1977.

Liu, Yuan-tu. "The Second Wave of Hong Kong Emigrants." *Nineties Monthly,* June 1987.

Long, Sin. *A Shadow Government of Hong Kong.* Hong Kong: Hai-san, 1985.

Lu, Fangzhi. *Hong Kong: From a Colony to a Special Administrative Region.* Hong Kong: Wide-angled Mirror, 1982.

Lu, Keng. *The Era of Deng Xiaoping.* Hong Kong: Pai Hsing, 1990.

Lu, Wen. "The Development of Xinhua's Hong Kong Branch." *Wide-Angled Mirror,* August 16, 1987: 82–97.

Mainland China Materials. *Unveiling the CCP's "One Country, Two Systems" Conspiracy.* Taipei: Mainland China Materials, 1987.

Mao, Zedong. *Selected Works.* Vols. 1–4. Beijing: People's Press, 1966.

———. *Selected Works.* Vol. 5. Beijing: People's Press, 1977.

Ng, F. Y., and Choy H. "The Outflow of People and Capital." *Hong Kong Economic Journal Monthly* 154 (1990): 19–22.

Ngai, Yum-cho. "Hong Kong File." *Nineties Monthly,* September 1989, pp. 50–51.

Pok, Shaofu. "Thank You, Mr. Xu Jiatun." *Newsdom,* 195 (August 17, 1985).

———. "My Pillow Testifies to My Serene Sleep Every Night." *Ming Pao,* January 7–9, 1986.

Qi Xin [Lee Yee]. "Analyzing the Xu Jiatun Affair." *Nineties Monthly,* June 1990: 24–27.

Research Office of the China News Publication Bureau. "A Summary of the Survey Results on Legislating Press Law." December 15, 1988.

Selection from the Document on the Question of Hong Kong. Beijing: People's Daily, 1985.

Shi, Junyu. "1.1 Billion People Shouted the Same Slogan." *Ta Kung Pao,* May 24, 1989.

Shi, Hua. "Communist China's Allergy to Hong Kong Publications." *Nineties Monthly,* March 1990.

Shi, Yufei. "The *Hong Kong Times'* Quarrel in Taipei." *Nineties Monthly,* February 1985.

Sixty-four Hong Kong Reporters. *The People Won't Forget: An Account of the 1989 Student Movement.* Hong Kong: Journalists Association, 1989.

Sun, Lung-chi. *The Deep Structure of the Chinese Culture.* Hong Kong: Lungmeng, 1983.

The Moving and Tragic Student Movement: Most Peaceful Beginning, Most Bloody Ending. Hong Kong: Ming Pao, 1989.

Tong, Chung-Han. "Recent Activities of Pro-Taiwan Forces in Hong Kong." *Pai Hsing Semimonthly,* Novemember 16, 1985.

Tsang, Wai-Yin. *Days and Nights in Beijing.* Hong Kong: Publications Ltd., 1984.

"Xinhua in the Aftermath of June 4." *Contemporary Weekly,* no. 1, November 25, 1989: 14–17.

Xu, Jiatun. "Reconsider Capitalism and Build Socialism Consciously." *Qiu Shi Magazine,* no. 5, 1988.

Xuan, Yuan-lo. *Xinhua in Perspective.* Hong Kong: Wide-angled Mirror, 1987.

———. *Looking Closely at Xinhua.* Hong Kong: Wide-angled Mirror, 1987.

Yu, Mang. "Pok Shaofu, Har Kung and Freedom of Speech in Hong Kong." *Cheng Ming Monthly,* October 1985.

Yu, Giwen. "The Chinese Communist Party's Work System in Hong Kong." *Nineties Monthly,* October 1985: 56–59.

Index